Beyond Church and State
Democracy, Secularism, and Conversion

Secularism is often imagined, in Thomas Jefferson's words, as "a wall of separation between Church & State." *Beyond Church and State* moves past that standard picture to argue that secularism is a process that reshapes both religion and politics. Borrowing a term from religious traditions, the book goes further to argue that this process should be understood as a process of conversion. Matthew Scherer studies Saint Augustine, John Locke, John Rawls, Henri Bergson, and Stanley Cavell to present a more accurate picture of what secularism is, what it does, and how it can be reimagined to be more conducive to genuine democracy.

Matthew Scherer is Assistant Professor of Government and Politics at George Mason University.

Beyond Church and State

Democracy, Secularism, and Conversion

MATTHEW SCHERER
George Mason University

CAMBRIDGE UNIVERSITY PRESS
Cambridge, New York, Melbourne, Madrid, Cape Town,
Singapore, São Paulo, Delhi, Mexico City

Cambridge University Press
32 Avenue of the Americas, New York, NY 10013-2473, USA

www.cambridge.org
Information on this title: www.cambridge.org/9781107026094

© Matthew Scherer 2013

This publication is in copyright. Subject to statutory exception
and to the provisions of relevant collective licensing agreements,
no reproduction of any part may take place without the written
permission of Cambridge University Press.

First published 2013

Printed in the United States of America

A catalog record for this publication is available from the British Library.

Library of Congress Cataloging in Publication Data
Scherer, Matthew, 1977–
Beyond church and state : democracy, secularism, and conversion
pages cm
Includes bibliographical references and index.
ISBN 978-1-107-02609-4
1. Secularism. 2. Religion and politics. I. Title.
BL2747.8.S26 2013
322'.1–dc23   2012036776

ISBN 978-1-107-02609-4 Hardback

Cambridge University Press has no responsibility for the persistence or accuracy of URLs
for external or third-party Internet Web sites referred to in this publication and does not
guarantee that any content on such Web sites is, or will remain, accurate or appropriate.

For my parents,
Patricia Scherer and Oscar Scherer

Contents

Acknowledgments		*page* ix
	Introduction: Beyond the Separation of Church and State – Secularism as Conversion	1
1	Authorized Narrative and Crystalline Structure: Conversion in Augustine's *Confessions*	30
2	Toleration and Conversion in Locke's Letters: It Is "Above all Things Necessary to Distinguish"	71
3	The Crystalline Structure of Conversion: Henri Bergson's *Two Sources*	97
4	Saint John (Rawls): The Miracle of Secular Reason	132
5	The Wish for a Better Life: Stanley Cavell's Critique of the Social Contract	168
	Conclusion: From *Supernovas* into *The Deep* – Secularism as Conversion, a Conversion of Secularism…	219
Index		237

Acknowledgments

This book wouldn't be anything like it is without William E. Connolly: thanks, Bill, for everything your work makes possible, and for showing me something new every time we talk. Jane Bennett and Dick Flathman are two of the most original and creative voices in political theory; while I was their student, they taught me a lot about trusting my own ideas and following them wherever they lead. I could not have had better teachers. Paola Marrati and Hent de Vries welcomed me with extraordinary graciousness in their seminars in the Humanities Center – I'm immensely grateful for the privilege of studying with them and for the time I have spent with each of them. Johns Hopkins was a wonderful place to be a graduate student – in large part because of the people there with me – and I thank in particular Jennifer Culbert, Frances Ferguson, John Marshall, Lars Tønder, Paulina Ochoa, Smita Rahman, Rob Watkins, George Oppel, Simon Glezos, Bhrigupati Singh, John Olson, and Patrick Peel for the important and timely interventions they made in my work, for their sustained and continuing friendship, or for both.

The two years I spent as a postdoctoral Fellow at UC Berkeley were enriched by the generous influence of many people. My thanks especially to Wendy Brown, Judith Butler, Charles Hirschkind, Saba Mahmood, David Bates, Pheng Cheah, Niklaus Largier, Bob Sharf, Felipe Gutterriez, Shalini Satkunanandan, Marianne Constable, Yves Winter, Katherine Lemons, Michael Allan, Karen Feldman, Ramona Naddaff, Ivan Ascher, Nancy Weston, Vicky Kahn, Ron Hendel, Victoria Frede, and Samera Esmeir.

Talal Asad read the entire manuscript of this book – I can't thank him enough for taking an interest in my work and sharing his time and thoughts with me. José Casanova, George Shulman, James Martel, Terrell Carver, John Seery, Mort Schoolman, Stephen White, Kennan Ferguson, Steve Johnston, Char Miller, Mike Gibbons, Simon Stow, Jason Frank, Sam Chambers, Davide Panagia, Tracy Strong, Roxanne Euben, Kirstie McClure, Andrew Norris, David Alvarez, Tom Dumm, Lori Marso, Chris Nealon, Joshua Dienstag, Sara Rushing, David Gutterman, Andrew Murphy, Barbara Arneil, Emily Nacol, Danielle Allen, David Kim, Lisa Ellis, Ted Miller, and Brad Bryan made invaluable comments on this manuscript and/or were indispensable partners in conversation. Thank you all. I benefited greatly from invitations to share my work in progress by giving lectures or participating in workshops at Johns Hopkins, Berkeley, Maryland, Columbia, and George Washington – my thanks especially in those contexts to Ingrid Creppell, Derek Malone-France, Abe Newman, Robert Adcock, John Sides, Fred Alford, Jim Glass, and Ian Ward. My thanks to Tom Banchoff for appointing me as a research Fellow at Georgetown's Berkley Center for Religion, Peace, & World Affairs. Thanks are also due to the Nuttle family for endowing the Patrick Henry postdoctoral fellowship in early American politics at Johns Hopkins, and to the Mellon Foundation for funding my postdoctoral fellowship in the humanities at Berkeley – both fellowships supported the research and writing of this book.

Libby Anker, my most cherished critic, read each chapter many, many times – she also made me rewrite each many, many times. I am very lucky to have such a tireless and incisive interlocutor; more lucky still to have such an amazing and beloved life partner.

Finally, love and thanks to my family – who are everything: Elisabeth Robin, Daniel Jay, Lilah Eve, Pat, Oscar, Carol, Billie, Shell, Annie, Berkeley, Mark, Jon, David, Dara, Christie, Bridget, Bella, Charlotte, Madeline, Elias, Everett, Noah, and Nathan.

An earlier version of Chapter Four was published as "Saint John: The Miracle of Secular Reason" in *Political Theologies: Public Religions in a Post-Secular World*, eds. Hent de Vries and Lawrence E. Sullivan (New York: Fordham University Press, 2006), 341–62. Part of the Introduction appears in my entry on "Secularism" in *The Encyclopedia of Political Thought*, eds. Michael Gibbons, Diana Coole, and Lisa Ellis (Hoboken, NJ: Wiley-Blackwell). I am grateful for permission to reprint these here. My thanks also to Barbara Takenaga, DC Moore Gallery, and Henry V. Heuser for permission to reproduce "Nebraska Painting, EL 1" on the cover of this book.

Introduction

Beyond the Separation of Church and State
Secularism as Conversion

This book's thesis can be stated in three parts: First, secularism is not now, and in fact never has been, primarily a matter of separating religion and politics, despite the prevalence of that authorized view. Second, secularism has been, and continues to be, a process that transforms religion and politics. Third, in a Euro-American context, in a global context even, if done carefully, it will be useful to think of that process of transformation as a process of crystalline conversion. To develop this thesis, I draw upon a figure of conversion that is inscribed in the margins of the Augustinian tradition; that is expressed in minor trajectories within the writings of the great early modern and contemporary proponents of secularism, John Locke and John Rawls; and that recurs as a major theme in the work of two of the past century's most salient philosophical critics of secularism, Henri Bergson and Stanley Cavell. I argue that the commonplace image of secularism as the separation of church and state presents an obstacle to the development of a more genuinely democratic politics, and that refiguring secularism as a process of conversion may open new possibilities for democracy within the condition of deep pluralism that marks contemporary global politics.

Insofar as this book aims to move its readers toward a new perspective on a familiar problem, its objective, and thus to some extent its writing, reflects its subject matter: it is a book about secularism and conversion that aims to produce a certain kind of conversion in its readers' view of secularism. Such a prospect is worth entertaining, I submit, because secularism is a central and an essentially contested component of modern democracy – precisely because arguments over the very meaning of this term can be expected to persist, it is of critical importance to engage them.[1]

Secularism is a moving target, for its forms change over time, but it consistently names the processes that continuously recontour both religious and political life. The metaphor of a "wall of separation between church & state," for example, most famously employed in the early nineteenth century by Thomas Jefferson, although it long predates him, is currently the authorized emblem of modern secularism.[2] It actively shapes American constitutional jurisprudence and circulates widely within public debates, within popular consciousness, and even within contemporary theoretical analyses.[3] The idea of separation lies at the core of many of today's most important debates about secularism: whether political discourse can be separated from religious discourse, whether political institutions are separate from religious institutions, whether modern Western secularism is separate from the religious traditions that have conditioned it, whether and how the West's apparent secularism separates it from the non-Western world.[4] The separation of church and state remains a fundamental and persistent part of the modern secular imaginary, to be sure, but it is also just as certainly an imperfect characterization of modern secularism. Secularism today is neither primarily a matter of separating religion from the major domains of modern life – including politics, economics, science, morality, and the arts – nor has it ever primarily been a matter of separating religion from these domains. Secularism has instead always been a crystalline process of transformation that produces and reshapes key dimensions of political and religious life. If the idea of "a wall of separation between church & state" presents an insufficient image of secularism, and if it would be more accurate to say that secularism is instead a process of transformation, the figure of conversion shows how and why this process produces such an image. In the language this book

---

[1] The term "essentially contested concept" was introduced by W. B. Gallie, but I borrow from William E. Connolly's discussion and use of it in *The Terms of Political Discourse*.
[2] For a history of Jefferson's phrase, see Daniel Dreisbach's *Thomas Jefferson and the Wall of Separation between Church and State*.
[3] Thomas Jefferson, "A Letter to the Danbury Baptists."
[4] Carl Schmitt, *Political Theologies*; William E. Connolly, *Why I Am Not a Secularist*; John Rawls, *Political Liberalism*; Jürgen Habermas, "Religion in the Public Sphere"; Winnifred Fallers Sullivan, *The Impossibility of Religious Freedom*; Philip Hamburger, *Separation of Church and State*; Max Weber, *The Protestant Ethic and the Spirit of Capitalism*; Hans Blumenberg, *The Legitimacy of the Modern Age*; Marcel Gauchet, *The Disenchantment of the World*; Charles Taylor, *A Secular Age*; Samuel Huntington, "The Clash of Civilizations"; Gil Anidjar, "Secularism"; Saba Mahmood, *The Politics of Piety*.

will develop, figuring secularism as conversion shows how the image of separation constitutes the authorized surface of a deeper, crystalline process of transformation. Figuring secularism as conversion accounts for the persistent appeal, even the necessity, of conceiving secularism as the separation of church and state despite the inadequacy of that conception.

The modern secular imaginary isolates a single part of a much larger, multifaceted process that reshapes the specific practices, institutions, and discourses that condition experience in both political and religious domains when it promotes the principle of separation to a central place. This larger process has produced a series of variable boundaries between politics and religion throughout history – and not only modern and Western history. In the context of modern Euro-American secularism, this process unfolds as a process of conversion; ironically, it is a process of conversion in which modern secularism emerges by excluding religious conversion from public life, and from its own narrative self-identity. Within the Augustinian tradition from which I draw this figure, conversion refers to a transformational process of ethical character formation and communal reorientation that is retrospectively consolidated through the production of a new narrative self-identity. Such a figure foregrounds the transformation of individuals in relation to communities mediated by narrative, which is by no means merely a religious phenomenon, but occurs instead within politics generally, and within the politics of modern secularism specifically.

Figuring the emergence of modern secularism as a process of conversion shows how secularism has in fact emerged in new, distinctly modern forms by reshaping institutions, practices, sensibilities, communities, and discourses. It also shows how these transformations are catalyzed and obscured by a simplifying figure of secularism as the separation of church and state. One already sees in Augustine's writings a conversion, which involves the complex disciplinary process of ethical character formation, represented and refigured by a conversion narrative, which obscures, simplifies, and consolidates this work. The social transformations that produced modern Euro-American secularism entailed a long, slow, and quiet conversion of political and religious sensibilities, which underpinned the exclusion of forced conversion from politics, a process that has since been obscured by conversion narratives that simplify and consolidate its outlines. Modern secularism is bound to the problem of conversion in a historical sense, and the figure of conversion can illuminate the contours of secularism as a process of transformation in a theoretical sense.

The connection proposed here between the problem of modern secularism and the figure of conversion – a figure of *religious* conversion it must be noted – should be surprising insofar as religious conversion was explicitly excluded from the purview of political institutions, and from the conceptual vocabulary of political thought, precisely as a concept of separation became ascendant in early European modernity. A constitutive moment, it is widely held, of the modern separation of public and private spheres consisted in excluding religious conversion from public life and consigning it to the private – such is a plausible way of understanding the core of the seventeenth century's debates over toleration. Although this exclusion formed a precondition for a more tolerant politics, it also restricted the theoretical vocabulary within which processes of social transformation could be described – toleration becomes possible when new strictures are successfully imposed upon the public sphere and upon speaking subjects, and it can be cogently argued that such strictures compromise the possibility of a deep, genuinely pluralistic democratic politics.[5] This book returns to the figure of conversion in part to reconsider the limitations placed on aspirations for a more democratic politics by the legacies of modern secularism, and to reopen the question of how elements of what we now think of as "the religious" can and should figure within politics.

To figure secularism as a process of conversion is also to propose a new way of thinking about the connection between secularism and Christianity; it represents one way of drawing on the resources of "religious" and "spiritual" traditions to rethink problematic categories of "the political." To say that secularism is a form of conversion strongly suggests that Euro-American secularism cannot be cleanly separated from the forms of Christianity that dominated the context in which it emerged, but it also helps to account for secularism's perceptible distance from Christianity (and other religions). Conversion is both a process that unfolds slowly through the continuous amendment of habits, dispositions, and communal attachments, and an outcome enabled by a retrospective narrative that posits an instantaneous moment of separation between old and new.[6] Conversion therefore transforms sensibilities and retrospectively represents this transformation as a clean separation between past and present. As a figure for secularism, it suggests that this formation is

---

[5] For these latter claims, see Wendy Brown, *Regulating Aversion*; Talal Asad, *Formations of the Secular*; William E. Connolly, *Why I Am Not a Secularist*.

[6] Augustine, *Confessions*; Peter Brown, *Augustine*; John Freccero, *Dante*.

sustained by retrospective narratives that intensify and consolidate the changes it introduces by imposing a categorical difference between a secular modernity and a religious past. A theory of secularism based on the figure of conversion registers multiple forms of connection between Christianity and secularism, and it explains why narratives about the emergence of secularism nonetheless posit a series of clean separations between secularism and its others. More precisely, the formal demands of the Christian conversion narrative that contribute to the identity of modern Euro-American secularism impose a series of clean breaks between politics and religion, secularism and Christianity, and Christianity and non-Christianity that belie the processes of transformation connecting each of these terms. This book aims to show how dominant conceptions of modern secularism as the separation of church and state emerge as part of a multifaceted process of transformation, which suppresses conversion on the one hand, but itself unfolds as a process of conversion on the other. This introduction will treat the problem of modern secularism and the figure of conversion in turn and then explain how the figure of conversion can be used to address the problem of secularism. It concludes by previewing the arguments of coming chapters.

The Problem of Modern Secularism

The figure of conversion presents the problem of modern secularism in a new light, but it is important at the outset to present a relatively uncontroversial view of this terrain before introducing the figure of conversion. It is widely agreed that modern secularism is a broad rubric under which to group a series of more precisely formulated problematics, most importantly "secularization," "secularity," and "secularism" proper.[7] What follows immediately are the outlines of commonplace approaches to these three problematics.[8]

Theories of "secularization" are largely the provenance of sociology thanks in large part to the foundational work of Émile Durkheim and Max Weber. In its strongest form, the secularization thesis posits a long-term and large-scale historical process of differentiation in which major

---

[7] William Connolly and Talal Asad go further, isolating "secularists" and disinterring "the secular," respectively. See William E. Connolly, *Why I Am Not a Secularist*; Talal Asad, *Formations of the Secular*; and Matthew Scherer, "Landmarks in the Critical Study of Secularism."

[8] This introductory overview draws from my entry on "secularism" published in *The Encyclopedia of Political Thought*.

areas of human activity such as politics, law, economics, science, and art have been effectively separated from religion. More specifically, this process is presented as unfolding with respect to Christianity in Europe in three interlocking dimensions: the retreat of religion from public life, the restriction of religion to individual belief, and the general decline of belief. The theory of "disenchantment" sketched in Weber's *The Protestant Ethic and the Spirit of Capitalism* provides a classical locus for the theory of secularization. Durkheim's claim in *The Elementary Forms of Religious Life* that "the Sacred" lies at the core of primitive religion and that a functional analogue underpins modern social integration represents a different but equally classic locus for the concept of secularization, in which modern society replaces the content of the sacred while retaining its formal structure. Despite its prominence, two central problems with a strong form of the theory of secularization are commonly cited: the first is that these theories are undermined by empirical research; the second is that they produce an ambiguity with respect to the relation between the secular and the religious.[9] In Weber's account, for example, it is unclear whether the spirit of capitalism that grows from the Protestant ethic emerges freestanding and independent of its religious foundation or represents instead a more profound continuity between the secular modern present and its religious past. In Durkheim's account, the functional equivalence of the sacred and the social transforms this ambiguity into a formal identity, such that there is no effective difference between the sacred and the social or the religious and the secular.

The indeterminacy left in such theories of secularization has become the object of fierce debate, the key positions of which were marked out by the mid-twentieth century when Hans Blumenberg advanced the thesis that the modern age is freestanding and self-legitimating against Carl Schmitt's contention that modernity is dependent upon and derived from a prior Christianity.[10] More recently, a movement known as Radical Orthodoxy has taken over a position in debates about secularism comparable, although not reducible, to Schmitt's. From the perspective of Radical Orthodoxy, it is philosophy that constitutes secularism by claiming adequate knowledge of an immanent world independent of any transcendent creator and by claiming its independence from theology. Once more, in this story, secularism is constituted through a break with

---

[9] José Casanova's *Public Religions in the Modern World* is a landmark statement of the relatively recent wave of empirical criticism of the secularization thesis.

[10] Hans Blumenberg, *The Legitimacy of the Modern Age*; Carl Schmitt, *Political Theology*.

Christianity. And in this view, secular modernity is an extremely arrogant but nonetheless heretical offshoot of Christianity: secularism is synonymous with nihilism and necessarily consigned to spiritual, moral, and social decline. Radical Orthodoxy attempts to turn the tables on both modern social theory and modern theologies, which it views as complicit in the assumptions of modern social theory, by undermining philosophy's claims to independence and reasserting the foundational position of theology, of early Christianity – and, ultimately, as it were, of God. On the one hand, Radical Orthodoxy's argument that the modern separation of philosophy from theology must be erased is disarmingly simple: because everything is created by and "participates in" God, everything must be countenanced within a theological framework; if God is everywhere, so too must be theology. On the other hand, however, it reinscribes the modern separation of philosophy from theology insofar as it constitutes itself as "radical" and "orthodox" through contrast with its modern and post-modern rivals. To put this another way, Radical Orthodoxy reverses the privilege of the secular over the religious in modern social theory and seeks to restore the privilege of the religious over the secular that it takes as characteristic of medieval and early Christian orders. But its polemical portrait of a modernity constituted by the division of an ascendant secular world from a beleaguered Christian Tradition does nothing to question the distinction between religious and secular.

Taking over a position comparable but again by no means reducible to Blumenberg's, Jeffrey Stout articulates a powerful critique of the religious traditionalism exemplified by Radical Orthodoxy – as well as by such thinkers as Alasdair MacIntyre and Stanley Hauerwas – and he offers an alternative interpretation of modern secular politics. Stout argues that the proponents of religious traditionalism misapprehend important dimensions of contemporary political life, and that they do so to the extent that they inherit insufficient understandings of both "religion" and "politics" from the "secularist" theories that they oppose. Stout takes John Rawls and Richard Rorty as key examples of the secularist position insofar as both argue that liberal democracies can and should exclude religion from public argument at key points. He joins the traditionalists in opposing that exclusion, but Stout argues that the traditionalists err by treating this secularist position as a sufficient characterization of modern liberal democratic politics. From Stout's perspective, both proponents and opponents of secularism are blinded by a secularist ideology that posits a clean distinction between religion and politics. Beneath a secularist ideology, Stout maintains, religion has always in fact played important public roles in the rich and variegated practices that constitute the "democratic tradition" as it has been lived historically – at least in the United States, the focus of his study. In the terms I develop here, Stout argues that secularists and their opponents are both captured within a modern secular imaginary that takes the separation of "politics" and "religion" as an accomplished fact, whereas contemporary politics is marked instead by the intersection of these fields. For Stout, as for me, the task in approaching secularism is to understand precisely how religion and politics intersect, constitute, and reconstitute each other within modern liberal democracies.

With such debates in mind, this book employs a relatively circumspect concept of secularization, in which secularization refers to a transformation of the multiple relations between religion and morality, politics, economics, science, and art. In this view, secularization does not refer to the emergence of a new secular order from a prior religious order. Instead it names a process whereby both "the religious" and "the secular" are constructed as opposed but nonetheless constitutively interrelated domains. The secular and the religious, in other words, form two sides of a single process of secularization that continuously shapes and recreates both. In the course of the Protestant Reformation, for example, Martin Luther argued for the importance of a strong secular authority but precisely with the understanding that such an authority would serve to manage and limit theological disputes. The Protestant Reformation, in such a view, did not simply remove religion from public life but rather redistributed power and authority between newly emerging forms of politics and religion. In this view, it is not the case that modernity is constituted as the overcoming of religion but rather that the very concepts of "religious" and "secular" are produced with distinctly modern grammars through a process of secularization.

If the secularization thesis is particularly at home in the discipline of sociology, "secularity" is more typically the subject of philosophy and increasingly of anthropology. Rather than a transformational process, secularity refers to the specific qualities that mark certain forms of thought, speech, and conduct in their difference from religious or pious forms. Enlightenment idioms stretching from Descartes to Kant emphasize the qualities of a mind that dares to think for itself, to produce knowledge with its own authority, and to criticize dogma and tradition, all of which are often taken to be constitutive of modern secularity (*avant la lettre*). To these are often added historical consciousness, worldliness, and self-reflectiveness. Although Jürgen Habermas and John Rawls have typically shifted attention to the public or intersubjective dimensions of secularity, their arguments are nonetheless consistent with an enlightenment heritage that marks public or communicative reason in its difference from religious or theological discourses. In counterpoint to philosophical valorizations, similar qualities of speech, thought, and conduct have been construed in a variety of religious or theological idioms as incoherent, ungrounded, naive, faithless, corrupt, debased, egotistical, self-glorifying, bankrupt, mutilated, and nihilistic.[11] The precise nature and value of modern secularity remain topics of research and debate, and the anthropologist Talal Asad has persuasively argued that the study of secularity is only now at its very beginning.[12] Insofar as it is aligned with modern social and philosophical developments, it is difficult to disentangle secularity from the process of secularization – for if there is such a thing as modern secularity, it must be intimately bound with the process of secularization.

In Euro-American contexts, "secularism" is often framed alongside political liberalism as an outgrowth of the regimes of religious toleration, and in such commonplace narratives, secular liberalism appears on the world stage as part of the political resolution to the wars of faith that followed the Protestant Reformation in the sixteenth and seventeenth centuries.[13] By way of contrast with "secularization" and "secularity,"

---

[11] Charles Taylor, *A Secular Age*; Stanley Hauwerwas, *The Hauerwas Reader*; Alasdair MacIntyre, *After Virtue*; John Milbank, *Theology & Social Theory*.
[12] Talal Asad, *Formations of the Secular*.
[13] The emergence of modern secularism, however, may also be framed within a number of competing historical narratives. It has, for example, been analyzed as a function of state formation. In such a view, the imperatives of neutrality toward religious differences emerged in the seventeenth century as responses to the turmoil of confessionalization begun in the sixteenth century. Superseding the principle of *cuius regio eius religio* (roughly, "who rules a territory decides its religion"), a nascent secular state emerged blind to its subjects' religious beliefs and practices and foreswore forcible interference with the individual consciences of its subjects in pursuit of its own interests. The state would also intervene to prevent religious associations from exercising forms of coercive power, reserving that prerogative for itself. Secularism has been cast as the product of changing political discourses. In this view, faced with the obstinate fact of religious difference, a sociopolitical vocabulary free of the principles of heresy, schism, apostasy, and scandal evolved, thereby obviating the options of persecution and forced conversion as a resolution for the forms of deep doctrinal conflict named by these principles. Shifting to still another perspective, broad patterns of sociability shifted as a correlate of this transformed political discourse. And in this view, secularism emerged as truth began to enter public contests in a different fashion, aligned with probability, tempered by skepticism, and mediated by the toleration of difference. As a result, civility flourished as a regulative norm for public intercourse as modern republican theories, practices, and sensibilities were invented and disseminated. From a theological- or church-historical perspective, the Protestant Reformation has been

secularism is ordinarily taken as the proper name for political doctrines and institutional ensembles that impose and enforce barriers between religion and the other domains of social life largely in accord with the patterns differentiating the public and the private. It is reducible neither to secularization nor to secularity but is enmeshed with both: secularism is both a cause and an effect of processes of secularization; it both depends upon and reproduces secularity. The points at which secularism mediates the relation between religion and other spheres of social life are myriad: Secularism shapes the development of law by determining which authorities will decide which questions in accordance with which canons of reason based on the interpretation of which texts (disputes are particularly acute, for example, in the case of laws regulating marriage in places such as Israel and Egypt but also in the United States). Secularism shapes education by determining which institutions will receive state funding, and which texts and traditions will be taught, by whom and in which manner. Secularism shapes social policy by determining what will count as legitimate factors in decision making, and which areas of society will be open for or closed to intervention. Secularism shapes religion itself by determining which of its practices and claims will be entitled to public respect and protection, which of its denominations will be recognized as legitimate and permissible, and which of its functions will be assimilated within the larger apparatus of governance.

Alexis de Tocqueville's account of secularism in *Democracy in America* is pertinent at this point. Tocqueville was one of the few pioneering social scientists of the nineteenth century to depart from the secularization thesis, and his analysis of American political culture dwells on its "marvelous combination" of what was elsewhere irreconcilable, namely "the spirit of religion and the spirit of freedom."[14] Far from declining, Tocqueville understood Christianity to be a key and ascendant force in American political culture, noting that "the religious atmosphere of the country was the first thing that struck me on arrival in the United

---

seen as independently initiating a shift in Christianity's focus away from community and sacrament toward the individual's unmediated and private relation to God, thus enabling the public and private distinction that underpins modern secularism. On these various approaches, see Kirstie McClure, "Difference, Diversity, and the Limits of Toleration"; John Marshall, *John Locke, Toleration and Early Enlightenment Culture*; Norbert Elias, *The Civilizing Process*; JGA Pocock, *Machiavellian Moment*; Quentin Skinner, *Foundations of Political Thought*; Ian Hacking, *Probability*; Patrick Collinson, *The Reformation*.

[14] Tocqueville, *Democracy in America*, Lawrence trans., 46.

States."[15] In Tocqueville's view, Christian mores provided the foundation of American democracy, but their power and durability were paradoxically derived from the lack of direct interference between religion and politics. "One cannot therefore say," in Tocqueville's view, "that in the United States religion influences the laws or political opinions in detail, but it does direct mores, and by regulating domestic life it helps regulate the state."[16] Tocqueville concluded that "religion, which never intervenes directly in the government of American society, should... be considered as the first of their political institutions, for although it did not give them the taste for liberty, it singularly facilitates their use thereof."[17] In Tocqueville's view, American politics is secular, in the sense of being devoid of direct religious influence, but the secularism of American institutions is rooted within a deeply religious culture.

The power of Tocqueville's analysis of nineteenth-century America, and the complexity of his appraisal of its democratic practices notwithstanding, his view that American secularism necessarily rests on Christian foundations is difficult to sustain – it is no longer clear that American political culture ever rested on the moral foundations of Protestant Christianity as he imagined; if it did, it is no longer clear that such a foundation could be found now, or that it would be desirable to do so. Nonetheless, it is worth noting that his analysis clearly differentiates a process of secularization (which unfolded with disastrous consequences in Europe, but has not unfolded in America), a condition of secularity (exemplified by the pragmatism and business sense typical of Americans), and institutions of secularism (which separate the activities and public authority of churches and the state). Tocqueville considers each of these dimensions individually, but he also understands that they are related and argues that they are of critical importance to American politics.

As much as it differs from Tocqueville's account, this book similarly alternates between disaggregating the disparate components of the problem of modern secularism and considering them in conjunction with one another. Although I refer to "the problem of secularism" or simply "modern secularism," this should be taken as a reference to a multifaceted process. The figure of conversion helps to acknowledge the different facets of the problem of secularism, as well as the importance of treating them in their mutual relations, of understanding them to be suspended in what

---

[15] Tocqueville, *Democracy in America*, 295.
[16] Tocqueville, *Democracy in America*, 291.
[17] Tocqueville, *Democracy in America*, 292.

will be called crystalline formation. Figuring secularism as a process of conversion suggests that certain dimensions of secularity depend upon narrating the process of secularization in specific ways, and that this dependence in turn conditions approaches to secularism's contemporary institutional forms. These loose outlines can be traced more clearly after introducing the figure of conversion.

The Figure of Conversion

It would be a mistake to deny the polysemy of conversion, for there are in fact many different kinds of conversion. Conversion takes place between religions, between denominations, and as the intensification of practice within a single tradition. Conversions may be quick, slow, forced, chosen, feigned, and partial. Conversion varies in medieval monasticism, in Puritan New England, in philosophy, in contemporary American mega-churches, in the course of scientific revolutions, and so on.[18] Nonetheless, from the disparate range of experiences collected under the idea of conversion, this book will develop a figure of conversion that has three key dimensions. First, it entails a significant transformation of the self. Second, it re-situates an individual in relation to a community, or a community in relation to a larger tradition or collective; it entails joining, leaving, affirming, or rearticulating a collectivity. Third, it requires the production of a new self-narrative, which both catalyzes and consolidates the experience of conversion by retrospectively marking a moment of discontinuity, change, or rebirth within the convert's life course, and naming this as the moment of conversion.[19] As developed here, a theory of conversion foregrounds a significant – even radical – transformation of individuals and collectivities, in their relation to communities, mediated by retrospective narratives that contribute to the formation and undoing of these individuals, collectivities, and communities. As developed here, these three dimensions of conversion are

---

[18] Some of this variety is captured in the following exemplary studies: Susan Harding, *The Book of Jerry Falwell*; Comaroff and Comaroff, *Of Revolution and Revelation*; Gauri Viswanathan, *Outside the Fold*; Hefner, *Christian Conversion*; Eliza Kent, *Converting Women*; Rob Wilson, *Be Always Converting, Be Always Converted*; Michael Warner, *The Evangelical Public Sphere in Eighteenth-Century America*.

[19] Incidentally, this third dimension may differentiate the modes of conversion documented by Hadot in the context of ancient philosophical schools from the Christian practices of conversion that would follow; as the next chapter argues, Augustine's *Confessions* made a pivotal contribution to the figure of conversion in its powerful rearticulation of the conversion narrative.

distributed across two distinct layers: conversion adjusts the complex, composite structures of identity through the amendment of habit as a deep, crystalline process of transformation; conversion narratives project a simplified image of this transformative process upon an authorized surface.[20]

Although a figure of conversion could be abstracted from the religious traditions to which it is often consigned, maintaining an appreciation for the connection between this concept and the religious archive from which it is drawn helps to reframe the larger problem of secularism's relation to religious traditions, and its relation to what has been called the theological-political problematic. It is important to note that many traditions have developed and deployed concepts of conversion and to ask at the beginning why, for example, a medieval Islamic figure of conversion would not serve as well for the analysis of modern secularism?[21] Or why not the conversion of Jews in Europe or of colonial subjects outside of Europe? Or why not use all these cases to open up the problem of secularism comparatively? It is not sufficient to answer that such territory is explored elsewhere or to plead that any book, this one included, must limit its scope – although both are true. This book is about the modern Euro-American secular imaginary because this formation dominates Euro-America and because it is often presumed to be appropriate globally. I draw from Augustine because he articulates the pivotal concept of conversion for the traditions of Christianity that have been of decisive importance for the emergence of modern secularism. That modern secularism is Euro-American, and that Euro-America is Christian, are doubtless assumptions strongly tinged by ideology, but it is this very ideological, or imaginary, dimension that the concept of conversion is meant to probe. To put this another way, this book argues that secularism can no longer be understood as a separation from religion, but it seeks to avoid the most obvious alternative to this commonplace understanding, which is that secularism is merely an outgrowth or continuation of religion. To argue that secularism does not simply continue European Christianity, one might look for alternative sources or influences and pursue the comparative gesture by looking at alternative connections between

---

[20] For a full explanation of the "crystalline" structures, see Chapter Three. For a full explanation of the work of narrative in producing an "authorized" surface, see Chapter One.

[21] I thank Roxanne Euben for suggesting a comparative approach; although I do not ultimately follow this suggestion, the invitation to consider why one would or would not proceed this way has been very helpful.

modern secularism and Judaism, Islam, Buddhism, or Confucianism, for example – to be sure, European Christianity has been made and remade in connection with non-European traditions. Or one might pursue this book's strategy, which is to accept the connection between secularism and Christianity, to say that secularism *is* conversion, and conversion in Augustine's sense, but to insist that religion, Christianity, and conversion themselves be redefined. To figure secularism as a process of conversion is not to disinter the encrypted Christian origins of modernity. It is rather to rethink the ways in which the categories of "the secular" and "the religious" are continually reconstructed, and to rethink the contemporary contents of both categories as well. It is not a question of secularism's being Christian or not Christian (religious or not religious) but a question rather of deconstructing the very opposition between the secular and the Christian (the secular and the religious) that authorizes the figure of separation and underpins the modern secular imaginary in the hope of imagining and practicing secularism in new, less restrictive ways.

This is not merely a formal argument about concepts and categories and not simply an exercise in literary or philosophical deconstruction; it is concretely and historically grounded in tradition and practice. If Christianity is at best a family-resemblance concept in Wittgenstein's sense, within this family, theology, practice, spirituality, and rhetoric tend to be intimately bound up with the figure of conversion.[22] Pauline theology, in which the essence of religious experience lies in the transformative capacity of the Christ's death and resurrection, is grounded upon conversion. Likewise, Augustine's pivotal articulations of personal sin, will, and faith, as well as the appropriate disciplinary functions of the church, are lodged in his own personal conversion story and in his experience enforcing conversion as the bishop of a fractious church. Conversion formed the basis for medieval monasticism and the rite of entry for early Christian communities as well as many modern formations.[23] It has also played a pivotal role in missionary activities and in religious persecutions. Like those of Paul and Augustine, Martin Luther's biography and theology would be tied strongly to the reimagination and reactivation of conversion, a turn that would be fateful for the modes of protestant Christianity that followed. It is no exaggeration to say that conversion

---

[22] See Ludwig Wittgenstein, *Philosophical Investigations*, para. 67.
[23] St. Bernard of Clairvaux, *On Conversion*; Talal Asad, *Genealogies of Religion*; Jean Leclercq, *Monks and Love in Twelfth-Century France*; Karl F. Morrison, *Conversion and Text*, vol. 1–2.

permeates the historical and contemporary textures of Christianity. *The Oxford Companion to Christian Thought*'s entry for *conversion* provides the following lucid summary of its central place:

> Conversion is at once the most common and the most controverted of Christian concepts... There is no account of saintly (or model) Christian life that does not include an account of that life's beginning – that is, of conversion to Jesus Christ and to his rule or Kingdom... [All the] apostles, saints, mystics, and martyrs not only had to endure to the end but had also to begin the life of faith, and the name of that beginning is conversion... Typically, it involves a change in the self over a period of time, though recognition that one is converted may focus upon a few inner choices or outward events. It is more than a mere development or series of developments, however. It is a transformation of the human self and its world that issues in a change of course and direction... For the individual, conversion shapes the convert's world-view, directing judgements and forming character. As a communal and historical phenomenon, conversion imparts to a group or movement a thematic character by which it explores its origins and measures its developments, successes, and failures.[24]

Although the history of Christianity is bound up with the concept of conversion, the concept of conversion was neither produced by Christianity nor has it been it exhausted by it.

The classicist Pierre Hadot places the concept of conversion in a longer view by attending to Christianity's birth in the collision of Jewish, Greek, and Roman traditions and by recovering the importance of practices of conversion within each of these traditions. Hadot reminds his readers that ancient philosophy was not constituted primarily as a body of knowledge but rather as a distinct "way of life" requiring an individual's "existential decision" to enter upon it as well as a series of practices undertaken to cultivate his or her commitment to it. Bodies of knowledge were key elements of ancient philosophical traditions, but practices of philosophy extended well beyond any systematic collection of doctrines. "The [ancient] philosophical school thus corresponds," for Hadot, "to the choice of a certain way of life and existential option which demands from the individual a total change of lifestyle, a conversion of one's entire being, and ultimately a certain desire to be and to live in a certain way."[25] According to Hadot, ancient philosophical schools required an existential decision and a conversion from their adherents: "if they were genuine philosophers... they must have been converted – that is, they had to profess philosophy, and make a choice of life which obliged

---

[24] Adrian Hastings, *Encyclopedia of Christianity*.
[25] Pierre Hadot, *What Is Ancient Philosophy?*, 3.

them to change all aspects of their behavior in the world, and which, in a certain sense, separated them from the world."[26] Those who practiced philosophy in pre-Christian Greece and Rome relied upon discipline and technique to effect a turn from worldly affairs sufficient to constitute their conversion. Far from representing a radical innovation, Hadot argues that many of the practices devoted to enabling Christian conversions were inherited from the spiritual exercises that enabled earlier practices of philosophy.

The interrelation of Christian practice and ancient philosophy stands in need of careful articulation; Michel Foucault, for example, dissented from a number of the specific connections Hadot draws between Christian and pre-Christian practices.[27] Translating Hadot's arguments about ascetic and spiritual practices from pre-Christian antiquity to early modernity, Ian Hunter's *Rival Enlightenments* investigates the competition between schools in the German university system. According to Hunter, "attending to the self-formative functions of the enlightenment philosophies provides an appropriate setting for a theme long discussed by historians of theology and, more recently, by cultural and intellectual historians: namely, that there is no sharp break between these philosophies and Christian theology, and no epochal shift from a religious age to a secular 'age of reason.'"[28] Hunter finds it more accurate to emphasize the entanglement of enlightenment and religion than the emergence of one from the other. More to the point here, where Hadot shows conversion to precede Christianity, Hunter shows it to appear within enlightenment practices that attend the decline of Christian intellectual, spiritual, and cultural hegemony in Europe. He argues that understanding the reconfiguration of early modern religious and political culture depends in part on understanding the practical cultivation of specific dispositions by adherents of divergent philosophical schools.[29]

---

[26] Pierre Hadot, *What Is Ancient Philosophy?*, 247.
[27] Michel Foucault, *Hermeneutics of the Subject*, 205–29; see also Talal Asad, *Genealogies of Religion* and *Formations of the Secular*.
[28] Ian Hunter, *Rival Enlightenments*, 25.
[29] See Hunter, *Rival Enlightenments*, 24. Without dissenting from the results of Hunter's remarkable study, my own argument here differs not only in historical context but also in emphasis. Where Hunter is concerned primarily with the "means through which certain individuals forge the relation to the self – that is, as different forms in which individuals cross the threshold of subjectivity and learn to deport themselves as subjects of particular kinds," the problem of conversion focuses attention on social and public formations rather than the individual and private formations highlighted in Hunter's analysis.

The general thrust of Hadot's argument, at any rate, is shared by Foucault and Hunter: important strains of the Christian, Hellenistic, and Enlightenment traditions employed practices of conversion to cultivate certain intellectual, spiritual, and ethical characteristics within individuals and collectivities. These traditions employed a range of techniques directed toward transforming the self, including but not limited to critical introspection and spoken confessions, the use of written journals, meditations, and especially letters between friends that extended the possibilities of introspection while turning this practice toward public view. They also employed more expressly communal practices such as carefully staged encounters with exemplary figures and the application of comprehensive disciplinary regimes that incorporated the discouragement of some habits and the encouragement of others within daily life.[30] Across these formations, which are in many respects vastly different, practices of conversion were understood to shape certain types of individuals and enable particular forms of community.

Hadot argues quite plausibly that attention to conversion as self-transformation, which formed a central concern in ancient and early Christian ethics, has been relegated to the place of a minor tradition within modern philosophy, and I would add within the modern secular imaginary as well. In Foucault's terms, "Cartesian modernity" has privileged "knowledge of the self" at the expense of a larger category of practices of "care for the self," which encompass it, and which would include conversion. Hunter's study is premised on the claim that "attending to the self-formative functions of rival philosophies" requires a "shifting of the methodological axis of the history of philosophy" from its current general orientation to include the problem of conversion.[31] These theorists suggest that the conceptual vocabulary of conversion has been displaced as part of the process of transformation that produced the formation of modern secularism, to which I would add that the displaced figure of conversion presents an important key to understanding this transformation. According to what could be called an authorized historical narrative, political modernity emerges along with powerful, centralized, bureaucratic states, which secure territories, regulate commerce, and manage populations but which sever ties to religious authorities and cease to

---

[30] Two recent anthropological studies of character formation in Islamic traditions provide invaluable insight into these processes in contemporary non-Christian contexts; see Charles Hirschkind, *The Ethical Soundscape*, and Saba Mahmood, *The Politics of Piety*.
[31] Hunter, *Rival Enlightenments*, 23.

intervene in religious matters. In this authorized narrative, that is, the modern state emerges at the same time that political power ceases to be exercised for the purpose of forcing religious conversion; the liberal state emerges along with the protection of conscience and the ascendance of toleration. Along with the practices of forced conversion, the very idea of conversion is excluded from modern theories of politics but, ironically, the very transformations that produce modern states, nations, publics, and religions, in their distinctive forms, can and should be described as a process of conversion, and as a process that obscures its own nature as a process of conversion.

The modern secular imaginary is impoverished once by excluding conversion from consideration, for the concept of conversion presents an important way of thinking about the transformation of individuals and communities in general, but it is impoverished a second time insofar as the concept of conversion presents an important key for thinking about the specific transformations that produce and sustain modern secularism itself. The chapters of this book move back and forth between two tasks, therefore, describing conversion itself in a new way and describing secularism as conversion – my hope is that readers will come, by the end of the book, to think about conversion differently and that they will also come to think about secularism a bit differently as well. To put that somewhat less modestly, this book tries to think past one of modernity's most familiar distinctions, the distinction between the secular and the religious, because that distinction seems to get in the way of answers to important questions, because it seems to be more ideological and misleading than it is helpful, and because the mode of secularism it sustains often seems to stand in the way of more genuinely democratic practices. It tries to get past this distinction by willfully violating it, by borrowing the language of religion to redescribe the secular, and by using the idea of religious conversion to better understand the secular itself, more precisely, both the politics of the secular, as the politics that produce and sustain secularism, and also secular politics, as the kind of politics most commonly associated with contemporary democratic institutions.

The Structure of the Book

The following chapters present a series of engagements with two complex and multifaceted problems: "conversion" and "secularism." Throughout, however, the figure of conversion is subservient to the problem of secularism, and the importance of conversion lies in its capacity to show something new and important about secularism, so that one problem is introduced in the service of another. This book's ambition – to develop a new view on secularism – should be balanced against an acknowledgment that its scope is necessarily limited and that the claims it makes are clearly contestable even within its scope. Insofar as the refigured version of secularism as a process of crystalline conversion that I imagine here moves strongly toward what William E. Connolly has described as a deep and multidimensional pluralism, a sense of modesty about one's arguments is not only intellectually important but important too in an ethical-political register.[32] My argument is not intended to be comprehensive – there is a good deal more to say about conversion and secularism. Nor is it intended, necessarily, to be definitive, to be what Charles Taylor has called a "knock-down argument" – the perspective proposed here does not necessarily preclude or obviate other approaches, but it does seek to present an important alternative to the authorized discourses of secularism.[33]

If this book's argument is in some ways unusual, there is a definite reason: *Secularism as we now know it has to do in large part with the ways in which we conduct public arguments* – including the texts and authorities that can be invoked, the extent of the commitments that are opened to contestation, the rhetorical forms that are employed, and the skills and practices of critical thought or reasoning that will count as legitimate.[34] To think about the problem of secularism suggests, in my view, thinking again about the ways in which we can and should argue with one another. Because so much of the problem of secularism concerns the ways in which we argue, two of the chapters that follow are devoted explicitly to analyzing the complex rhetorics of modern secularism developed in an early case by John Locke and in a late case by John Rawls. But as important as that kind of work is, analyzing the rhetoric of authorized secular discourses does not yet get to the bottom of the problem as I see

---

[32] Rethinking and deepening the problem of "pluralism" is one of the central themes throughout Connolly's work – his arguments here are perhaps most accessible in *The Ethos of Pluralization, Why I Am Not a Secularist*, and *Pluralism*.

[33] Charles Taylor, *Philosophical Papers*.

[34] In addition to the key contemporary theories of secular public discourse, see John Rawls's *Political Liberalism* and Jürgen Habermas's *Theory of Communicative Discourse*; for a range of approaches to this point, see Amanda Anderson, *The Way We Argue Now*; Victoria Kahn, *Wayward Contracts*; Saba Mahmood, *The Politics of Piety*; Michael Warner, "Uncritical Reading."

it, and it is important for me to say a few words about the rhetorical construction of this text as well.

Answering the initial question, *How does one seriously and responsibly make an argument about the ways in which we in the modern secular world make arguments?*, then, is anything but a tangential or minor concern.[35] This question reappears throughout the text, most prominently in discussions of Locke, Rawls, and Cavell, but also noticeably in discussions of Augustine and Bergson. The discipline of political theory suggests a few ready-made ways of constructing an argument. With only a bit of caricature: One possibility is to write a "history of political thought," which demands synchronic attention to arguments in their discursive contexts and allows a survey of their diachronic development across carefully controlled fields of dispersion. This is to ask who has written what, what those writings meant to say, and how they have shaped or been shaped by what somebody else has written. Another possibility is to develop a "normative political theory," which would focus instead on what we *should* say and do now. Holding to the spirit if not the letter of David Hume's fateful injunction that none of its desired "oughts" can be derived from what "is" ready at hand, normative theories tend to dispense with any serious treatment of history, seeing it as a species of "is" – a subaltern species at that, a mere "has been." Histories of political thought, for their part, often seem to suggest that it is presumptuous or obtuse (or both) to make claims about what one *should* do. Responding in part to pressure that comes from its subject – taking on the burden of making an argument about argument – and in part simply following the example of those many scholars whose work does not fit this caricatured division of labor, this book tries to do things a third way. It aims to take stock of present historical circumstances; to think about how things have gotten to be the way they are and about where they seem to be going; and to try to intervene critically, in a way that suggests how things might be made to go somewhat differently. In a very minimal sense, conversion too implies the necessity of finding out where one is, as a condition for moving in another direction. Most roads are probably bumpy – this third road certainly was, and it has taken years of reading and talking across disciplines – traces of research in such fields as religious studies, anthropology, sociology, comparative literature, history, philosophy, and

---

[35] An exchange between Richard Rorty and Nicholas Wolterstorff brings this point to light very clearly. See Rorty, "Religion as a Conversation-Stopper," and Wolterstorff, "An Engagement with Rorty."

of course a bit of political science are strewn along the way. My hope is that the result might interest readers from these disciplines as well.

All told then, this book neither presents a detailed account of how discourses on secularism got to be the way they are nor makes an ambitious case about what secularism should be – although it engages with both ways of thinking. The argument consciously avoids reproducing a narrative of the emergence of modern secularism in the manner of G. W. F. Hegel, Marcel Gauchet, Owen Chadwick, and Charles Taylor.[36] Nor does it attempt to say what secularism should be in the manner of Immanuel Kant, John Rawls, Jürgen Habermas, and Robert Audi.[37] Although this book engages a series of thinkers in a chronological order, it produces neither a narrative history of secularism nor arguments for or against the positions advocated by the philosophers it engages. It tries instead to make a number of pointed interventions that draw from a minor tradition of thought about secularism – within the writings of Augustine, Bergson, and Cavell – and that draw out the minoritarian trajectories in theories of secularism proper – within the writings of Locke and Rawls. What holds these chapters together, then, is not a single story line, a single historical process, a single tradition, or a single line of argument but instead a figure – conversion – and the ways in which this figure can help us to think in different ways about one of today's problems: secularism.

To say that secularism is an essentially contested concept is to acknowledge more broadly that contemporary secular practices and institutions are troubled by the sociological conditions in which they are situated, and that theories of modern secularism are generally compromised by the complex historical and philosophical inheritances they seek to comprise.[38] But that is only a premise, and this book goes further to suggest something concrete about the ways in which secularism is compromised and the kind of trouble in which it finds itself. To suggest that secularism is a process of conversion is to argue that the commonplace image of secularism as the separation of church and state, and the

---

[36] Charles Taylor, *A Secular Age*; Marcel Gauchet, *The Disenchantment of the World*; G. W. F. Hegel, *Lectures on the Philosophy of History*.
[37] John Rawls, *Political Liberalism*; Jürgen Habermas, *Between Naturalism and Religion*; Immanuel Kant, *Conflict of the Faculties* and "An Answer to the Question."
[38] José Casanova's *Public Religions in the Modern World* served as an important reminder to sociologists and scholars more broadly of religion's persistence in defiance of the classical "secularization thesis," and Hent de Vries's recent edited volume, *Religion The Concept*, gives some sense of the complex terrain marked out by contemporary philosophical engagements with religion.

commonplace narrative that presents secularism as it emerges through a break with the premodern, religious past, both contribute to the constitution of secularism in its modern form and at the same time obscure the larger processes that reshape "religion," "politics," and "secularism," the larger processes that demand, enable, and in turn grow from the contribution of image and narrative. A modern secular imaginary, which projects an authorized image of secularism as the separation of church and state, catalyzes, falsifies, propels, and undermines the crystalline process of modern secularism. Conversion narratives, which project a "new man" separate from the "old man," catalyze, falsify, propel, and undermine the process of conversion. Explaining the work of conversion, this book argues, can help to explain the work of modern secularism.

The concept of conversion, drawn as it is from a specifically religious archive, opens new insight into the predicament of modern secularism, and it may also open unexpected possibilities for thinking about its future. Part of what the concept of conversion contributes is a certain savvy about the work of narrative in constructing identities (individual and group alike). Although the work of narrative in shaping a secular identity is in many ways akin to the problem of fetishization identified by Marx, as he is interpreted by Lukacs, and familiar to theorists working in the critical tradition, I will argue that this work is more precisely captured in Augustine's *Confessions*, Bergson's *The Two Sources of Morality and Religion*, and Cavell's *The Claim of Reason*. Lukacs' famous argument about reification in *History and Class Consciousness* was, after all, inspired by Bergson. Without denying that the concepts of "fetishization" and "reification" drawn from a Marxian archive open important dimensions of the problem of modern secularism to view, my claim is that the figure of conversion discloses new and important facets of the problem; the process of conversion, as Augustine, Bergson and Cavell show, depends upon and exceeds the work of narrative in a very particular fashion. My claim is that the process of conversion they describe maps the process of modern secularism, and the engagements with Locke and Rawls serve both to explain and to verify that claim. Beyond thematizing the work of narrative, however, to invoke the concept of conversion is to challenge assumptions about secularism at a more fundamental level. To figure secularism as conversion is to foreground and in some sense to challenge the fundamental gesture of separating "the secular" and "the religious."

This argument unfolds across five chapters: The first, third, and fifth chapters engage Augustine, Bergson, and Cavell, respectively, as exemplary philosophers of conversion – these chapters work to present a new way of thinking about conversion. Conversion occupies a place at the center of each thinker's work, and these studies each draw a different dimension of the figure into focus – the study of Augustine brings narrative into focus, the study of Bergson highlights transformation, and my reading of Cavell foregrounds the problem of community. The second and fourth chapters engage Locke and Rawls, respectively, as representatives of the main stream of secular theory – together with the fifth chapter, these chapters work to present secularism as conversion. Chapters Two and Four develop a rhetorical analyses of their texts that draw out the often suppressed role of conversion in the articulation of their pivotal contributions to the authorized theory of modern secularism as the separation of religion from politics.

Chapter One focuses on the importance and limitations of the narrative dimension of conversion in Augustine's *Confessions*, and translates this discussion into a critique of narrative accounts of the emergence of modern secularism through an engagement with Charles Taylor's *A Secular Age*. *Confessions*, the single most important and influential conversion narrative across Christian traditions, presents two contending images of conversion. It projects an authorized image of conversion, written in a smooth hand, which traces a narrative arc that leads Augustine from the condition of a sinner to that of a saint. But it also registers another form of conversion that punctuates and escapes this narrative structure. This second form, the crystalline form of conversion, appears in the margins, omissions, and contradictions of Augustine's text, testifying to the continuous oscillation between piety and sin, Christianity and paganism, holiness and carnality. This second form is more fugitive and complex than the authorized image of conversion. Where the first image is reducible to a narrative of instantaneous transformation through the grace of God, the second testifies to an unsteady modification of habit based on a repetitive, recurrent pattern and modulated by relations of kinship and community. This tension in the text of *Confessions* illustrates a more general feature of conversion: there can be no conversion experience without a conversion narrative, which retrospectively narrates and consolidates the experience, but conversion nonetheless depends on more complex transformations than the narrative form can accommodate. This chapter touches on the dimensions of transformation and community, but its central concern is to open to view the importance, as well as the necessary distortion, of conversion narratives, a point that the following chapters will carry on and develop further.

Chapter Two traces the authorized figure of separation back to an early document from the seventeenth century's debates about toleration, John Locke's *A Letter Concerning Toleration*.[39] Locke's text provides an influential articulation of the principle of separation in arguing that it is "above all things necessary to distinguish exactly the Business of Civil Government from that of Religion." However, closer inspection of Locke's writings on toleration show that these texts work to transform key dimensions of both political and religious life in a fashion that extends far beyond their mere separation. In addition to articulating a principle of separation, therefore, they serve as a register of modern secularism as a crystalline process that transforms religion and politics through the conversion of both. Tracing the figure of conversion through Locke's writings shows how they both recommend the exclusion of religious conversion from politics but also seek to enable a new form of conversion that would transform both religious and political practices. I argue that the rhetorical strategies embodied in Locke's *Letter* are key elements of a larger project of converting political and religious dispositions particular to secularism. This chapter begins to argue that grasping the importance of the often obscured transformational dimension of secularism can lead to better political judgments in contemporary politics.

Chapter Three turns to the work of Henri Bergson – a mathematician, philosopher, winner of the Nobel Prize for literature, and subject of a complex conversion to Christianity; the world's most influential intellectual at the beginning of the twentieth century; and now a somewhat obscure name in the history of philosophy – in order to pursue conversion as a transformation of the self. My reading of Bergson's largely neglected late work, *The Two Sources of Morality and Religion*, develops the more complex image of crystalline conversion introduced in the text of Augustine's *Confessions* by embracing the productivity of time; the multiplicity of the self; the articulacy of affect; and the deep pluralisms of the world of images, language, and thought. A range of highly specific Bergsonian concepts – which are key to the earlier writings upon which his fame rests – of emergent causality, sheets of time, memory-perception-affection circuits, and intuition contribute to an image of conversion as part of a multilayered, refractive, and crystalline process, the complexity and possibilities of which far exceed what is suggested by the linear form of the

---

[39] I by no means claim that Locke's text is the origin of the figure of separation (although it is sometimes treated this way) but argue instead that it represents an important and influential reiteration of this figure.

authorized conversion narrative. I turn to *The Two Sources*, however, to show how Bergson uses this philosophical apparatus to challenge the very distinction between religious and moral-political life at the core of the modern secular imaginary. In this same text, Bergson articulates a figure of conversion as the key to the spiritual, moral, and political innovations and transformations necessary for coping with the modern tendencies that would rend Europe in his lifetime, many of which continue to produce turmoil in global politics today.

Chapter Four, like the second chapter, turns to a rhetorical analysis, this time of near-contemporary texts, John Rawls's *A Theory of Justice* and *Political Liberalism*, to draw out the work of conversion within these paradigmatic texts of secular theory. Following the suggestive fact that Rawls appeared as "a saint" to many of his students and admirers, I show how his own conception of public reason as stripped of religious commitments and affects is insufficient to account for the forms of attachment stirred by his own personality and theory of justice. Rawls's texts are as central to the modern secular imaginary as Locke's texts, and close inspection shows once more that they mobilize a range of rhetorical, cognitive, and affective resources that secular theories purport to avoid or to consign to religious life. Focusing on the work of conversion registered in these texts suggests how certain aspects of religious conversion are reproduced within secularism as conversion, and perhaps within any moment of serious intellectual and social change. Here, the conceptual lens of conversion brings into focus affective attachments to secular principles and communities, as well as the transformative power and narrative complexity of these attachments.

Chapter Five engages the work of Stanley Cavell to pursue the connection between conversion and political community. Building again on a more complex figure of crystalline conversion drawn out in Augustine's and Bergson's writings, my reading of Cavell focuses on his injunction to wrestle with the forms of skeptical doubt peculiar to modern selves – doubts about the humanity of oneself and others; doubts about the intelligibility of one's own desires, commitments, claims, and responsibilities; doubts about the efficacy of communication; *and, most centrally, doubts about the very possibility of a genuinely democratic politics*. Similar in spirit to Bergson but much different in important details, Cavell's work foregrounds the narrowly intellectualist conception of political or public reason that is central to the main stream of secular theory, and it suggests that periodic reorientations, reaffirmations, and revisions of our fundamental commitments provide a necessary supplement to public reason.

Such reorientations are figured as moments of conversion, in which not only the self but also extant forms of community are called into question, and even radically reformulated.

Beginning with the counterintuitive suggestion that Cavell's work is continuous with the critical spirit of the early Marx, Chapter Five concludes by suggesting that a critical theory of politics might take new bearings today from the writings of John Locke. I follow Cavell's reading of Locke's *Second Treatise on Government*, which translates the problem of conversion from the field of toleration to that of potentially radical, democratic social change. I argue that the open-ended processes of conversion elaborated by Bergson and Cavell might present key insights into the possibility of stimulating more democratic modes of engagement and collective action. Such processes of conversion are not reducible to the play of religious faith, but neither are they articulable from within a contemporary secular vocabulary premised upon the disavowal of all ties to "the religious."

In conclusion, I briefly review the book's argument, show how it differs in fundamental ways from other accounts of modern secularism, and explain why the alternative I propose should be more conducive to fostering a genuinely democratic politics in the global condition of deep pluralism. I suggest that the very idea of secularism is in crisis today and that we may stand poised to move in a new direction toward a secularism beyond the separation of church and state. I conclude by arguing that refiguring secularism as a process of crystalline conversion may open this formation to a more genuinely democratic politics that acknowledges difference as the necessary and ineliminable basis of collective political action rather than marking difference as a condition to be regulated, contained, or overcome through the establishment of a single authoritative mode of public reason or through a single authoritative image of secularism.

Bibliography

Anderson, Amanda. *The Way We Argue Now: A Study in the Cultures of Theory*. Princeton, NJ: Princeton University Press, 2006.

Anidjar, Gil. "Secularism." *Critical Inquiry*. vol. 33, no. 1, 2006: 52–77.

Asad, Talal. *Formations of the Secular: Christianity, Islam, Modernity*. Palo Alto, CA: Stanford University Press, 2003.

Asad, Talal. *Genealogies of Religion: Discipline and Reasons of Power in Christianity and Islam*. Baltimore, MD: Johns Hopkins University Press, 1993.

Augustine. *The Confessions*. New York: Vintage, 1998.

Bernard of Clairvaux. *On Conversion, A Sermon to Clerics*. Kalamazoo, MI: Cistercian Publications, 1981.
Blumenberg, Hans. *The Legitimacy of the Modern Age*. Cambridge, MA: MIT Press, 1983.
Brown, Peter. *Augustine of Hippo: A Biography*. Berkeley: University of California Press, 2000.
Brown, Wendy. *Regulating Aversion: Tolerance in the Age of Identity and Empire*. Princeton, NJ: Princeton University Press, 2006.
Casanova, José. *Public Religions in the Modern World*. Chicago: University of Chicago Press, 1994.
Collinson, Patrick. *The Reformation: A History*. New York: Modern Library, 2004.
Comaroff, Jean, and John L. Comaroff. *Of Revelation and Revolution*. Chicago: University of Chicago Press, 1991.
Connolly, William E. *Pluralism*. Durham, NC: Duke University Press, 2006.
Connolly, William E. *The Ethos of Pluralization*. Minneapolis: University of Minnesota Press, 1995.
Connolly, William E. *The Terms of Political Discourse*. Princeton, NJ: Princeton University Press, 1983.
Connolly, William E. *Why I Am Not a Secularist*. Minneapolis: University of Minnesota Press, 2000.
Dreisbach, Daniel L. *Thomas Jefferson and the Wall of Separation between Church and State*. New York: New York University Press, 2002.
Elias, Norbert. *The Civilizing Process*. New York: Wiley-Blackwell, 2000.
Foucault, Michel. *The Hermeneutics of the Subject: Lectures at the Collège de France, 1981–1982*. New York: Palgrave-Macmillan, 2005.
Freccero, John. *Dante: The Poetics of Conversion*. Cambridge, MA: Harvard University Press, 2003.
Gallie, W. B. "Essentially Contested Concepts." *Proceedings of the Aristotelian Society*, vol. 56, 1956: 167–98.
Gauchet, Marcel. *The Disenchantment of the World: A Political History of Religion*. Princeton, NJ: Princeton University Press, 1997.
Habermas, Jürgen. *Between Naturalism and Religion: Philosophical Essays*. Cambridge: Polity Press, 2008.
Habermas, Jürgen. "Religion in the Public Sphere." *European Journal of Philosophy*, vol. 14, 2006: 1–25.
Hacking, Ian. *The Emergence of Probability*. Cambridge: Cambridge University Press, 2006.
Hadot, Pierre. *What Is Ancient Philosophy?* Cambridge, MA: Harvard University Press, 2002.
Hamburger, Philip. *Separation of Church and State*. Cambridge, MA: Harvard University Press, 2002.
Harding, Susan Friend. *The Book of Jerry Falwell: Fundamentalist Language and Politics*. Princeton, NJ: Princeton University Press, 2000.
Hastings, Adrian. *A World History of Christianity*. Grand Rapids, MI: W. B. Eerdmans, 2000.

Hauwerwas, Stanley. *The Hauerwas Reader*. Durham, NC: Duke University Press, 2001.

Hefner, Robert W. *Conversion to Christianity: Historical and Anthropological Perspectives on a Great Transformation*. Berkeley: University of California Press, 1993.

Hegel, Georg Wilhelm Friedrich. *Lectures on the History of Philosophy 1825–26*. New York: Dover Philosophical Classics, 2004.

Hirschkind, Charles. *The Ethical Soundscape: Cassette Sermons and Islamic Counterpublics*. New York: Columbia University Press, 2006.

Hunter, Ian. *Rival Enlightenments: Civil and Metaphysical Philosophy in Early Modern Germany*. Cambridge: Cambridge University Press, 2001.

Huntington, Samuel P. *The Clash of Civilizations and the Remaking of World Order*. New York: Simon & Schuster, 1996.

Jefferson, Thomas. "A Letter to the Danbury Baptists." 1802.

Kahn, Victoria Ann. *Wayward Contracts: The Crisis of Political Obligation in England, 1640–1674*. Princeton, NJ: Princeton University Press, 2004.

Kant, Immanuel. "An Answer to the Question: 'What Is Enlightenment?'" in *What is Enlightenment?: Eighteenth Century Answers and Twentieth Century Questions*. James Schmidt, ed. Berkeley: University of California Press, 1996: 58–64.

Kant, Immanuel. *The Conflict of the Faculties = Der Streit der Fakultäten*. New York: Abaris Books, 1979.

Kent, Eliza F. *Converting Women: Gender and Protestant Christianity in Colonial South India*. Oxford: Oxford University Press, 2004.

Leclercq, Jean. *Monks and Love in Twelfth-Century France: Psycho-Historical Essays*. Oxford: Clarendon Press, 1979.

MacIntyre, Alasdair. *After Virtue: A Study in Moral Theory*. Notre Dame, IN: University of Notre Dame Press, 2003.

Mahmood, Saba. *Politics of Piety: The Islamic Revival and the Feminist Subject*. Princeton, NJ: Princeton University Press, 2005.

Marshall, John. *John Locke, Toleration, and Early Enlightenment Culture: Religious Intolerance and Arguments for Religious Toleration in Early Modern and "Early Enlightenment" Europe*. Cambridge: Cambridge University Press, 2006.

McClure, Kirstie M. "Difference, Diversity, and the Limits of Toleration." *Political Theory*, vol. 18, no. 3, 1990: 361–91.

Milbank, John. *Theology and Social Theory: Beyond Secular Reason*. Cambridge: B. Blackwell, 1991.

Milbank, John, Catherine Pickstock, and Graham Ward, eds. *Radical Orthodoxy: A New Theology*. New York: Routledge, 1991.

Morrison, Karl Frederick. *Conversion and Text: The Cases of Augustine of Hippo, Herman-Judah, and Constantine Tsatsos*. Charlottesville: University Press of Virginia, 1992.

Pocock, John Greville Agard. *The Machiavellian Moment*. Princeton, NJ: Princeton University Press, 2003.

Rawls, John. *Political Liberalism*. New York: Columbia University Press, 1993.

Rorty, Richard. "Religion as a Conversation-Stopper." *Common Knowledge*, vol. 3, no. 1, 1994: 1–6.
Scherer, Matthew. "Landmarks in the Critical Study of Secularism." *Cultural Anthropology*, vol. 26, no. 4, November 2011: 621–32.
Scherer, Matthew. "Secularism." *The Encyclopedia of Political Thought*. Hoboken, NJ: Wiley-Blackwell.
Schmitt, Carl. *Political Theology: Four Chapters on the Concept of Sovereignty*. Cambridge, MA: MIT Press, 1985.
Skinner, Quentin. *The Foundations of Modern Political Thought*. Cambridge: Cambridge University Press, 1978.
Stepan, Alfred C. "Religion, Democracy, and the 'Twin Tolerations.'" *Journal of Democracy*, vol. 11, no. 4, 2000: 37–57.
Stout, Jeffrey. *Democracy and Tradition*. Princeton, NJ: Princeton University Press, 2004.
Sullivan, Winnifred Fallers. *The Impossibility of Religious Freedom*. Princeton, NJ: Princeton University Press, 2007.
Taylor, Charles. *A Secular Age*. Cambridge, MA: Belknap Press, 2007.
Taylor, Charles. *Philosophical Papers*. Cambridge: Cambridge University Press, 1985.
Tocqueville, Alexis de. *Democracy in America*. New York: Harper Collins, 1969.
Viswanathan, Gauri. *Outside The Fold: Conversion, Modernity, and Belief*. Princeton, NJ: Princeton University Press, 1998.
Vries, Hent de, ed. *Religion: Beyond a Concept*. New York: Fordham University Press, 2008.
Warner, Michael. *The Evangelical Public Sphere in Eighteenth-Century America*. Philadelphia: University of Pennsylvania Press, forthcoming.
Warner, Michael. "Uncritical Reading," in *Polemic: Critical or Uncritical*. Jane Gallop, ed. New York: Routledge, 2004: 13–38.
Weber, Max. *The Protestant Ethic and the Spirit of Capitalism*. New York: Routledge, 2001.
Wilson, Rob. *Be Always Converting, Be Always Converted: An American Poetics*. Cambridge, MA: Harvard University Press, 2009.
Wittgenstein, Ludwig. *Wittgenstein: The Philosophical Investigations*. London: Macmillan, 1968.
Wolterstorff, Nicholas. "An Engagement with Rorty." *Journal of Religious Ethics*, vol. 31, no. 1, 2003: 129–39.

I

Authorized Narrative and Crystalline Structure
Conversion in Augustine's Confessions

> This is another way in which the story of how we got here is inextricably bound up with our account of where we are, which has been a structuring principle of this work throughout.
> – Charles Taylor[1]

> I don't profess to understand why my beliefs changed, or believe it is possible fully to comprehend such changes. We can record what happened, tell stories and make guesses, but they must be taken as such. There may be something in them, but probably not.
> – John Rawls[2]

Conversion has signified the radical transformation of a human life, splitting that life in two, a life before and a life after conversion, from the time of St. Paul's letters and, indeed, long before this time. In the wake of Paul's interpretation, conversion has attained a constitutive importance for Christian traditions, for any mode of Christianity figured as a religion of transformative faith in Jesus as the Messiah, quite possibly from the beginning of these traditions, and most certainly throughout many of their medieval and modern formations. Conversion is a Christian phenomenon, but theories of conversion – "metanoia" in Classical Greek of the Athenian age as well as the Koine of the *New Testament* – are at least coextensive with a much older tradition that begins with Plato, whose *Republic* allegorizes the life of the philosopher as a series of conversions,

---

[1] Charles Taylor, *A Secular Age*, 772.
[2] John Rawls, "On My Religion," 261.

so that conversion is not only a Christian phenomenon.³ A complete genealogy of conversion in Western thought would pass down through the beginning of Christian time into its prehistory, and it would extend outward to trace the connections between Western Christianity and its historical others; it would take many volumes to even begin to follow these connections and transformations. Instead of tracing its historical connections, this book takes the centrality of conversion to "religious" experience as uncontroversial; given that, it argues that the figure of conversion may also be important today for understanding "secular" experience, as well as the fraught relation between the secular and the religious.

This chapter begins by examining the intersection of conversion, secularism, and narrative in an important recent text, Charles Taylor's *A Secular Age*. Taylor has intervened at a fundamental level in unfolding debates about modern secularism, arguing that secularism cannot be understood as the separation – what he calls the "subtraction" – of religion from modernity but that it represents rather the continuation of the Western Christian tradition.⁴ Within Euro-America, this must be true in some sense, but it makes every difference how the continuity that Taylor posits and, indeed, how Christianity itself is understood. This chapter engages Taylor's account of modern secularism by turning to the intersection of conversion and narrative in a classical text of the Christian tradition – Augustine's *Confessions*. A close reading of *Confessions* reveals dimensions of the relationship between conversion and narrative that complicate the continuous relation between Christianity and secularism presented by Taylor. Indeed, this chapter uses the text of *Confessions* to show how the category of "modernity" deployed by contemporary theories of secularism is produced and sustained by a special kind of conversion narrative, and it suggests that the modernity in which we actually live is produced by a much more complex and multifaceted process of conversion than this narrative can capture. It takes a detour through a

---

³ See the beginning of book seven of Plato's *Republic* (514a–519d) for the "allegory of the cave," in which Plato repeatedly figures education as turning the soul around, that is, as conversion.

⁴ Such an interpretation is at least as old as G. W. F. Hegel's *Lectures on the Philosophy of History*, which argues that *"the last stage in History, our world, our own time"* is one in which "Secular life is the positive and definite embodiment of the Spiritual Kingdom" such that "what has happened, and is happening every day, is not only not 'without God,' but is essentially His Work" (442, 457). Its broad rubric includes the otherwise diverse work of Max Weber, Carl Schmitt, Karl Löwith, Hans Blumenberg, John Rawls, Jurgen Habermas, Marcel Gauchet, Robert Bellah, David Martin, Samuel Huntington, and many more.

key early Christian text to loosen Western Christianity's hold on modern secularism and to rethink the possibilities and limitations imposed by the historical connections between Christianity and secularism.

There are three critical steps to this argument. First, an overarching conversion narrative shapes the modern secular imaginary, which permeates popular consciousness and public discourse, and which is embedded in the key texts of the modern secular tradition by Taylor, John Rawls, and John Locke, which will be considered here and in the following chapters. Second, the particular figure of conversion that shapes the modern secular imaginary is a partial and, in many ways, a deficient representation of the process of conversion. Third, the modern secular imaginary can and should be revised to incorporate a more complex figure of conversion, which I call *crystalline conversion*.[5] The figure of conversion that shapes conventional theories of secular modernity – that of a break and a rupture through which the new is separated from the old and the old is consigned to the past – may be essential to the process of conversion, but it represents only a relatively small part of the complex, crystalline process of conversion as it has evolved within the Western tradition. The idea of a crystalline process of conversion is not new, for its outlines are traced in the text of Augustine's *Confessions*. However, the crystalline structure of conversion is obscured by the partial image of conversion that informs today's secular imaginary: indeed, *Confessions* prefigures and discloses this irreducible tension between the crystalline process of conversion and the conversion narratives that represent this process in a simplified form. This tension is a chief characteristic of modern secularism, which is in part, but not in whole, a matter of separating religion from politics. Although contemporary theories present secularism as the outcome of a process of conversion, they do so tacitly and on the basis of an insufficient figure of conversion; this chapter begins to argue expressly that modern secularism should itself be understood as a process of conversion, provided that this is understood as a process of crystalline conversion.

This chapter is divided into four parts. The first part shows the importance of narrative to the process of conversion and argues that Taylor's *Secular Age* narrates the story of modern secularism as a story of conversion. The second part identifies what I call an *authorized figure of conversion*, which is written in the smooth narrative hand of Augustine's

---

[5] "Crystalline" here suggests a process that is multifaceted and layered. For fuller explanation of the concept of crystalline structure, see Chapter Three.

Confessions. It suggests that this authorized figure is recapitulated by contemporary theories of secularism, including Taylor's. The third part outlines the more complex figure of crystalline conversion introduced immediately before, as it is inscribed within the rough texture and margins of *Confessions*' smooth narrative. It suggests that this more complex figure might provide the basis for a more accurate theorization of modern secularism. The fourth part ties these threads together to show how a crystalline figure of conversion presents a theoretical basis on which to complicate and supplement key dimensions of the leading theories of modern secularism, exemplified here by Taylor's *Secular Age*.

Conversion, Narrative, and Secularism: A *Secular Age* as Conversion Narrative

While narration is simply a matter of telling stories, or perhaps because it is such a rudimentary phenomenon, there seem to be endless approaches to narrative – indeed, the humanities could be conceived as the study of narrative, and perhaps also the social sciences, as well as the sciences proper. Given the complexity of the field, Aristotle's *Poetics* is no more absurd a starting point than any other for a brief introductory discussion of narrative. According to *Poetics*, a narrative follows a single action through its beginning, middle, and end. Based on that elemental structure, narration is a human activity that creatively represents events for an audience in a form that comprises plot, character, thought, and diction.[6] Although plot is the most conspicuous element of narrative, as Aristotle already recognized – and this is important – plot is certainly not the only element. A narrative, in other words, depends on but clearly exceeds the bare representation of events in a plotted sequence (of words, pictures, or actions). In a fundamental sense, narration points both below and above the events comprised by its plot toward a layer of experience that precedes representation, and toward a layer of experience that follows as a response to this representation.[7] More specifically, each plot is enacted by characters whose capacities, desires, and personal histories are established

---

[6] Although I present it as a simple starting point, the account in *Poetics* is far more complex than I can indicate here. It could already be added, for example, that Aristotle situates the problem of narrative within the larger problematics of "imitation" (*mimesis*) and "poetics" (*poesis*), and that he acknowledges that narratives may be both "historical" and "fictional," depending on whether their referent is actual or imagined.
[7] Paul Ricoeur gives a lucid account of this problem in *Time and Narrative*, where he distinguishes between what he calls "$mimesis_1$," "$mimesis_2$," and "$mimesis_3$."

before and often continue to develop beyond the plot's horizons. It is enriched and complicated by thought, which remains invisible for the most part, screened in art as in life from the audience, if not from the characters themselves, but registered periodically in their speeches and displays of passion. Plot, character, and thought are in turn given form by the stylized language in which they are expressed and which employs technical means such as meter, metaphor, and the use of uncommon or unexpected words. The narrative recounting of events as a single action through an emplotted sequence with beginning, middle, and end, then, is complicated by characters whose histories and traits exceed the story's horizon, compounded by hidden thoughts made only partly manifest, and expressed in a stylized or technically mediated language – language that in one sense provides the medium for representation and in another sense militates against and undermines the purity of the *present* implied by the notion of re*present*ation.

Aristotle's *Poetics* was concerned primarily with the dominant modes of artistic representation of its time, the tragic drama and epic poem. Sophocles' tragedies, and *Oedipus the King* in particular, were the highest achievements of narrative art, according to *Poetics*, and the narrative ideal therefore suggests the representation of a single action that draws its protagonist through a crisis before reaching a decisive resolution – Oedipus' pursuit of the "trail of ancient guilt," identity-shattering discovery, and conclusive act of violence. *Poetics* cannot be expected to have anticipated the importance of conversion narratives for Christianity, which would emerge through such texts as *Acts of the Apostles* and *Confessions*, but it nonetheless predicts their contours and suggests the basis of their appeal. Insofar as conversion narratives depict (1) an individual who (2) faces crisis and (3) finds resolution, they meet the requirements of Aristotle's ideal narratives quite precisely. In other words, it is as though the inventors of the converssion narrative (if one can imagine such a thing) had taken the *Poetics* as their guidebook for narrative artistry: formally speaking, following Aristotle at least, conversion narratives are perfect stories.

If narration is simply a matter of telling stories, conversion can provisionally be imagined as a process through which an individual comes to tell a new story about him- or herself. More specifically, conversion can be imagined as a process in which one learns to tell not just any story but rather a specific kind of story about oneself in which one's experience of conversion occupies a decisive place. In this provisional view, to convert is to tell one's life story as a story of conversion. At its simplest, the process of conversion represented in these stories consists of three irreducible parts, a transformation of the self, in relation to a community, mediated by narrative. This chapter begins by isolating conversion narratives and examining them apart from the processes of conversion they represent: an artificial procedure, but one necessary initially to manage the complexity of the argument. By its conclusion, however, the chapter reintroduces the narrative to its context and argues that the relation between conversion narrative and conversion process is of the utmost importance for understanding conversion and therefore for understanding modern secularism.

The text of Taylor's *A Secular Age* allows us to draw together the problems of conversion, narrative, and secularism in extraordinarily sharp and sustained focus. *A Secular Age* follows Marcel Gauchet's earlier work, *The Disenchantment of the World*, in arguing that the present secular age must be understood as a mutation of an earlier order, and Taylor self-consciously sets out to tell a new story about the emergence of modern secularism from an age of naive faith. Gauchet and Taylor reflect on the roles they adopt as storytellers, and their arguments are particularly attentive to the importance of narrative in crafting and sustaining identity. Human beings are narrative creatures, for Taylor, both in the terms of interpretative social science, because they unfold their lives and world in words, and in the terms of the Christian theology most clearly expressed in *John*, because they owe their lives and world to the Word (of God, and the Word as God).[8] For Taylor, the present is denied, disfigured, or "mutilated" when the sedimentation of the past within it is ignored or obscured: insofar as "our past is sedimented in our present... we are doomed to misidentify ourselves, as long as we can't do justice to where we come from."[9] *A Secular Age* is premised on a claim that the significance of secular modernity cannot be comprehended without producing a historical narrative, and that a modern secular identity is incomplete or necessarily confused without appropriate narratives with which to fashion and sustain itself. According to Taylor, individuals cannot attain "full lucidity" about their place in the cosmos, moral order, or social structure without elaborating a historical narrative for themselves.

Western modernity, for Taylor, can be characterized by a shared, civilizational frame of reference, which is self-enclosed and anchored firmly to the inheritance of Latin Christendom, and thus he refers to the

---

[8] See Taylor's *Philosophical Papers*, where he develops the theme of man as "a self-interpreting animal," and *John* 1:1, "In the beginning was the Word, and the Word was with God, and the Word was God."

[9] Taylor, *A Secular Age*, 29.

Euro-American world as "ex-Latin Christendom." Taylor claims that we consciously register only part of our cultural condition, and he sets out to articulate an explicit narrative of our emergence from a previous one because this "past is sedimented in our present, and we are doomed to misidentify ourselves, as long as we can't do justice to where we come from. This is why the narrative is not an optional extra, why I believe that I have to tell a story."[10] *A Secular Age* rests on the claim that translating background assumptions into narrative form does significant work upon them – he argues that we need stories about Western modernity; more precisely, he argues that a secular identity is partly composed of and maintained through the kinds of stories that secular individuals tell about themselves.[11]

Taylor would no doubt acknowledge the significance of the concrete differentiation of social institutions and practices that followed in the wake of the Protestant Reformation (a period coextensive with his story), but he insists on the importance of the collective narration of this transformation and focuses exclusively on the contribution of narrative to a secular identity. "We have undergone a change in our condition," he claims, "involving both an alteration of the structures we live within, and our way of imagining these structures."[12] If the concept of a social fact or structure, which is irreducible to the ideas or beliefs held by individuals, but which shapes society, can be attributed to Durkheim, and the different idea that "man is an animal suspended in webs of significance he himself has spun" can be attributed to Weber, one might say that Taylor's story is like Durkheim's insofar as it engages the inarticulate background structures or "social imaginaries" that pattern social interactions in a secular age, but that Taylor adds a twist like Weber's by insisting that the narratives we produce – and the meanings we share – emerge from, evolve with, and feed back into these background structures in a transformative manner.[13] The structural transformations in the background conditions of thought – "social imaginaries" – condition individual possibilities of belief, and Taylor highlights the transformation in these conditions of belief and their self-reinforcing, looping, and cascading effects.

---

[10] Taylor, *A Secular Age*, 29.
[11] Taylor does not theorize the relation of identity and narrative at any length in *A Secular Age*, but it is a leitmotif of his work; see particularly his work on interpretive social science in his *Philosophical Papers*. See also Wendy Brown's response to Taylor's text in *Varieties of Secularism* for a careful consideration of the significance of "idealist" and "materialist" perspectives in the analysis of secularity.
[12] Taylor, *A Secular Age*, 594.
[13] Following Clifford Geertz, *Interpretation of Cultures*, 5.

A Secular Age submits the present condition of Western modernity to a historical reconstruction because the problems of modern secularism bear an internal relation to their historical articulation. To some extent, the secular age is portrayed as a distinctive age of history, neither reducible to the modern image of unlimited linear progress nor consigned to the images of the naive past in which time either moved in circles or was inscribed within a divine-eschatological frame; the secular age might be defined as the age that comes after all this. In Taylor's own words, "it is a crucial fact of our present spiritual predicament that it is historical; that is, our understanding of ourselves and where we stand is partly defined by our sense of having come to where we are, of having overcome a previous condition."[14] According to Taylor, the story of Western modernity should no longer be told as one of the gradual diminishment of faith but rather as one of the emergent possibility of a qualitatively different faith experienced from within a natural frame of immanence. This is a twofold claim that modern subjectivity is conditioned by a historically extensive narrative or, in other words, that the lives of individuals are inseparable from the stories they tell about themselves and their communities, and that these stories are inseparable from the accretion of past time that is narrated as the past.

Although the argument of *A Secular Age* is ambitious, it nonetheless follows a relatively simple trajectory across the book's three main sections. The first section narrates the last five hundred years of European cultural history. The category of nature plays the leading role in this part of the story; when nature arrives on stage, it appears as coextensive with an immanent frame of reference, within which society is cast as an association established to promote the flourishing of its individual members by enabling them to benefit one another. The second section follows the emergence of a multiplicity of pictures of the universe and of human nature that develop within this immanent frame of reference. Taylor calls this proliferation of worldviews the "supernova" effect of modernity. The third section shows how these rival pictures run up against, and "fragilize," one another, thereby pressing individuals to acknowledge the existence of conflicting interpretations of the world and the possibility of multiple moralities and religions.[15] In sum, this narrative portrays a shift from the formation of "Latin Christendom" – which it presents as dominated by a single, hierarchical picture – to a fragmented modern

---

[14] Taylor, *A Secular Age*, 28.
[15] Taylor, *A Secular Age*, 299–300.

formation. In the former, individuals were embedded in societies, societies in a larger cosmos, and this cosmos in a providential order ordained and anchored by God, whereas in the latter, individuals are disembedded from society, societies placed within a natural universe, and this universe detached from a providential order.[16] Within the specifically modern formation of an immanent natural frame, Taylor argues, faith in a transcendent God remains possible, but it is now possible as a self-reflective option rather than as an unquestioned and therefore naive assumption, such that while modern "faith is not the acme of Christianity," it is also far from a failed or "degenerate version" of it.[17]

Taylor is extremely reflective about the role of narrative in sustaining a modern secular identity, but he does not reflect on the extent to which his story follows the form of a conversion narrative. He is not alone in this: on the contrary, the emergence of modern secularism is generally framed as a conversion narrative, although this fact is seldom if ever remarked upon. To appreciate the modern condition, according to Taylor, we need to tell a story in which modernity breaks away from its premodern form, in which Western modernity both remains Christian and breaks from Christianity. This is once again a story in which the old man dies and is reborn anew. It is this structure, in which a compound protagonist – here Latin-Christendom/Euro-America – leads a split life, that repeats the form of a conversion narrative. To begin exploring the importance of that repetition, I turn next in this chapter to the text of Augustine's *Confessions* to articulate the canonical form of the Christian conversion narrative – the authorized form – and to begin exploring the alternate image of conversion that attends it – the crystalline form. I will return to Taylor briefly at the end of the chapter to suggest the consequences of the authorized form's prominence in his narrative. I return once more to Taylor in the concluding chapter to fully articulate my criticism of his theory of secularism and to draw more clearly the contours of the alternative I suggest.

The Smooth Surface and Authorized Narrative of Augustine's Conversion

Acts of the Apostles, with its accounts of Paul's conversion in particular, and *Confessions* are among the most important narratives of conversion

---

[16] Taylor, *A Secular Age*, 152.
[17] Taylor, *A Secular Age*, 754.

in the Christian canon. Both tell stories in which their protagonists' lives shift course from a wayward path toward the true direction: Saul the zealous persecutor of Christians is transformed into Paul, the chief theologian and evangelist of Christ, whom later generations would know as *The* Apostle. Aurelius Augustine emerges from the carnality and pagan learning of his youth into a chaste, mature, pious, and serene Christianity. Both are stories of regeneration whose end is a faith enabled, enacted, and sustained by the grace of God. As Paul would figure conversion time and again in his letters, and as Augustine would reiterate this figure in his own writings, just as the Christ died and was reborn, the old man perishes in conversion and is born again as a new man. The stories of *Acts* and *Confessions* would come to constitute what might be called an "authorized image of conversion" through which every Christian must pass or against which, at least, any Christian life might be measured. They would become types for stories of Christian lives that would be told and written thereafter. Indeed, Christian conversion is a literary event through and through, and it would be difficult to overstate the importance of such stories to the patterns of conversion that have been developed within Christian traditions.[18]

If Paul de Man suggests that the trope of irony is the "trope of tropes," one might add that the figure of conversion is the figure of figures. Where irony turns meaning away from itself, it might be said that conversion turns the self away from itself, producing, sustaining, or figuring a new man in distinction from the old man. Like irony, which de Man would ultimately argue cannot be given a stable conceptual definition, the figure of conversion is protean, elusive, and perhaps even necessarily impossible to pin down. And because the figure of conversion is so protean, again like irony, one can recount a long history of theories and figurations of it. The figure of conversion elaborated in *Confessions* already depends on a history of conversion, including but irreducible to *Acts of the Apostles*. Augustine's text cannot therefore mark the beginning of this history, but it marks an important junction as a conversion of conversion: Augustine represents his experience of conversion with unprecedented lucidity,

---

[18] The title of Karl Morrison's *Conversion and Text* suggests the importance of this connection, and it explores the literary dimensions of conversion in a medieval context. Molly Murray's more recent *The Poetics of Conversion* makes out a different argument about the connection between conversion and literature in early modern English poetry. These are but two ways of thinking through a point made by *Confessions* itself, namely that conversion depends not only on the circulation of texts but also on the literary practices of reading and writing presupposed by the circulation of any given text.

insight, and nuance, so much so that experiences of Christian conversion thereafter would be marked by his hand. The problem of conversion in *Confessions* is extraordinarily complex, but to engage that complexity, it is important to begin by tracing the outlines of the simple, authorized image of conversion that governs the text.

An authorized figure of conversion, in which a sinful man is redeemed by the grace of God and delivered to true faith, is inscribed in a smooth hand on the shimmering surface of Augustine's *Confessions*. This authorized figure, which is cast within the text's first nine books, translates a theological perspective developed in Paul's letters to the *Ephesians*, *Colossians*, and *Romans* into a narrative of personal transformation. In the Pauline perspective, conversion is figured as *a putting off of the old* and *a putting on of the new* through imitation of the Christ: "Do not lie to one another," Paul writes, "seeing that you have put off the old nature (*ton palaion*) with its practices and have put on the new nature (*ton neon*), which is being renewed in knowledge after the image of its creator."[19] In his exegesis of the *Psalms*, Augustine would echo this idea, writing that "the new man knows, the old man does not know. The old man is the old life and the new man is the new life."[20] In *Confessions*, Augustine recasts his own life as a process of transformation from the old man to the new. To say that his treatment is "allegorical," which is to say that Augustine is only apparently writing of his own life, and truly writing of a more general spiritual predicament, however, forecloses some of the problems this chapter seeks to open. Let it only be said at this point that the question of what Augustine was doing in writing *Confessions* hints at a complex underside of the simple, authorized image of transformation presented on the surface of his text.

According to the common historiography of Augustine studies, the authorized image of conversion was accepted as common coin by the readers of *Confessions* from the time of its publication for more than 1,500 years until Pierre Courcelle's *Recherches sur les "Confessions" de Saint*

---

[19] *Colossians*, 3:5–11; RSV. Paul's letters alternately conjoin conversion with the imitation of God in whose image man is created, and with the imitation of the Christ whose crucifixion and resurrection figures the death and rebirth of conversion. The centrality of mimetic activities that seek to repeat the passion of the Christ in each convert, and to restore each individual convert to the proper image of God, as well as the insistence upon the centrality of restaging the rebirth of the Christ (traveling both through crucifixion and resurrection) to the experience of conversion within the medieval Christian tradition, are convincingly argued in Karl Morrison's two volumes, *Understanding Conversion*, and John Freccero's *Dante: The Poetics of Conversion*.

[20] Augustine, *Exposition of the Psalms*, 97.1.

Augustin complicated the question of its authenticity. Courcelle's text cracked open the surface of *Confessions* to suggest that it cannot be read naively as an immediate report on Augustine's experience of conversion.[21] Through meticulous comparative textual scholarship, Courcelle argued that the authorized image of conversion in *Confessions* had been prefigured by a host of precedents, tropes, types, and figures disseminated by its author with persuasive intentions that extend beyond disclosing the facts behind his life's story. Although this argument did not render the common coin counterfeit, it does suggest a more complicated theory of conversion in the text of *Confessions* than that presented in the authorized image, a theory based on a deeper appreciation of the complexities of literary production in general and autobiography in particular. But precisely because they take no cognizance of the problematics of literary production, pre-*Rescherches* studies of *Confessions* are immensely helpful in presenting the authorized image of conversion. My claim is not that the authorized image is unimportant: although it presents only a part of the narrative work conversion, this is a deeply significant part. Studies of conversion by William James and Arthur Darby Nock, two of the most often-cited modern ones in English, derive their working concepts of conversion in large part from the authorized image of conversion recovered from the text of Augustine's *Confessions* read as a transparent and immediate account of the experience of conversion. These accounts are worth considering in turn for what they show about the authorized image.

Nock describes the central figure of his study *Conversion: The Old and the New in Religion from Alexander the Great to Augustine of Hippo* as "the reorientation of the soul of an individual, his deliberate turning from indifference or from an earlier form of piety to another, a turning which implies a consciousness that a great change is involved, that the old was wrong and the new is right."[22] In Nock's image, the "turning" at the center of conversion issues from a "deliberate" and "conscious" choice between clear alternatives, that is, between "right" and "wrong." At a pivotal point in developing his own theory of conversion, Nock presents the following discussion of the experience of conversion in Augustine's *Confessions*:

---

[21] Although I think it is an overstatement to say that before Courcelle, *Confessions* had only been read as an accurate autobiographical report (to cite only one example, in her own *Confessions*, St. Theresa maps out a much more complicated devotional relation to Augustine's text), it is important to note how such a reading was possible immediately before Courcelle's intervention and how it has been foreclosed since.

[22] Arthur Darby Nock, *Conversion*, 7.

He reached a state of conviction in which he just could not act: he had desired continence but not yet. And then came the critical moment in the garden. As Augustine wrestled in thought he heard a child say, 'Take up and read, Take up and read'; tolle lege, tolle lege. He took up the volume of Paul which he was reading and found Romans xiii, 13, 'Let us walk honestly, as in the day; not in rioting and drunkenness, not in chambering and wantonness, not in strife and envying.' Such a sudden voice was to a pagan as to a Christian guidance from without. To Augustine it meant the certainty which he had almost but not quite reached: it was like a long convalescence at the end of which it is sometimes some casual circumstance which at last enables a man to realize that he is well. All was now plain and settled and he could meditate on the Psalms and go to Ambrose and at his direction read Isaiah... Adolescence brought to him, as to so many, not only its welter of vague inquisitive desire which does not exactly know what it wants, but also its generous if incoherent aspirations after new truths. So his quest ran its way to an intellectual conviction, and this conviction gradually acquired an emotional strength sufficient to bring him to decisive action.[23]

In this interpretation, Augustine reaches an intellectual acceptance of the doctrines of Christianity, characterized as "conviction" without ethical consequences, that is, without actions, or conviction without piety. At a "critical moment" by means of "guidance from without," this conviction is translated into "certainty," bolstered by "emotional strength" that enabled "decisive action," namely a profession of faith and the assumption of a pious life. The causality and temporality of conversion here are relatively straightforward: after "a long convalescence," figured also as "adolescence," a "sudden voice" precipitates the "circumstance" in which Augustine can "realize" or recognize the truth, structurally mirroring the moment of peripety or tragic recognition identified in Aristotle's *Poetics*. It is clear for Nock that Augustine's conversion entails the attainment of intellectual certainty bolstered by a proper arrangement of the emotions, a public profession of his new faith, a rejection of his former life, and an entrance into a Christian community all cast in the form of a decision between right and wrong and premised upon a clean break or separation between the old and the new.

Conversion occupies a similarly pivotal position in William James's classic study *The Varieties of Religious Experience*. Where Nock focuses centrally on experiences that follow from deliberate choice, James supplements the consideration of voluntary conversions with an account of the impersonal and involuntary processes that might also contribute to the transformation of the self. The text of *Varieties* is itself extremely

---

[23] Nock, *Conversion*, 265–6.

nuanced and complicated: it is a deeply polyvocal text, composed largely of quotations from a wide range of speakers, as is hinted by the insertion of text from Paul's *Letter to the Romans* within the discussion of Augustine that follows. Nonetheless, like Nock, in the midst of developing his theory of conversion, James presents the following relatively straightforward account of Augustine's *Confessions*:

> Wrong living, impotent aspirations; "What I would, that do I not; but what I hate, that do I," as Saint Paul says [*Romans* 17:15]; self-loathing, self-despair; an unintelligible and intolerable burden to which one is mysteriously the heir. // Let me quote from some typical cases of discordant personality, with melancholy in the form of self-condemnation and sense of sin. Saint Augustine's case is a classic example... You all remember his half-pagan, half-Christian bringing up at Carthage, his emigration to Rome and Milan, his adoption of Manicheism and subsequent skepticism, and his restless search for truth and purity of life; and finally how, distracted by the struggle between the two souls in his breast, and ashamed of his own weakness of will, when so many others whom he knew and knew of had thrown off the shackles of sensuality and dedicated themselves to chastity and the higher life, he heard a voice in the garden say, "Sume, lege" (take and read), and opening the Bible at random, saw the text, "not in chambering and wantonness," etc., which seemed directly sent to his address, and laid the inner storm to rest forever... [James punctuates his reconstruction of the narrative at this point with a quotation from book 8 of Confessions before concluding that] there could be no more perfect description of the divided will, when the higher wishes lack just that last acuteness, that touch of explosive intensity, of dynamogenic quality (to use the slang of the psychologists), that enables them to burst their shell, and make irruption efficaciously into life and quell the lower tendencies forever.[24]

In contrast with Nock, James – with an apparently ironic wink at the "slang of the psychologists" – suggests the insufficiency of the model of decision, using the problem of conversion to highlight the importance of intensities that circulate below the threshold of thought and conscious decision making. He nonetheless uses Paul's and Augustine's texts to support a theory in which conversion consists primarily in the effective exchange of one creed for another, and in which it is manifest as an instantaneous event (even if this event required a preparatory process of discipline).

Later in *Varieties*, when James generalizes over the conversion narratives, such as *Confessions*, that form the subject of his study, he posits the following two-part schema as an essential model for the experience of conversion:

---

[24] William James, *The Varieties of Religious Experience*.

1. An uneasiness; and

2. Its solution.

1. The uneasiness, reduced to its simplest terms, is a sense that there is something wrong about us as we naturally stand.

2. The solution is a sense that we are saved from the wrongness by making proper connection with higher powers.

It is this formal scheme that would be echoed in Nock's definition, "a deliberate turning... which implies a consciousness... that the old was wrong and the new is right." In this, James and Nock pinpoint rather precisely the structure of *Confessions'* authorized image of conversion. But in doing so they have not outlined the structure of conversion so much as they have fixed the key plot points in Augustine's construction of a conversion narrative. Aristotle already suggests that such plots are complicated by further dimensions of narrative, and the next section will consider more precisely how the authorized image of conversion emerges from and is folded back within Augustine's text and within the process of conversion it represents.

Within a process of conversion, multiple layers of sedimented habit are reconfigured, individual and collective identifications are repatterned, and new possibilities are consolidated – indeed, as theorists in dialogue with the work of Michel Foucault have long accepted, the formation of ethical subjects is a complex and multifaceted process.[25] James acknowledged some of these dimensions in his discussions of habit and character without making them a central point of concern, and the questions of ethical character formation were central for Augustine himself. It is important nonetheless to trace the limitations of the authorized narrative of conversion, considered both as a narrative and as a single element within the process of ethical subject formation. The problem is not only that the study of narrative is insufficient to the problem of conversion. That is true, for conversion entails more than simple re-narration, but to go a few steps further, this very insufficiency is in fact a part of the productive work of conversion narratives, and this work takes highly specific and predictable forms. It will follow from this argument that narratives of the emergence of modern secularism are likewise insufficient to the problematic of modern secularism, and that they produce specific, predictable, *and perhaps also contestable* effects.

[25] See especially Talal Asad, *Genealogies of Religion*, and Peter Brown, *The Self and the Body*.

The Rough Texture and Crystalline Structure of Augustine's Conversion

There are two central figures of conversion in Augustine's *Confessions*: the first appears as a luminous surface on which is traced an ascending arc from venery, through philosophy, to the security of Christian faith; on the obverse side of this image, a pattern of conversion is traced as an uneven process in which habits accrete, and in which discourses, memories, texts, and attachments are interwoven, a trajectory that doubles back upon itself constantly, just as it is punctuated by lacunae. Augustine's *Confessions* is not simply an austere and luminous surface, and part of its complexity inheres in the combination of discourses that comprise it. Where pre-*Rescherches* studies such as those of Nock and James have accepted the image presented on the surface of *Confessions* as a complete account of conversion, since 1950 scholars have submitted the text of *Confessions* to much more extensive literary analyses, including contextualization, historicization, and deconstruction. Such approaches detect the traces of a more complex process of conversion inscribed in the margins, reversals, elisions, transpositions, and aporias of the text, a process that is obscured by the authorized image. This section will trace out the more complex process of crystalline conversion that is recorded in the hesitations, redoublings, erasures, substitutions, and conjunctions of the text itself, and that stands at odds with the official, authorized narrative.

In this second image, Augustine's conversion appears as a continuous process through which the past is conserved in the present, and the future is rendered indeterminate. In this second view, there is no single moment of change but instead a long process of transformation, of becoming otherwise, of the self's differing from itself, without definite end.[26] The subject formed within this more complex process of conversion endlessly wrestles with the crosscurrents and folds of language, habit, desire, and identity as the text itself moves through layers of citation from the Hebrew Bible, the Greek Gospels, the Pauline Epistles, the Latin Rhetoric of Cicero, and the diffuse neoplatonism of Plotinus and Porphyry. This subject takes shape in the words of *Confessions* before its readers in the resistances, elisions, transpositions, and conflicts inscribed between the

---

[26] Although it is not reducible to the practices of Hellenistic philosophy, this second image of conversion shares more with such practices than with the Pauline image of conversion. See Michel Foucault, *The Hermeneutics of the Subject*; Pierre Hadot, *Philosophy as a Way of Life*; and Talal Asad, *Genealogies of Religion*.

episodes that compose the narrative life of Augustine presented in the authorized image. But if the crystalline and the authorized images present two facets of conversion, both are indispensable to the process that produces them. The interaction between crystalline process and authorized image will be brought into focus in what follows.

Pierre Hadot argues that Courcelle's *Recherches* revolutionized the study of Augustine's *Confessions* by identifying the preexisting types that patterned its narrative of conversion.[27] As Hadot puts the matter, this text "almost caused a scandal, particularly because of the interpretation Courcelle proposed for Augustine's account of his own conversion." In more general terms, Courcelle's scholarship threatened the authenticity of the authorized image of conversion by drawing attention to the literary and rhetorical techniques employed in the construction of Augustine's narrative. Hadot summarizes the scandal as follows:

> Augustine recounts that as he was weeping beneath a fig tree, overcome with pressing questions and heaping bitter reproaches upon himself for his indecision, he heard a child's voice repeating, "Take it up and read." He then opened Paul's Epistles at random, as if he were drawing a lot, and read the passage that converted him. Alerted by his profound knowledge of Augustine's literary procedures and the traditions of Christian allegory, Courcelle dared to write that the fig tree could well have a purely symbolic value, representing the "mortal shadow of sin," and that the child's voice could also have been introduced in a purely literary way to indicate allegorically the divine response to Augustine's questioning. Courcelle did not suspect the uproar his interpretation would unleash. It lasted almost twenty years.

Hadot continues to gloss Courcelle's argument as follows:

> I would like to stress how interesting his position was from a methodological point of view. Indeed it began with the very simple principle that a text should be interpreted in light of the literary genre to which it belongs. Most of Courcelle's opponents were victims of the modern, anachronistic prejudice that consists in believing that Augustine's *Confessions* is primarily an autobiographical account. Courcelle on the contrary had understood that the *Confessions* is essentially a theological work, in which each scene may take on a symbolic meaning.[28]

---

[27] Pierre Hadot, Peter Brown, and Gary Wills, for example, all support this interpretation of the scholarship.

[28] Pierre Hadot's inaugural lecture at the College de France (February 1983), "Forms of Life and Forms of Discourse in Ancient Philosophy." This assessment is echoed by Brian Stock, "Courcelle's studies marked a turning point in historical research on the *Confessions* by replacing 'the subjective reconstitution' of Augustine's 'intellectual or religious development' with 'an inquiry...carried out in a methodical manner' [here citing Courcelle's own text] which made use of the entire corpus of his autobiographical writings" (*Augustine the Reader*, 19).

Insofar as James and Nock accepted Augustine's text as a direct autobiographical report in a gesture of modern anachronistic naiveté, as Hadot's argument goes, Courcelle's re-characterization would seem an important revision. And yet, even if Courcelle and Hadot are right to say that *Confessions* does not simply fit within the genre of autobiography as an immediate report upon experience (if, indeed, such a genre exists; John Freccero, to whom we shall turn in a moment, suggests that this is in turn a dangerously naive way of imagining autobiography), their claim that *Confessions* is "essentially a theological work" is problematic in a new sense.

The distinction that Hadot posits here between the genres of autobiography and theology opens onto a key component of the more general problematic of secularism insofar as "the secular" is conceived as a ground for authoritative argument and interpretation distinct from "the religious." The problem of interpretive authority is a key issue within the formation of modern secularism, and almost all commentators would agree that it has been so since Spinoza's *Theological-Political Treatise* submitted the text of the Bible to scrutiny based on his new methods of textual criticism based in the procedures of collation, comparison, and grammatical analysis. Indeed, most commentators would allow that this has been the case since Martin Luther rendered the Bible in the German vernacular and refigured the problematic of authority with respect to scriptural interpretation. And many would be willing to find this problem implicit in Augustine's guidelines for interpretation of scripture and elaboration of Christian doctrine. Arguably, it is the theme of the letters Paul addressed to the various congregations he had established, in which he put forth the parameters of orthodoxy and set to correcting the interpretations of his wayward brethren. And plausibly, it is well before this as the prophetic writers of the Hebrew Bible invoked their interpretation of Israelite tradition to challenge existing political authorities. If secularism involves the distribution of authority between "the religious" and "the secular" – implied by a dispute over whether a text is in fact "theological" or "autobiographical" – it is unclear that the distribution of authority is best mapped by a clean and absolute distinction between these fields. If, in other words, Hadot's and Courcelle's approaches to *Confessions* show the limitations of James's and Nock's approaches to the text as purely autobiographical, it remains to move beyond the limitations imposed by treating *Confessions* as "purely theological."

More directly to the point here, an interpretation of *Confessions* as either immediate autobiography or pure theology obscures an important dimension of the problem of narrative and of conversion narratives in particular. A conversion narrative is produced after the event of conversion that it represents, but it is only through the narrative reconstruction of this event that the event in question becomes an event of conversion. A conversion narrative takes up the raw material of experience and emplots this material in a selective and intelligible pattern. To be more precise, if experience never consists of raw material but is instead articulated with narrative all the way down, the construction of a Christian conversion narrative folds experience once more to produce a new pattern such that theretofore unconnected events are brought into connection through the plot of a theological/christological/biographical story: the old man dies in sin, and a new man is reborn in faith. The narrative of conversion, therefore, comes after the event of conversion, but it also retrospectively produces this event as an event of conversion.

In reading Augustine's *Confessions*, the literary critic John Freccero complicates the boundary between the theological and the autobiographical proposed by Courcelle and Hadot. Building on Paul de Man's analyses of the split subject of autobiography, and working primarily with Dante and Augustine, Freccero argues that all self-narration takes the form of a conversion narrative.[29] According to Freccero, "in theological terms, conversion is the separation of the self as sinner from the self as saint, but in logical, or narratological, terms, this separation founds the possibility of any self-portraiture, a separation between the self as object and the self as subject when the two are claimed to be the same person."[30] The autobiographical and the theological are then entangled in deep and complicated ways according to Freccero, and this argument about the relation between conversion and narrative appears analogous to my argument about conversion and secularism. It is not, according to Freccero, that narrative practice secularizes a prior theological account of conversion but rather that the structure or theory of conversion itself describes the activity of self-narration; conversion figures self-narration for Freccero, much as I will argue that it figures secularism.

Let us consider this argument in somewhat greater depth in relation to Dante (the same argument applies to Augustine). "As in all spiritual autobiographies," Freccero writes,

> [S]o in the *Confessions* and in the *Divine Comedy* there is a radical division between the protagonist and the author who tells his story. The question of the relative "sincerity" of such autobiographies is the question of how real we take

---

[29] See Paul de Man, "The Rhetoric of Temporality" and "Autobiography as De-Facement."
[30] John Freccero, "Autobiography and Narrative," 16–7.

that division to be. Augustine and Dante took it to be almost ontologically real, for it was their conviction that the experience of conversion, the subject matter of their respective stories, was tantamount to a death of their former selves and the beginning of a new life. // For Dante, the distance between protagonist and author is at its maximum at the beginning of the story and is gradually closed by the dialectic of poetic process until pilgrim and poet coincide at the ending of the poem, which give a unity and a coherence to all that went before. From the outset, the poet's voice expresses the detached point of view toward which his pilgrim strives, while the journey of the pilgrim is history in the making, a tentative, problematic view at the last moment that the metamorphosis of the pilgrim's view of the world is completed, when he himself has become metamorphosed into the poet, capable at last of writing the story that we have read.[31]

According to Freccero, then, a theological figure of conversion as the instantaneous moment of transformation enabled by God's grace in which an individual dies to sin and is born again in faith serves as the condition of possibility of any spiritual autobiography. Telling a story about oneself, according to Freccero, requires a decisive distance from the self whose story is to be told – the distance, that is, between protagonist and author. The subject of autobiography must be a split subject, and a figure of conversion splits the subject by positing an "almost ontologically real" distinction between a protagonist as the old man and the author as a new man. In such an account, it is not merely the case that figures are displaced or transferred from theological to biographical registers but instead that the theological is constitutive of the autobiographical. Freccero's is a strong argument, the limitations of which will have to be considered in what follows; I introduce it here, however, to begin to open some distance between conversion narratives and processes of conversion, and to suggest that narrative and process remain importantly related despite their nonidentity or distance from one another.

In Augustine's case, there is a temporal gap of roughly ten years between the event and the narrative of conversion. It is sometimes said that Augustine waited ten years from the event in the garden to compose the text of *Confessions*, but to say this is to credit the authorized story; a more skeptical, perhaps more prudent, formulation would be to say that when Augustine wrote *Confessions* in Northern Africa in the year 397, he represented events that took place more than ten years before in Italy. By the time he writes *Confessions*, Augustine had traveled from Africa to Italy and back, converted to Christianity, been twice ordained, first as a

---

[31] Freccero, *Dante*, 25.

priest, then once more as a bishop, in Hippo, where he would spend the rest of his life tending to an eclectic and tumultuous flock on the edges of a declining empire. By the time he writes *Confessions*, Augustine is a reluctant bishop in a reluctantly Christianizing city living in fellowship with recent converts such as himself and in society with all manner of pagans and heretics. Although such simple biographical data indicates the literal displacement of the writing of *Confessions* from the events it represents, the text itself draws the authorized narrative and the process of conversion into a complex relation.

Augustine does not seem inclined to honor the boundaries between autobiography and theology proposed by Hadot and Courcelle, nor does he seem inclined to fit the pattern depicted by Freccero, although this comes closer – the text of *Confessions* complicates the clean distinctions these theorists draw at every turn. Rather than marking the text as purely theological as opposed to autobiographical, or as depending on a "radical division" that is "almost ontologically real," it may be better to say that the text of *Confessions* develops an authorized narrative of conversion that works as part of an ongoing process of conversion. In conjoining these two facets, it shows how identity and experience are infused with certain doctrines (philosophical, ethical, and theological), articulated in connection with communities (e.g., fellow Northern Africans, reading citizens of the Roman world, Catholics), and enhanced by intimate human relationships (e.g., family, friends, recent converts living in quasi-monastic community).

This line of argument is borne out in recent literature on Augustine, particularly in the work of Peter Brown and Brian Stock. Brown's seminal *Augustine Bishop of Hippo: A Biography*, for example, helps to situate Augustine within contexts of intimate friendships and loyalties supported both by epistolary communication and communal living arrangements, in which the parties involved worked together to cultivate what were for many newly adopted Christian ethical dispositions.[32] Stock's *Augustine the Reader* impressively documents the importance that Augustine attributed to reading and writing as processes of self-formation, and it is worth citing at length for the contrast in argument and perspective it produces with respect to James and Nock but also Courcelle, Hadot, and Freccero:

---

[32] Peter Brown, *Augustine of Hippo*, and see also Carolinne White's more specialized study on *Christian Friendship in the Fourth Century*.

In the *Confessions* Augustine linked the experience of narrative and memory through ethics, stressing the role of personal obligation in attaining a way of life that is improvable, if never perfect... [Augustine unites] study, remembering, and self-examination in a plan for disciplining the body... Moral precepts are read (or heard); they are then transformed from thought to practice as they are recalled... As this proceeds, the study of scripture gradually becomes a form of life (*forma uiuendi*)... By the time Augustine wrote, reading and writing had for some generations been united with oral habits in producing a "technology" of self-reform [citing Foucault, Hadot and Brown]... In moving from life to text and back to life, his concern was ethical before it was literary, and it was literary only in combination with ethics... He saw a potential fit between the inner and outer "readings" of the self as an instrument for bringing about personal improvement... he stamped his personal interpretation on Paul's statements concerning the transition from the "old" to the "new," [i.e., conversion] delicately positioning the student of the Bible in the ontological space between the inner and outer person... Living "according to the inner man," as Paul recommended, was like an advanced literary exercise: it was a "reediting" of the self in which one narrative, a life to come, was traced over another, a life already lived.[33]

As these passages demonstrate, Stock's work carefully traces the connections among doctrine, narrative, and the practices of self-formation. Finally, Brown's more recent *The Rise of Western Christendom: Triumph and Diversity, A.D. 200–1000* situates Augustine's cultural milieu – what Charles Taylor calls "Latin Christendom" – within a much larger (and, as its title suggests, more diverse) ancient and early medieval world, suggesting the polyglot and poly-cultural complexity of this context.[34]

Brown and Stock show Augustine awash in a sea of traditions, a welter of communities, a complex intersection of languages as he dictates the books, composes letters, and delivers sermons that remain for us to read but which were crafted by him to cultivate the life of a community and as part of a process of ethical self-formation. From such a vantage, Augustine does not seem inclined to honor many clean distinctions at all. The resistance of the text of *Confessions* to clear characterization is also well remarked in the literature, for as Gillian Clark puts it, "The Confessions, in places, are almost a cento of biblical texts – literally a 'patchwork', a

---

[33] Brian Stock, *Augustine the Reader*, 14, 17.
[34] In this case, Brown is representative of the larger tendencies in contemporary scholarship to reconceive history in truly global terms – a tendency explicitly refused by Taylor in his singular focus on "Latin Christendom" in exclusion of its connections to the wider world. It could be useful and important to complicate Taylor's historiography, as historiography, but this chapter aims instead to develop a theoretical critique focused on the construction and work of narrative within the theory of secularism.

fabric made by sewing together pieces of material."[35] According to Clark, "The different 'voices' in Augustine's style can be heard in other authors; but although Virgil and Cicero and Plotinus and the Latin Bible spoke to others besides him, no one else achieved a personal tone in which all of them could be heard. Because the Confessions is so 'polyphonic', it is particularly difficult to extract a passage for more detailed examination, and once the choice is made it is difficult to stop quoting and to resist making more and more cross-connections."[36] This complex textuality serves as the basis for Courcelle's argument against taking *Confessions* as a direct report, but it also overruns the distinction he proposes between such a report and a pure theology.

To draw upon these considerations for the purposes of constructing a more nuanced theory of conversion, it might be said that alongside the authorized narrative of conversion, read with some attention to its literary diversity and its practical and its cultural contexts, *Confessions* registers moments of extreme doubt, disruption, disjuncture, transition, and incompleteness throughout. This is to say that the text of *Confessions* complicates the authorized image of conversion, in which doubt precipitates the experience of conversion and certainty follows it. Augustine's hesitations, reversals, and transformations are fomented at least in part by the circulation of texts (of conversion narratives, more precisely) and *Confessions* itself foments the further circulation of texts, touching and rerouting memory and perception as well as habits of speech, action, affiliation, and commitment, both for its author and for his readers.[37] At least as important as the relations Augustine describes and enacts toward God through his prayer and confession are the relations that Augustine describes and enacts among his life, his life's story, the lives of his coreligionists, and the scriptures they hold sacred.

In a fine-grained analysis, within the whirlwind of voices conjured in the text of *Confessions*, which Stock refers to as a "web of interlocution" (citing Taylor), it is not surprising to find Augustine negotiating between the Greek theologico-philosophical and Jewish traditions insofar as such negotiations have presented continual dilemmas for Christian, Jewish, and secular intellectual traditions from their inceptions to the present.[38]

---

[35] Gillian Clark, *Augustine*, 73.
[36] Clark, *Augustine*, 83.
[37] For a relatively recent study of Augustine's reading practices, see Brian Stock, *Augustine the Reader: Meditation, Self-Knowledge, and the Ethics of Interpretation*.
[38] Ironically, Stock follows Taylor in selecting this locution. He writes, "If language, from which reading and writing derive, is definable through a community of speakers, then

One finds numerous instances of conversion here at the level of the sentence, with neoplatonic concepts, for example, being turned toward and completed by scriptural references. Negotiation of this sort is continuous; consider just one example from book ten's pivotal meditation on memory. Augustine invokes a parable recounted in *Luke* (15:8–10), "A woman had lost a coin; she searched for it with a lamp." The scriptural passage that Augustine cites here opens with these words: "What woman having ten silver coins, if she loses one of them, does not light a lamp, sweep the house, and search carefully until she finds it?" Augustine compresses this opening verse, but that does not noticeably alter its meaning. Because the parable is invoked in the context of a meditation on memory, it is not surprising to see that Augustine supplies this conclusion for the parable:

[U]nless she had had some memory of it she would not have found it, for when it was found, how could she have known that this was it, if she did not remember it?

However, the parable is concluded in *Luke* as follows,

When she has found it, she calls together her friends and neighbors, saying, "Rejoice with me, for I have found the coin that I had lost." Just so, I tell you, there is joy in the presence of the angels of God over one sinner who repents.

The discrepancy between Augustine's source text and his own meditation, then, is enormous at this point: where *Luke* conveys Jesus's admonition to "repentance," *Confessions* substitutes the neoplatonic figure of "recollection."

Augustine's continuing commitments to the neoplatonism of his youth, however, do not tally well with Freccero's theory of conversion as a radical division between old and new selves, nor are they well met by his

selves, souls, or minds, which depend on language for their human expression, have to have their communities too. Their lives consist of what Charles Taylor calls a 'web of interlocutions' [citing *Sources of the Self*, pp. 35-6, a point at which Taylor cites Wittgenstein, who famously begins his *Philosophical Investigations* by citing Augustine...]. It is this intersubjective quality that makes Augustine's *Confessions* unique in the ancient literature of the soul rather than the doctrine that the inner self is veiled, mysterious, or inaccessible" (*Augustine the Reader*, 16). Daniel Boyarin's *Border Lines, A Radical Jew*, and *The Jewish Gospels* are recent and accessible texts on the complex interrelation of early Christianity and (Rabbinic) Judaism that also survey a great deal of scholarly literature; Jacques Derrida's engagement with Augustine in his "Circonfession" argues the necessity of modern Judaism's passing through Christianity, much like Emanuel Levinas's "Between Two Worlds" had earlier argued in connection with Franz Rosenzweig's *The Star of Redemption*.

characterization of *Confessions* as a "polemic against neoplatonism,"[39] for Augustine writes more or less comfortably in the language of neoplatonism throughout *Confessions*. It is furthermore not clear that one discourse has priority over the other: in recrafting the parable of the lost coin, does Augustine begin with the canonical *New Testament* and slide into Plotinus' *Enneads*. Or does he punctuate an overarching neoplatonic reflection with an outburst of scriptural reference? It may be better to say that although the text of *Confessions* borrows liberally from the canonical texts of the Christian Bible (leaning heavily on the poetry of the *Psalms of David*), it crystallizes these texts with other discourses. There are countless junctures between philosophical and scriptural texts in Augustine's *Confessions* that trace a consistent background pattern of multiple dissonant voices, which I follow Bergson in calling a crystalline structure.[40]

The text of Augustine's *Confessions* and, by extension, Augustine himself are neither simply neoplatonic nor Catholic/Christian, and this presents a critical key to understanding the work of conversion within this text. In other words, it would seem that Augustine does not cross from one stable and complete identification to another; the opening, middle, and closing stages of this text instead present a voice composed of multiple, partial identifications, which strive toward a regularity, a consolidation, or a monological condition that they never attain. Augustine writes of certainty, resolution, and consistency at many points, but the voice in which he writes hesitates, doubles back, and belies itself throughout. In counterpoint with the authorized image of conversion, Augustine faces irreconcilable discourses and commitments in the process of his conversion, but he does not so much choose between them as he is forced to speak and live both alternatives together, uneasily and transformatively.

The text of *Confessions* complicates its own authorized narrative of conversion, and the clean distinctions proposed by Courcelle, Hadot, and Freccero at a larger structural level of composition as well. *Confessions* is famously divided between books one through nine, which present a narrative account of Augustine's life from birth to the time of his conversion, and books eleven through thirteen, which consist of meditations on time and *Genesis*. These halves of the text can be subsumed under different literary genres, and Augustine himself marks out the distinction between them in the pivotal tenth book when, referring to what is to follow, he

---

[39] Freccero, *Dante*, 19.
[40] See Chapter Three for a full explanation of Bergson's concept of crystalline structure.

writes, "I will disclose myself not as I have been but as I am now, as I am still."[41] This creates a division that can be neatly mapped by Freccero's argument that all spiritual autobiographies (i.e., conversion narratives) must present two "I"s: the unconverted I whose story is narrated, and the narrating "I" who has emerged from the process of conversion to look back upon his or her own story. According to Freccero, the disjunction between the narrative that leads to Augustine's conversion and the meditations that follow this event testify to the difference in Augustine himself before and after conversion: if Dante's pilgrim becomes the poet himself at the conclusion, Augustine's youthful self is to be divided from his mature self at the center of the text. Furthermore, the meditations on time and scripture in the second half of the text, insofar as they pertain to recollecting and reinterpreting experience, resonate with and recapitulate the task of transforming the will as narrated in the first half of the text. Following Freccero again, a reader sees in these last four books of *Confessions* how Augustine and Dante after him "used scriptural exegesis in order to structure their experience, superimposing (or discovering, they would insist) a biblical pattern of meaning upon their own history."[42] Augustine's reading of the fall in *Genesis* at the conclusion of *Confessions*, in other words, presents an argument about free will, sin, and redemption that can be seen to have structured the narrative account of Augustine's life as a young man. The text of *Confessions*, then, would allegorically translate providential history to a biographical plane.

Although there is something right about Courcelle's and Freccero's arguments that theological figures shape the narrative of Augustine's text, Stock's account of Augustine as a reader helps to press their interpretations in a more subtle direction by placing a practice of reading between the old man and the new that brings the process of conversion into focus. This implies that the old man never truly departs and the new man never truly arrives, and that Augustine's literary practice opens a space in which the old man is forever departing and the new man always arriving. In other words, as closer inspection reveals, the hesitations, discontinuities, incompletions, lacunae, confusions, and indirections of Augustine's text are spread across all thirteen of its books; it is in hesitation, uncertainty, and transition that the authorized image of conversion is conjured and from which it is projected. Turning directly to Augustine's composition of the authorized image will show this more clearly.

---

[41] Augustine, *Confessions*, X, 6.
[42] Freccero, *Dante*, 13.

Chapter seven of *Confessions*' eighth book presents the focal point of the authorized image of Augustine's conversion, and it is this book that is quoted at length by Nock, James, and virtually every student of *Confessions*; it is this book that narrates the event that in Freccero's view would separate Augustine's life. Recalling James's formal schema, a reader looking for a conversion event in this book is prepared to find "1. An uneasiness; and 2. Its solution... by making proper connection with higher powers." The first criterion is certainly met in what can be called the "shame episode," which *Confessions* narrates as follows:

> Lord, even while he spoke you were wrenching me back toward myself, and pulling me round from that standpoint behind my back which I had taken to avoid looking at myself. You set me down before my face, forcing me to mark how despicable I was, how misshapen and begrimed, filthy and festering. I saw and shuddered. If I tried to turn my gaze away... you set me before myself once more, thrusting me into my sight that I might perceive my sin and hate it... a huge storm blew up within me and brought on a heavy rain of tears.[43]

This seems to indicate clearly enough the state of crisis prior to conversion: Augustine is ashamed and collapses in tears. Resolution, indeed, follows this crisis in what can be called the "garden episode," thus filling James's second criterion:

> Suddenly, I heard a voice from a house nearby – perhaps a voice of some boy or girl, I do not know – singing over and over again, "Pick it up and read, pick it up and read"... I snatched it up, opened it and read in silence the passage on which my eyes first lighted: *Not in dissipation and drunkenness, nor in debauchery and lewdness, nor in arguing and jealousy; but put on the Lord Jesus Christ, and make no provision for the flesh or the gratification of your desires* [Romans 13:13–14]... No sooner had I reached the end of the verse than the light of certainty flooded my heart and all dark shades of doubt fled away... and now indeed I stood there, no longer seeking a wife or entertaining any worldly hope, for you had converted me to yourself.[44]

If Augustine himself reports a crisis and its instantaneous resolution through the intervention of a higher power, ending in certainty and conversion, why insist that conversion in *Confessions* is reducible neither to the authorized image accepted by James and Nock nor to the structural bifurcation suggested by Freccero?

One reason is the prominence of passages in *Confessions* for which the authorized image cannot account. There are a number of utterances

---

[43] Augustine, *Confessions*, VIII, 7.
[44] Augustine, *Confessions*, VIII, 29–30.

voiced by Augustine-the-converted-author that deny the suggestion of the authorized image that Augustine has put his "inner storm to rest forever." An important example comes in the tenth book, at a point clearly past what was to be the dividing line between narrative and meditation, between old and new self. "When at last I cling to you with my whole being there will be no more anguish or labor for me, and my life will be alive indeed, because filled with you," Augustine writes firmly within his meditative present, rather than his narrative past, and he continues,

> But now it is very different. Anyone whom you fill you also uplift, but I am not full of you, and so I am a burden to myself. Joys over which I ought to weep do battle with sorrows that should be matter for joy, and I know not which will be victorious. But I also see griefs that are evil at war in me with joys that are good, and I know not which will win the day. This is agony, Lord, have pity on me! It is agony! See, I do not hide my wounds; you are the physician and I am sick; you are merciful, I in need of mercy. Is not human life on earth a time of testing? . . . Is not human life on earth a time of testing without respite?[45]

This requires little interpretation: Augustine describes himself as sick, wounded, anguished, and "not full" of God. But it deserves some comment. Emphatically, this statement cannot be attributed to the unconverted Augustine whose life is narrated in books 1–9. Instead, in Freccero's terms, it is Augustine the new and converted man, Augustine who stands in the same place in *Confessions* as Dante the poet in the *Divine Comedy*, who speaks these words about himself in the present, not in recollection of his past life of sin. Although Augustine presents himself as laying quiet forever the inner storms that torment him upon conversion in the "garden episode," he nonetheless goes on to show himself as remaining subject to these same torments in the meditative present. Although James and Nock ignore or repress this contradiction, and Freccero seeks to reconcile these positions, I would like to suggest that the simple authorized narrative and the complex process of crystalline conversion stand in a more intricate pattern of relation than their theories suggest.

Freccero seems right to a point in claiming that Augustine's *Confessions* presents a "division" between narrated and narrating selves that Augustine may well have understood as "almost ontologically real." It helps a great deal to see that the narrating Augustine stands in a special, distanced relation to the narrated Augustine of the past. However, this clear structure is complicated by the dimensions of *Confessions* that exceed the plot of the authorized narrative, such that the

---

[45] Augustine, *Confessions*, X, 28.

division is as much imagined as it is "almost ontologically real." As we shall see, this almost-real line to which Augustine's narrative draws its readers' attention mirrors the line drawn between naive religiosity and secular reflectiveness in the modern secular imaginary, represented here by Taylor's *Secular Age*. Replacing "almost ontologically real" with "fictive, fabricated, artificial, imagined but nonetheless effective," however, may more accurately present the importance of narrative in the process of conversion, and in a theory of secularism as a process of transformation.

A second reason for supplementing the authorized image can be found within book eight itself, for this book not only narrates Augustine's conversion, but it also reports upon at least seven conversions. Many of these narratives of conversion are nested and interlocked with one another; some reflect each other, creating a citational hall of mirrors, or perhaps better a layered, crystalline structure. To begin untangling these reports, consider the portion of Augustine's text elided in my previous quotation of the "garden episode":

> I stemmed the flood of tears and rose to my feet, believing that this could be nothing other than a divine command to open the Book and read the first passage I chanced upon; for I had heard the story of how Antony had been instructed by a gospel text. He happened to arrive while the gospel was being read, and took the words to be addressed to himself when he heard, Go and sell all you possess and give the money to the poor: you will have treasure in heaven. Then come, follow me. So he was promptly converted to you by this plainly divine message. Stung into action, I returned to the place where Alypius was sitting, for on leaving it I had put down there the book of the apostle's letters. I snatched it up.[46]

At the moment considered decisive in the authorized image, Augustine folds one conversion narrative told in *The Life of St. Antony* into his own narrative, and along with it a second conversion narrative told about a reading of this same text. Augustine presents himself as converting upon picking up and reading a passage of scripture. Earlier in book eight, Augustine had recounted that a certain Ponticianus had told him a story about the conversion of two friends; these friends converted upon picking up and reading *The Life of St. Antony*. St. Antony himself is presented in that text as converting upon picking up and reading a chance passage of the gospel according to *Matthew*.

Before the "shame episode," Augustine reports:

> Ponticianus went on talking and developing the theme, while we listened spellbound... he and three of his colleagues went out for a walk in the gardens...

---

[46] Augustine, *Confessions*, VIII, 29.

Authorized Narrative and Crystalline Structure 59

There they found a book which contained *The Life of Antony*. One of them began to read it... began to mull over the possibility of appropriating the same kind of life for himself... [and with another of the friends] they abandoned all their possessions and followed you [God].

Ponticianus' narrative incites the "shame episode," but the heavy rain of tears that follows Augustine's experience of shame does not properly belong to that episode. Placing tears there creates a bridge between the "shame episode" and the "garden episode," so in the previous citation, I took the liberty of transposing the former episode so that it abuts the latter. The text of *Confessions* (i.e., Augustine's narrative) does not indicate how much time has elapsed between the "shame episode" and the "garden episode," between shame, tears, and conversion; between Ponticianus's visit and Augustine's and Alypius's conversions in the garden. Alypius is present at both events, but this does not ensure that they followed one another immediately; Alypius is at Augustine's side throughout his life. How many readers make the same transposition? Does Augustine the presbyter in Hippo, writing his *Confessions*, know how much time has elapsed? As Courcelle points out, Augustine presented the critical moments leading up to his conversion in at least three different ways in his *De beata uita, De utilatate credendi*, and *Confessiones*.[47] Is there a continuous chain of transposition between the lucan evangelist's story in *Acts*, between St. Antony's story in *The Life of Saint Antony*, between Ponticianus' story recounted by Augustine, between Augustine's own story that enfolds these, between the stories of those who would read this most famous of late antiquity's conversion narratives? Freccero sees one: "The interpretive process does not stop here, however, for he passes the book to his friend Alypius, who reads on and is also converted. That touch has the effect of extending the trajectory of the reading proleptically to us, the readers of a text about someone who was interpreted by a text after someone was interpreted by a text in a regress that for Augustine goes back to the Gospels."[48] The event of conversion all but dissolves within the swirling stream of conversion narratives – more precisely, the singularity of experience is refracted into a multiplicity, which can be figured as a layered, crystalline structure. Conversion, in other words, is not only an event within an individual's life story but also an open process through which an individual passes.

---

[47] "*Il est curieux de noter comment il a successivement traduit de manière très différente, selon les époques, cette crise décisive.*" ("It is curious to note how he successively treats this decisive crisis in very different ways at different times.") Courcelles, *Recherches*, 188.
[48] Freccero, "Autobiography," 26.

A reader informed by modern criticism knows that Augustine must have transposed at least a few things, and that *Confessions* shapes its narrative and meditative stretches not only with the rhetorical resources of the Latin language but also with citations from the Hebrew and Greek scriptures, with the tropes of neoplatonic philosophy, and with those of Christian allegory. A critical contemporary reader, in other words, cannot be satisfied with the authorized image as a complete account of the experience of conversion. But that does not diminish the importance of *Confessions* as an account of conversion; it is rather the source of its importance for this study. In my reading, the text of *Confessions* – against its surface testimony – indicates that there is no single moment of turning in the course of Augustine's conversion, nor in the process of conversion in general insofar as we can speak of conversion in general. Instead, the text marshals a multiplicity of sentences turned from pagan to Christian sentiment, from theological reflection to personal narration, from the present voice to the memory of past actions, from the praise of God to the blame of the self, from narratives heard to the narrative written. Enfolded within the grand narrative arc of the turn from old life to new, falling outside the field of vision open to James and Nock, are a series of minor folds and turns; when this series of microscopic gestures attains a certain degree of consistency, as it seems to in *Confessions*, an observer can be justified in claiming that a process of conversion has been consolidated in new habits of speech, thought, and being. *Confessions* lends itself to a double view, most strongly perhaps in the eighth book, which also presents the apex of the authorized image, the very moment at which Augustine is said to convert to Christianity: there is no single conversion event in that book but instead an involuted narrative structure and at least seven interrelated conversions of Victorinus, Ponticianus, St. Antony, Ponticianus's first friend, Ponticianus's second friend, Augustine, Alypius, and so forth. Better yet, there is a multiplicity of conversions, no one conversion.

If *Confessions* is an account of Augustine's conversion, this conversion is a literary event, in the sense that it is represented as depending on Augustine's reading, and in the sense that is written in a text that knows itself to be about writing. This in no way detracts from or diminishes the authenticity or significance of Augustine's experience of conversion; it only emphasizes the extent to which there is no conversion event without a conversion narrative, and the extent to which these two – event and narrative – are irreducible to each other. The narrative of Augustine's conversion is a narrative of narration, and it is crucial not to let this dimension slip from sight. When is Augustine converted? It does not seem unreasonable to suggest that his conversion – in an important sense – takes place as he fits his account of these events together in writing *Confessions*. A series of propositions might follow from this: There is no conversion experience without a conversion narrative. The conversion narrative is not adequate to the conversion experience and does not exhaust this experience. The lapse between experience and its representation is ineliminable. This lapse falsifies neither experience nor narrative. Experience feeds into narrative and narrative feeds back into experience. The process of conversion depends upon but exceeds its narrative representation.

The Authorized Narrative and Crystalline Structure of Modern Secularism

Conceiving *Confessions* as part of a long and complex process of crystalline conversion shows how the writing of this text allows Augustine to refashion his identity in partial steps on numerous planes. The authorized narrative portrays an Augustine on a timeless spiritual journey through a series of conversions through Cicero's *Hortensius* to philosophy, hence to Manicheanism, hence to neoplatonism, and hence once more to Christianity. The text of *Confessions*, however, also served to introduce a very particular man, Aurelius Augustine, Bishop of Hippo, to a fourth-century North African audience eager to know where he had come from and what he stood for.[49] *Confessions* also records the sense in which Christianity, in Augustine's milieu, was lived in community with others, and it both records and participates in a process whereby newly converted Roman Christians shared with one another their stories as part of a life of spiritual community. The authorized narrative of conversion, then, projects Augustine's figure into an agonistic political field at the same time that the publication of his *Confessions* enmeshes him in a sympathetic network of communal organization.

Confessions records a process in which Augustine's experience at the time of writing, his remembered experiences at the time about which he writes, and the narratives that traverse and recompose these layers of time were interwoven with the scriptures, doctrines, authorities, disputes,

---

[49] These audiences may be drawn more or less tightly; for a striking way of conceiving Augustine's audience, see Peter Brown's *The Body*, in which Augustine is presented as introducing himself to the community of sexually abstinent Christian men.

narratives, and lives of the fellow members of an emerging community of Christian faith in the Roman and North African milieus of late antiquity, itself unfolding within a complex temporality, redoubled by the typological/allegorical elaboration of a Christian/eschatological structure of time. Conceived as such, this text opens a view to a more general problematic in which political arguments are set within historical and cultural contexts but also received by and incorporated within the lives of those individuals and communities who are party to them. Here, conversion registers the encounter between arguments and networks of resistance, misunderstanding, enthusiastic acceptance, and so on as they are taken up, reformulated, circulated, adopted, and rejected by the individuals whose lives they touch. Furthermore, this process is consciously registered, mediated, displaced, and repeated in the distinctive form of a conversion narrative that at various moments enables, extends, and completes the process of conversion with which it is enmeshed. *Confessions* is a special case insofar as it self-consciously foregrounds and thematizes these dimensions, but these dimensions nonetheless permeate practices of argumentation much more generally, although they are not always as readily visible.

Peter Brown notes that Augustine was

[T]he only Latin philosopher in antiquity to be virtually ignorant of Greek. As a young man, he will set out, pathetically ill-equipped... A cultivated Greek audience would have treated this exclusively Latin-speaking student from the university of Carthage as "a dumb fool", acquainted as he was only "with the opinions of Greek philosophers, or rather, with little snippets of these opinions, picked up, here and there, from the Latin dialogues of Cicero"; not "with these philosophical systems as they stand, fully developed, in Greek books."[50]

When he arrived in Rome and in Milan, he arrived from the provinces, and what Brown has noticed could not have been lost on Augustine himself: the individuals around him, who had been raised in the imperial center, such as the towering Milanese bishop Ambrose, "had enjoyed all the advantages of an upper-class education in Rome itself," and in Ambrose's case, "There was nothing 'provincial' about him. Thus, unlike Augustine, he could read Greek fluently. He could comb the books of a brilliant new generation of Greek bishops and a whole tradition of Greek Christian scholarship" that would forever remain unavailable to Augustine. "Such a man would have had little interest in Augustine," Brown concludes. Augustine, the last of the Latin Fathers, was a foreigner in the heart of the Roman Empire, just as much as he entered the milieu of Christianity

[50] Brown, *Augustine of Hippo*, 36.

as a foreigner, and just as he would find the seat of his bishopric in Hippo, a foreign city. The text of *Confessions*, despite the pure poetic continuity of the authorized image of conversion it projects, carries traces of this foreign outside, and the resounding certainty of Augustine's arrival at faith is circumscribed by a process in which he wrestles with doubts that he would never finally lay to rest. The authorized image and its more complex shadow exist in tension, each impossible without the other, neither reducible to the other, both contributing to a fuller picture of what "religious" conversion may entail as well as a fuller picture of the problem of secularism itself figured as a process of conversion. The presence of two images of conversion in Augustine's *Confessions* suggests an important way in which the problematic of modern secularism might be refigured by suggesting how a conversion narrative might be supplemented by a more complex account of the narrated process of conversion.

Just as a more complex process of conversion underlies the authorized narrative of *Confessions*, a more complex concept of transformation might be adduced to accompany authorized narratives of the emergence of modern secularism. Where secularism appears as a matter of clean separation, dividing the old from the new as Paul had put it, in the authorized narratives this might be supplemented by a more complex image that suggests how the old and the new stand in a resonant, dependent, and transformative relation to one another. To put this another way, the process of conversion secretes a stable image of conversion that reenters the process as the chief visible layer of a much deeper crystalline structure. Insofar as secularization can be figured as a process of conversion, it too would be composed of a two-tiered process characterized by a stable image that covers a deeper and more complex structure. Modern secularism could be seen, therefore, not simply to have emerged from a religious past with which it has broken but instead as both divided from a religious past and yet also locked in continuous and shifting patterns of interrelation with religion in the present.

To some extent, the retrospective production of a conversion narrative serves to cover the open, underdetermined, and creative dimension of conversion, but the prospective projection of the possibility of conversion also serves as a proleptic catalyst for this process. Narration, therefore, complicates the temporality of the conversion process. In the text of *Confessions*, as Peter Brown notes, "one constantly senses the tension between the 'then' of the young man and the 'now' of the bishop. The past can come very close: its powerful and complex emotions have only recently passed away; we can still feel their contours through the thin layer of new feeling that has grown over them."[51] Although this is evocative, it is an incomplete characterization: for Augustine, the process of conversion consisted in redirecting the habits acquired from an immemorial past – his account moves from infancy, with the acquisition of language through the cavernous and boundless expanses of memory – that continues to figure the present. In conjoining the old habits with new ones, Augustine comes to speak the languages of the *Psalms*, the Gospel, and the Pauline epistles, along with those of Cicero and Plotinus, and to speak all of these with the controlled cadences and well-developed tropes of a trained rhetorician. The language of Christianity that Augustine comes to speak, then, always retains foreign elements and incomplete identifications, even when it has become his second nature. When Augustine produced his *Retractiones*, in which he poured over his works, reviewing what he had written, correcting errors, commenting, and setting them in order, he would say this about *Confessions* as a whole, "Thirteen books of my *Confessions*, which praise the just and good God in all my evil and good ways, and stir up towards Him the mind and feelings of men: as far as I am concerned, they had this effect on me when I wrote them, and they still do this, when now I read them." Augustine does not seem to understand his good ways to be confined to books eleven through thirteen, and his evil ways to books one through nine, as Brown and Freccero would seem to suggest. Instead, he seems to acknowledge that his good and evil ways are mixed throughout the text and throughout his life.

Possidius, who knew Augustine, although we do not know how intimately, wrote a *Life of Saint Augustine* shortly after the bishop's death, which suggests what Augustine must have witnessed as the Roman empire collapsed in Africa. "The man of God saw whole cities sacked," he writes,

[C]ountry villas razed, their owners killed or scattered as refugees, the churches deprived of their bishops and clergy, and the holy virgins and ascetics dispersed; some tortured to death, some killed outright, others, as prisoners, reduced to losing their integrity, in soul and body, to serve an evil and brutal enemy. The hymns of God and praises in the churches had come to a stop; in many places, the church-buildings were burnt to the ground; the sacrifices of God could no longer be celebrated in their proper place, and the divine sacraments were either not sought, or, when sought, no one could be found to give them.[52]

Possidius also tells us that Augustine, knowing he would soon die, "ordered the four psalms of David that deal with penance to be copied

---

[51] Brown, *Augustine*, 157.
[52] Possidius, *Vita*, XXVIII, 6–8; cited in Brown, *Augustine*, 430.

out," so that "from his sick-bed he could see these sheets of paper every day, hanging on his walls, and would read them, crying constantly and deeply."[53] He reports that Augustine spent his last ten days alone praying along with the psalms of repentance, interrupted only for meals and the visits of his physicians.

Peter Brown borrows Possidius' image of Augustine praying on his deathbed for the penultimate image in his own biography, *Augustine of Hippo*. And he adds an image of Possidius standing alone in Augustine's "huge library" a year after the bishop's death, surrounded by the works Augustine had only recently collated, corrected and commented upon so that "his works as a whole... might be read, in the future, by men who had reached the same certainty as himself, by mature Catholic Christians," although Brown imagines Possidius confessing doubt that anyone would ever be able to read so many books.[54]

One last image can be placed alongside those of Augustine's penitence, and the library of books written by him for mature Catholics, certain in their faith. Possidius tells us that amid the degeneration of Roman Africa, throughout the siege of Hippo, and to his own death, Augustine, "was comforted by the saying of a certain wise man: 'He is no great man who thinks it a great thing that sticks and stones should fall, and that men, who must die, should die.'"[55] I follow Brown, who follows Courcelle, in attributing these words to Plotinus's *Enneads*. As Courcelle summarizes, then, "Augustine, the Catholic bishop, will retire to his deathbed with these words of a proud pagan sage" continuously on his lips.[56]

The text of Augustine's *Confessions* presents an image of conversion as an instantaneous transformation of the self, which delivers certainty in a new faith sprung from a repudiation of the old, and which is echoed by Nock and James. Freccero's theory of conversion refines this authorized image, complicating its temporality by introducing the problem of retrospective narration but retaining the absolute distinction between sinner and saint within the structure of self-narration in the form of an "I" who is the object of narrative and an "I" who is the subject of narration. But the text of *Confessions* hints at another image of conversion marked by hesitation and reversal, accompanied by layered commitments and

---

[53] Possidius, *Vita*, XXXI, 1–3. Cited in Brown, *Augustine*, 436.
[54] Brown, 433.
[55] Possidius, *Vita*, XXVIII, 11. Cited in Brown, *Augustine*, 430.
[56] Courcelle, *Hist. Littéraire*, 277–82; cited in Brown, *Augustine*, 430.

multiple identifications, and allowing for the persistence of the old man along with the new. The more complex image of crystalline conversion in the margins of *Confessions* extends the temporality of conversion by emphasizing the coexistence of multiple layers of time and the problem of repetition within the process of conversion, but it moves away from the figure of a strong central division between narrating and narrated, old and new, sinner and saint. This crystalline image stresses instead the coexistence and co-implication of these multiple levels within the process of conversion. The more complex image that emerges here supplements the authorized story by suggesting that the rejection of an old self, and the production of a new one, does not exhaust a process of conversion entailing a transformation of the self that retains the old as it enfolds and experiments with the new. In many cases, such experimentation proceeds in part by fashioning a narrative for oneself that posits an absolute break, a rebirth, or a decisive moment of conversion, but such a narrative does not constitute the complete truth of the process of conversion. There is more to conversion than the linear arc narrated in texts such as *Confessions*; indeed, even in *Confessions*, there is what can be called a crystalline structure of conversion.

Returning from conversion to modern secularism, this formation is likewise complex and multifaceted. I would agree with Taylor that narratives play an important role in determining its contours, but I would add that these narratives often take the form of conversion narratives, and my reading of Augustine's *Confessions* suggests that such narratives tend to flatten and simplify the complex processes they represent in predictable ways. Most important, they overemphasize the division between a past narrated self and a present narrating self, smoothing over their rough contours and attenuating the connections between them.

A Secular Age offers a narrative account of the emergence of modern secularism, but it is also more than a narrative account: it is evaluative, and it is normative. Taylor argues for the superiority of an ethical subject who maintains the Christian faith in a secular age. He also argues that this position is threatened on one side by naive and dogmatic believers who cannot accept the plurality of incompatible faiths around them, and on the other side by exclusive humanists who do not acknowledge a higher (moral) power beyond the "immanent frame" of the historically and scientifically knowable world. *A Secular Age* is also a polemical text at many junctures, engaging in skirmishes on civilizational, world historical scales as well as intramurally within the academy: trivially, the threat of exclusive humanism, for example, is embodied by "fashionable professors of comparative literature" and, more seriously, although they are never explicitly marked as such, within the contemporary global political climate references naive believers living in non-Western and non-Christian parts of the world might easily be taken as references to Muslims.[57] Despite the importance of thinking through that latter suggestion, *A Secular Age* refuses to engage either in a comparative study of secularism or in a study that acknowledges the West's relation to the rest of the world. In this, it carries on a tendency in the comparative study of world religions in which modern Christian scholars construe the world through a distinctive set of categories that tacitly privilege their own intellectual-cultural tradition – a tendency that is widely remarked and contested within the field of religious studies.[58]

To be sure, Augustine could likewise be a great polemicist, dogmatist, and Catholic-centric thinker. The text of *Confessions*, however, argues that this pillar of Latin Christendom practiced a more complex and reflective form of Christianity and exhibited a higher degree of "fragilized" provinciality and cosmopolitanism than Taylor suggests that we should be prepared to find prior to our own "secular age." Like Taylor, Augustine acknowledges that the past is sedimented in the present and that identity and narrative are interwoven. However, Augustine performs a feat of self-construction through narration within a community of converts that exceeds the expectations set by Taylor's account of the identity-narrative relation. Most important, in the context of reimagining secularism, my reading of Augustine's *Confessions* suggests that the contrast between secularity and naive religiosity is overdrawn in the text of Taylor's *Secular Age*, and that it is often overdrawn more generally. Like the authorized narrative of *Confessions*, stories about secularism's emergence from a religious past should be complicated by an acknowledgement of the more complex interrelation of a secular present and a religious past that remains copresent with it. Insofar as Augustine's own story suggests that his "Latin Christendom" was far from naive, it draws into question the standard contrast endorsed by Taylor between a self-reflective modern secularity and a naive pre-secular religiosity. Although doing so does not resolve important ethical and political questions about secularism, it may at least light one way beyond civilizational polemics that pit the secular West against its premodern, religious others.

---

[57] Taylor, *A Secular Age*, 637.
[58] See Wilfred Cantwell Smith, *The Meaning and End of Religion*; Talal Asad, *Genealogies of Religion*; Tomoko Masuzawa, *The Invention of World Religions*.

Taylor's *A Secular Age* presents a very subtle, nuanced, and self-reflective version of a commonplace narrative in which modern secularism emerges through a break with the religious past or, more specifically, in which the North Atlantic world enters modernity by breaking with its Christian past. Insofar as they narrate modernity's break from its own past from the perspective of the present, such accounts fit the pattern of Augustine's authorized conversion narrative – *necessarily*, Freccero would add. A theory of the work of narrative in conversion based on *Confessions* suggests how the image of secularism as separation from the religious past can be supplemented by an image in which secularism as a transformative process conjoins the past, present, and future in a complex, dissonant, and open-ended assemblage. Ironically, a more complex figure of conversion drawn from the text of Augustine's *Confessions* suggests that the break between Latin Christendom and secular Europe is not as sharp as Taylor claims. For just as *Confessions* suggests that the new man retains the old, and that the old man is constituted in part through striving toward the new, figuring secularism as a process of conversion would suggest both that the present retains more naive religion than Taylor's account allows but also that the past was itself far more reflective and much less naive that he presumes. Where many commonplace narratives about the emergence of modern secularism as a separation from the religious past function as triumphalist accounts of a Western civilization that is both Christian and secular, a theory of secularism as a process of crystalline conversion sketches the relation between Christianity and secularism in a more chastened and circumspect fashion, which may ultimately allow a more generous disposition toward difference both within Euro-American traditions and at their always porous and contested borders, and which may even allow for the translation of a reimagined secularism across these borders.

Bibliography

Aristotle. *The Complete Works of Aristotle*. Jonathan Barnes, ed. Princeton, NJ: Princeton University Press, 1984.
Asad, Talal. *Genealogies of Religion: Discipline and Reasons of Power in Christianity and Islam*. Baltimore, MD: Johns Hopkins University Press, 1993.
Augustine. *The Confessions*. New York: Vintage, 1998.
Boyarin, Daniel. *A Radical Jew: Paul and the Politics of Identity*. Berkeley: University of California Press, 1994.
Boyarin, Daniel. *Border Lines: The Partition of Judaeo-Christianity*. Philadelphia: University of Pennsylvania Press, 2004.

Boyarin, Daniel. *The Jewish Gospels: The Story of the Jewish Christ*. New York: New Press, 2012.
Brown, Peter. *Augustine of Hippo: A Biography*. Berkeley: University of California Press, 2000.
Brown, Peter. *The Body and Society: Men, Women, and Sexual Renunciation in Early Christianity*. New York: Columbia University Press, 1988.
Brown, Peter. *The Rise of Western Christendom: Triumph and Diversity, A.D. 200–1000*. Cambridge: Blackwell, 1996.
Brown, Wendy. "The Sacred, The Secular and the Profane: Charles Taylor and Karl Marx," in *Varieties of Secularism in a Secular Age*. ed. Michael Warner et al. Cambridge, MA: Harvard University Press, 2010: 83–104.
Clark, Gillian. *Augustine: The Confessions*. Cambridge: Cambridge University Press, 1993.
Courcelle, Pierre Paul. *Les Confessions de Saint Augustin dans la tradition littéraire: antécédents et poste*. Paris: Études Augustiniennes, 1963.
Courcelle, Pierre Paul. *Recherches sur les Confessions de saint Augustin*. Paris: E. de Boccard, 1950.
Derrida, Jacques. "Circonfession," in *Jacques Derrida*. Chicago: University of Chicago Press, 1970.
Foucault, Michel. *The Hermeneutics of the Subject: Lectures at the Collège de France, 1981–1982*. New York: Palgrave Macmillan, 2005.
Freccero, John. "Autobiography and Narrative," in *Reconstructing Individualism: Autonomy, Individuality, and the Self in Western Thought*. ed. Heller et al., Palo Alto, CA: Stanford University Press, 1986: 16–29.
Freccero, John. *Dante: The Poetics of Conversion*. Cambridge, MA: Harvard University Press, 2003.
Hadot, Pierre. "Forms of Life and Forms of Discourse in Ancient Philosophy," *Critical Inquiry*, vol. 16, no. 3, Spring 1990: 483–505.
Hadot, Pierre. *Philosophy as a Way of Life: Spiritual Exercises from Socrates to Foucault*. Malden, MA: Blackwell, 1995.
Hegel, Georg Wilhelm Friedrich. *Lectures on the History of Philosophy 1825–26*. trans. Sibree. New York: Dover Philosophical Classics, 2004.
James, William. *Varieties of Religious Experience*. New York: Library of America, 1990.
Levinas, Emanuel. "'Between Two Worlds'," in *Difficult Freedom: Essays on Judaism*. Baltimore, MD: Johns Hopkins University Press, 1990: 181–201.
Man, Paul de. "The Rhetoric of Temporality," in *Blindness and Insight: Essays in the Rhetoric of Contemporary Criticism*. Minneapolis: University of Minnesota Press, 1983: 187–228.
Man, Paul de. "Autobiography as De-Facement," in *The Rhetoric of Romanticism*. New York: Columbia University Press, 1984: 67–81.
Markus, R. A. *Saeculum: History and Society in the Theology of St. Augustine*. Cambridge: Cambridge University Press, 1970.
Masuzawa, Tomoko. *The Invention of World Religions, or, How European Universalism Was Preserved in the Language of Pluralism*. Chicago: University of Chicago Press, 2005.
Morrison, Karl Frederick. *Understanding Conversion*. Charlottesville: University Press of Virginia, 1992.

Morrison, Karl Frederick. *Conversion and Text: The Cases of Augustine of Hippo, Herman-Judah, and Constantine Tsatsos*. Charlottesville: University Press of Virginia, 1992.
Murray, Molly. *The Poetics of Conversion in Early Modern English Literature: Verse and Change from Donne to Dryden*. Cambridge: Cambridge University Press, 2009.
Nock, Arthur Darby. *Conversion: The Old and the New in Religion from Alexander the Great to Augustine of Hippo*. London: Oxford University Press, 1933.
Plato. *Republic*. Indianapolis, IN: Hackett, 1974.
Rawls, John. "On My Religion," in *A Brief Inquiry into the Meaning of Faith and Sin*. Cambridge, MA: Harvard University Press, 2009: 259–70.
Ricœur, Paul. *Time and Narrative*. Chicago: University of Chicago Press, 1984.
Rosenzweig, Franz. *The Star of Redemption*. New York: Holt, Rinehart and Winston, 1971.
Smith, Wilfred Cantwell. *The Meaning and End of Religion*. Minneapolis, MN: Fortress Press, 1991.
Stock, Brian. *Augustine the Reader: Meditation, Self-Knowledge, and the Ethics of Interpretation*. Cambridge, MA: Harvard University Press, 1998.
Taylor, Charles. *A Secular Age*. Cambridge, MA: Belknap Press, 2007.
Taylor, Charles. *Philosophical Papers*. Cambridge: Cambridge University Press, 1985.
White, Carolinne. *Christian Friendship in the Fourth Century*. Cambridge: Cambridge University Press, 1992.

2

Toleration and Conversion in Locke's Letters

It Is *"Above all Things Necessary to Distinguish"*

> I esteem it above all things necessary to distinguish exactly the Business of Civil Government from that of Religion, and to settle the just Bounds that lie between the one and the other.
> – John Locke[1]

> Believing with you that religion is a matter which lies solely between Man & his God, that he owes account to none other for his faith or his worship, that the legitimate powers of government reach actions only, & not opinions, I contemplate with sovereign reverence that act of the whole American people which declared that their legislature should "make no law respecting an establishment of religion, or prohibiting the free exercise thereof," thus building a wall of separation between Church & State. Adhering to this expression of the supreme will of the nation in behalf of the rights of conscience, I shall see with sincere satisfaction the progress of those sentiments which tend to restore to man all his natural rights, convinced he has no natural right in opposition to his social duties.
> – Thomas Jefferson[2]

Modern secularism, political liberalism, and religious toleration are entwined within Western history, and their relation is crystallized within the modern secular imaginary. True enough, secularism is not reducible to liberalism, and neither secularism nor liberalism are reducible to toleration. Secularism and liberalism, for example, include much more than toleration, and toleration itself need be neither secular nor liberal. But if they are by no means one and the same, being secular and being liberal

---

[1] Locke, *Letter*, 26.
[2] Jefferson, "A Letter to the Danbury Baptists," in *The Papers of Thomas Jefferson*.

today imply being tolerant, and modern secular liberalism is typically understood as an outgrowth of early modern toleration. This does not mean that the relation between liberalism, secularism, and toleration is straightforward or settled – they are crystallized, ranged in a layered pattern, indeed, but not identical, and not fixed. In fact, liberal theorists have long posed themselves a difficult question that touches on this relation: *Should a liberal society tolerate intolerant individuals?* In the twentieth century, for example, some form of this question famously appears in Karl Popper's *The Open Society and Its Enemies*, in John Rawls's *A Theory of Justice*, and in Michael Walzer's *On Toleration*. Theorists may favor this question about "tolerating the intolerant" because it implies further questions about the nature of individual rights, particularly the rights of conscience; questions about the nature of political power, particularly the justifiable uses of force within a political society; and questions about the nature of conflict between the members of a society, particularly the potentially tragic incompatibility of rights and interests. But it is not always pitched so abstractly, and it often arises apropos of the specific problem of religious toleration, in which case it quickly becomes a question about the meaning of secularism: *Should a secular liberal society tolerate people whose intolerance is rooted in religion?*

If the answers to this question are important in their own right, they also reveal something about the modern secular imaginary. According to Popper, Rawls, and Walzer, for example, toleration must be suspended in some cases, and tolerant individuals must then act to defend toleration itself. These theorists argue that there are limits to toleration: that intolerant individuals should not be tolerated when they threaten the liberty of certain others, or when they threaten to undermine the political order that sustains the liberty of all. Their answers must explain what makes a liberal individual's intolerance tolerant and makes an illiberal individual's intolerance mere intolerance. For Rawls and Walzer, the salient difference is that between a secular intolerance and a religious intolerance. There is a decided circularity to such arguments, for the difference between "the secular" and "the religious" itself is often imagined in terms of a properly secular capacity for, and a properly religious incapacity for, toleration. Answers to the question of "tolerating the intolerant," that is, typically impose a fundamental difference between secular liberal individuals and carriers of a certain kind of religion, adherents of what Rawls refers to as "intolerant sects," so that secular liberals are effectively tolerant because they are secular liberals, and the religious are effectively intolerant because they are religious.

Answers to the question of "tolerating the intolerant," in other words, typically posit a fundamental difference between "the tolerant" and "the intolerant," but the very distinction between "the secular" and "the religious," on which they also depend, itself tends to hinge on nothing other than the capacity or incapacity for toleration. The assumption of a fundamental difference (between tolerance and intolerance, between secular and religious) is based upon what I have been calling the cornerstone of the modern secular imaginary, namely the idea that secularism maintains the separation of religion from politics. This idea of separation, based upon the imposition of a fundamental difference between politics and religion, is so deeply rooted within the modern secular imaginary that it can be difficult to recognize it as an imposition. This chapter turns to early modern debates on toleration to show how the very distinction between religion and politics is constructed within a process of conversion.

If the idea that the secular and the religious are fundamentally separate is the most prominent part of the modern secular imaginary, the idea that the secular emerges as an evolutionary or dialectical overcoming of a prior, problematic, intolerant religious order comes next in line. With respect to the problem of "tolerating the intolerant," the secular can be at once tolerant and intolerant, while the religious are merely intolerant, the argument goes, because the secular has evolved beyond its religious precursors, has followed and improved upon its precursors, has added tolerance to mere intolerance. According to Rawls, for example, "the historical origin of political liberalism (and of liberalism more generally) is the Reformation and its aftermath, with the long controversies over religious toleration in the sixteenth and seventeenth centuries."[3] According to Jürgen Habermas, "The historical backdrop against which the liberal conception [of politics] emerged were the religious wars and confessional disputes in early Modern times."[4] According to Charles Taylor, "The origin point of modern Western secularism was the wars of religion; or rather, the search in battle-fatigue and horror for a way out of them."[5] The commonplace historical narrative that anchors the modern secular imaginary leads from the Reformation and religious war to toleration and secular liberalism, for the secular is imagined at a rudimentary level as the overcoming, the transformation, or the conversion of the religious.

---

[3] John Rawls, *Political Liberalism*, xxvi.
[4] Jürgen Habermas, "Religion in the Public Sphere," 4.
[5] Charles Taylor, "Modes of Secularism," 32.

In some sense it is obvious, and in some sense it is surprising, that such historical narratives about the evolution of modern secularism from a crisis within Christianity recapitulate the same formal pattern as Christian conversion narratives from *Acts of the Apostles*, through Augustine's *Confessions*, down to the present. These stories about the emergence of modern secularism tend to fit within the same formal outlines as the life-stories of Paul and Augustine insofar as they depict an agent passing through a definitive identity-shaking crisis from which it emerges transformed. In the Christian conversion narratives, Paul and Augustine find their identities shaken through God's intervention and are transformed into *the* Apostle and *the greatest* of Church Fathers, respectively. In the narrative accounts of modern secularism, Western Christendom passes through the crisis of religious warfare only to emerge anew, to break from this past as tolerant and secular liberal Europe. A critical dimension of all these authorized conversion narratives is the depth of the break they posit between the past and the present, in the case of the historical narratives, between the religious past and the secular present.[6] To recall John Freccero's argument, which was explored in the previous chapter, there may be narratological grounds for this feature if it is the case that all self-narration requires a split between a present *narrating*-self and a past *narrated*-self. This feature may also follow from the particular figure of conversion that informs the narratives, such as the authorized figure presented in *Confessions*, itself based on the figures of conversion that populate the New Testament, in which the "old man" is "born again" as the "new man" (*Ephesians* 4:22; *John* 3:3). Whatever its cause, the narratives that shape the modern secular imaginary create and maintain a series of absolute breaks between a Christian past and a secular present, between a politics pursued in public and a religion pursued in private, and between a secular-Christian West and a non-secular-Christian world.

Such historical accounts of modern Euro-American secularism reinforce the idea of separation as a mainstay of the modern secular

---

[6] For an introduction to narrative theory, see David Herman, *The Cambridge Companion to Narrative*; and, more particularly, for the split-subject of self-narration, see Paul de Man, "The Rhetoric of Temporality"; Paul Ricoeur, *Time and Narrative*; Gerard Genette, *Narrative Discourse*. On the structure of the conversion narrative, see in particular John Freccero, *Dante*, as well as Augustine, *Confessions*. Although my argument takes certain cues from literary theorists, it probes the convergences in narrative form between stories about the emergence of modern secularism and Christian conversion stories without taking "narratological" arguments in their strongest form. I am not positing a necessary connection among secularism, narrative, and conversion, in other words, but rather tracing the consequences of an observable convergence in narrative form.

imaginary, despite this concept of separation's failure to accurately map actually existing forms of secularism. The process of conversion that is fundamental to secularism entails the significant and ongoing transformation of fundamental sensibilities toward public life, and the reorientation of individuals in their relations to communities, which are not adequately captured by the idea of a break from the religious past or a separation of church and state. The process of conversion typical of secularism is pushed onward by this narrative, but the narrative circulates as an integral part of this process articulating and consolidating the ongoing transformation. Conversion narratives, in other words, affect the future by projecting a moment of discontinuity into the past from within a continuous process of transformation: they select and emphasize a moment of discontinuity, change, or rebirth at which the new self is decisively separated from the old, enabling a process of separation that will extend into the future by refiguring the past. Paul is struck by a vision on the road to Damascus; Augustine is overcome with tears in a garden in Milan; in "battle-fatigue and horror," Europe stumbles free of the wars of religion, chastened, tolerant, and ready to become secular. In each case, the narrative form imposes a separation between the past and the present as it facilitates a larger process that stretches between them, and into the future. That separation, however, is a narrative artifact that cannot be fabricated without obscuring other possible stories. In the margins of *Acts'* authorized account, it is noted that Paul would take some time to recover from and come to terms with the meaning of his vision, for example, and it would take him more time still to articulate the very framework of Christianity to which he would later be said to have converted.[7] A decade elapsed between Augustine's conversion experience and his description of it in *Confessions*, during which time the process of his conversion to Christianity continued and deepened considerably.[8] Toleration lagged the wars of religion, and secularism as we now imagine it lagged toleration. In each case, conversion narratives exaggerate the separation between the old and the new in service of a process at work differentiating the new from the old, a process that extends across the break between old and new as it reaches toward the future.

Although they are indispensable to the process of transformation that they describe, conversion narratives never correspond precisely to this process: in looking backward and representing the past, conversion

---

[7] Paul Fredriksen, "Paul and Augustine."
[8] Peter Brown, *Augustine*.

narratives intensify, consolidate, and participate in the late stages of a larger process of conversion. If early modernity is marked by the transformation of individuals and communities through the development of modern secularism, and if arguments about the separation of church and state were components of this process, the framework of the conversion narrative tends to accentuate the importance of separation at the expense of the larger processes that envelope it. This tendency helps to explain the emphases placed on a historical break between medieval Christendom and modern Europe, and a break between Europe and the rest of the world.[9] In order to present a multilayered account of the emergence of secularism, a more complete theory of modern Euro-American secularism would join analyses of the large-scale processes that reconstitute sensibilities in both religious and political registers with the narratives that simplify and consolidate such changes.

Beneath a narrative in which modern secularism as the separation of religion and politics emerged from the warfare of early European modernity, an ongoing process of secularism as transformation continues to unfold on a pitted field of contest, in which separation has seldom ruled in practice, and in which reversals and pragmatic alliances between religious and political forms have been and continue to be the norm. Initiatives to separate various dimensions of church and state have played important parts in this process, but the precise contours of the contested field on which these initiatives have been pursued are often obscured by the authorized narrative of separation, in which religion is imagined to have been evacuated from a newly autonomous sphere of politics, in which there is a categorical distinction between "the tolerant" and "the intolerant," and in which "the secular" and "the religious" reflect this distinction. It would be more accurate to say that the process of transformation, in which the idea of modern secularism as separation was produced, redetermined the nature of politics and religion simultaneously rather than merely separating them along a clear line of categorical distinction. Reframing secularism as a process of conversion can help to recapture a sense of the transformative process that constitutes secularism and that is retrospectively obscured and reduced within the modern secular imaginary to a moment of separation. Conversion provides a framework that

---

[9] On the former distinction, see Rawls, *Political Liberalism*, and Taylor, *A Secular Age*. For an excellent account of the historical construction and ideological deployment of the distinction between "Feudal" and "Modern" worlds, see Kathleen Davis, *Periodization and Sovereignty*. On the latter distinction, see Huntington, "Clash of Civilizations," and Anidjar, "Secularism."

explains how secularism as transformation produces and yet exceeds the principle of separation of church and state.

This chapter takes a new approach to the familiar question, *Should secular liberal societies tolerate the intolerant?*, by turning back to ask how the distinction between "the tolerant" and "the intolerant" is constructed, how that distinction grows into a critical component of the modern secular imaginary, and how it emerges within a field of public contestation. To do this, it takes up a key early modern text, John Locke's seventeenth-century *A Letter Concerning Toleration*, both because this text is of critical importance to the discourse of toleration but also because it illustrates the process in which the distinction between "the tolerant" and "the intolerant" is itself produced. Rather than answering the familiar question, this chapter shows how the very terms of this question are established and maintained within the modern secular imaginary, and how the sensibilities that sustain these categorizations are refashioned through public contestation. It shows how a very specific idea of secularism as the separation of church and state, based on the imperative to "distinguish exactly the Business of Civil Government from that of Religion," emerges from a process of crystalline conversion, and how this idea feeds back into the process of transformation that produces and exceeds it.

A Process of Crystalline Conversion in Locke's *Letter Concerning Toleration*

Viewed through the lens of conversion, Locke's writings on toleration frame a familiar image of secularism as the separation of church and state within larger processes transforming religion and politics. The *Letter* argues for the separation of church and state with respect to a wide range of questions, that much is clear, but its arguments are premised upon a transformation of political and religious sensibilities, and this transformation has been obscured by narratives that emphasize the importance of separation – narratives that simplify and consolidate the process of transformation in obscuring it. Locke's *Letter Concerning Toleration* still functions importantly today within these simplifying narratives: narratives of the emergence of secularism sometimes imply that modernity is born in the rapid transformation, the Enlightenment, of an intolerant premodernity along the lines of the authorized image of conversion, implying that Locke's arguments took hold much more rapidly than they in fact did. More subtly, the ongoing reception of Locke's *Letter* in successive centuries by Thomas Jefferson, the U.S. Supreme Court, and contemporary theorists draws this text into a multilayered conversion narrative that refigures, extends, and consolidates the crystalline process of conversion that originally produced it. Prior to their eighteenth-, nineteenth-, and twentieth-century reinterpretations and redeployments, Locke's writings originally participated in an earlier stage of a large-scale process of secularism as conversion, and they register a range of its vicissitudes in the seventeenth century. The reception of Locke's writings presents a number of important and complicated problems, which this chapter leaves largely aside in order to focus on the ways in which the *Letter*'s rhetorical construction reflects its participation within the ongoing processes of conversion that were reshaping religious and political sensibilities in its time. In this view, one can say that Locke's *Letter* emerged within a transformational process that converted sensibilities and reorganized public life in the seventeenth and eighteenth centuries, and that it contributed again from the late eighteenth century onward as part of the secular narrative of modernity. It is the transformational process itself, rather than the retrospective narrative, that will be the focus of analysis here.

The literature on Locke is imposing, but the following interpretation takes well-established approaches in new directions by showing how his letters on toleration negotiate a terrain of public life shared by religion and politics within a transformative process of secularism. It draws, for example, on John Marshall's contextualization of Locke within an "early enlightenment republic of letters" set against a background of profound theological and political controversy, but it diverges from Marshall's approach to draw the implications of Locke's works beyond this context and to show how religion and politics are continuously interinvolved within a process of secularism as transformation.[10] Within that larger context, this interpretation follows James Tully's focus on the regulation of individual conduct in early modern life.[11] It likewise follows Kirstie McClure's use of Locke's work to trace shifts in the "discursive terrain" of seventeenth-century politics.[12] It departs from their respective prioritizations of "juridical governance" and "political discourse," however, to focus on the inextricable links between the political and the religious discourses tied to the regulation of conduct. In line

---

[10] John Marshall, *John Locke, Toleration and Early Enlightenment Culture.*
[11] James Tully, "Governing Conduct."
[12] Kirstie McClure, "Difference, Diversity, and the Limits of Toleration."

with approaches developed by Paul de Man, William Walker, and Linda Zerilli, this interpretation depends on a close rhetorical reading of Locke's texts, but it presses the interpretation of Locke's rhetoric in a new direction by showing how the key tropes in Locke's writings on toleration serve to re-characterize the intersection of religion and politics as part of the conversion of political and religious sensibilities.[13] In short, the lens of conversion reveals in the texts of Locke's letters a nascent form of secularism that does not separate religion and politics so much as it seeks to reshape each by drawing them into new patterns of connection, by, in other words, crystallizing them within a new formation.

As the foregoing paragraph hints, there are a number of possible approaches to Locke's writings on toleration, but the following should serve as a relatively uncontroversial, preliminary presentation of the first *Letter Concerning Toleration*'s argument. Locke's *Letter* comprises four key movements, which (i) define and differentiate the commonwealth and the church; (ii) enumerate the duties of toleration for churches, private persons, ministers, and magistrates; (iii) set the outer limits of toleration; and (iv) make a pragmatic case against religious persecution. These arguments cohere to distinguish public from private concerns and to distance public political judgment from private religious conviction. Locke holds that civil government should not interfere with religious beliefs, insofar as possible, and that religious beliefs should not interfere with civil government. The reach of government into matters of religion is authorized by and limited to consideration of the public good, and the reach of churches is authorized by their concern for salvation but limited to means appropriate to a voluntary society. At first glance, the regime of toleration envisioned in the *Letter* differentiates civil government and religion; it implies that church and state should be separated, as far as possible.

With this cursory outline in place, it should be noted that Locke's *Letter* cannot be so easily paraphrased without distorting its more subtle claims; and it is the *Letter*'s more subtle registers that this chapter must bring into focus. Locke himself objected to such a reduction of his text, responding to an early critic of the *Letter* as follows,

[Y]ou tell us, "the whole strength of what that letter urged for the purpose of it, lies in this argument," which I think you have no more reason to say, than if you

---

[13] Paul de Man, "The Epistemology of Metaphor"; William Walker, *Locke, Literary Criticism, and Philosophy*; Linda Zerilli, "Philosophy's Gaudy Dress."

should tell us, that only one beam of a house had any strength in it, when there are several others that would support the building, were that gone.[14]

Although this retort was aimed at Jonas Proast's "The Argument of the Letter concerning Toleration Briefly Considered and Answered" (published in 1690), it might be taken as a general cautionary note, for Locke insists that the complex edifice of argumentation he develops on the question of toleration should not be reduced to a single line of argument. The reading that follows is intended to develop a sense for the multiple ways in which the *Letter* grapples with a complete architecture of interlocking presumptions about the will, the passions, the limits of reason, the governance of conduct, the shape of public life, and the dispositions of those who contribute to it. As part of an argument about modern secularism, this reading shows that although the *Letter* contains one line of argument declaring it "above all things necessary" to separate religion and politics, that line is but a single beam set in a crystalline structure that works to reshape both religious and political sensibilities.

A closer paraphrase of the *Letter* can begin to bring this structure into view. To begin again, the *Letter* argues that no one should be allowed to impose a particular orthodoxy on anyone else because "everyone is orthodox to himself" with respect to the proper forms of religious observance. Locke argued that the mind is apt to become inscribed with a host of ill-considered opinions by the time it reaches maturity, a condition that forms the epistemological-political background of the *Letter*, and from which follows the inconvenient consequence that one's own opinions are likely to conflict with the opinions of others. It is against his richly drawn background that he will develop his pictures of intolerance and toleration. The *Essay Concerning Human Understanding* paints this point with notable invective, arguing that "doctrines, that have been derived from no better original, than the Superstition of a Nurse, or the Authority of an old Woman may, by the length of time, and consent of Neighbours, grow up to the dignity of Principles in Religion or Morality."[15] The dire consequences of making opinion sacred by investing it with religious and moral standing were the apparent justification for this invective, for "all those propositions, how remote soever from Reason, are so sacred somewhere or other, that Men even of Good Understanding in other matters, will sooner part with their Lives, and whatever is dearest to them, than

---

[14] Locke, "A Second Letter Concerning Toleration," 67.
[15] Locke, *An Essay Concerning Human Understanding*, 81.

suffer themselves to doubt, or others to question, the truth of them."[16] The *Letter* thematizes the translation of this general epistemic condition into a politics of religious conflict for attributing a sacred status to opinion is not only the source of personal peril. "Whatsoever any Church believes, it believes to be true; and the contrary unto those things, it pronounces to be Error. So that the Controversie between these Churches about the Truth of their Doctrines, and the Purity of their Worship, is on both sides equal."[17] Outside the church there is only error, "for every church is Orthodox to itself," even though its practices rest on foundations as dubious as the "Superstition of a Nurse" or the "Authority of an old Woman." As there is not "any Judge, either at *Constantinople*, or elsewhere upon Earth, by whose sentence it can be determined," religious controversies will be both violent and endless.[18]

In order to comprehend an irreconcilable multiplicity of religious factions within a single polity, the *Letter* argues the necessity of creating some (epistemic) ground independent of that occupied by the churches on which to decide the affairs of the commonwealth. Its precise formulation would, therefore, fuse the doctrine of toleration together with the requirement of an impartial government, and the central assertion of this argument would be that it is "above all things necessary to distinguish exactly the Business of Civil Government from that of Religion, and to settle the just Bounds that lie between the one and the other."[19] The potential toxicity of religious and moral doctrines, because they rest on uncertain foundations and tend not to acknowledge their proper boundaries, required that these doctrines be distinguished absolutely from civil affairs, which were implicitly imagined to be governable in accordance with a limited, but sufficient, probabilistic rationality of their own.

As a statement of the main line of argument of the *Letter*, as Tully argues, this would seem a powerful and coherent position in which the compass of a public rationality of governance expands and in which the private domain of conscience is constrained.[20] Turning attention to the work of conversion within the *Letter*, however, foregrounds a different kind of negotiation between the claims of religion and those of politics. Although Locke's writings imply the privatization of religious conscience, which is the accepted hallmark of a Protestantized Western

---

[16] Locke, *Essay*, 81; emphasis in the original.
[17] Locke, *Letter*, 32.
[18] Locke, *Letter*, 32.
[19] Locke, *Letter*, 26.
[20] Tully, "Governing Conduct."

Christianity and of a secularized Western society, the letters also register a more subtle, persistent, and intimate relation between religion and politics than these terms suggest. If the separation of church and state forms the main line of argument, this main line is buttressed at every turn by arguments that acknowledge and even intensify the interconnection of religion and politics – arguments that crystallize their relation within a process of conversion.

These arguments are not commonly presented in such terms because the question of "toleration" so easily dominates, but Locke's letters were centrally concerned with imagining the proper form and place of conversion in public life. This may be most apparent in the second letter, which steps down from the universalist pitch of the first letter to address a specific interlocutor and a specific policy measure. The second letter directly addresses Jonas Proast and his proposal to impose penalties upon dissenters in order to induce their conformity to the Anglican Church. This was in effect a proposal to implement a policy of forced conversion, but Locke redoubles the significance of conversion by arguing that positions on both sides of the policy are so firmly entrenched that their reversal would require an experience of conversion. Locke stresses, however, the difference between the type of conversion he recommends and that favored by Proast:

> I am not without some hopes to prevail with you to do that yourself, which you say is the only justifiable aim of men differing about religion ... viz. carefully and impartially to weigh the whole matter, and thereby to remove that prejudice which makes you yet favour some remains of persecution: promising myself that so ingenious a person will either be convinced by the truth which appears so very clear and evident to me: or else confess, that, were either you or I in authority, we should very unreasonably and very unjustly use any force upon the other, which differed from him, upon any pretence of want of examination.[21]

The ingenious argument against forced conversion here could be paraphrased as follows: You may be freely persuaded to accept my position that coercion is wrong. Or you may maintain your own position. But if you choose to maintain your position, you must admit that you do not wish to be coerced from it. And, in either case, you must therefore admit the injustice of coercing another's position. But what may be more important than the argument itself is its acknowledgment of "that prejudice which makes you yet favour" certain positions over others, in the face of argument and evidence. Locke suggests that such prejudices may

---

[21] John Locke, "A Second Letter Concerning Toleration," 61–2.

be amenable to deliberation, which leads one "carefully and impartially to weigh the whole matter," and that they may also yield to other modes of persuasion. It would be fair to suggest that overcoming such prejudices in this context would have required a change sufficient to reconstitute one's identity, serious enough to reorient relations to one's community, and of such substantial importance to warrant narration. Imagine for a moment Locke or Proast switching sides on this issue, and consider what that would entail: overcoming such prejudices would in some cases entail conversion.

Although the doctrine of toleration proposed in Locke's letters was by no means unprecedented, it emerged in a context in which the forced conversion (or destruction) of dissenters was not only an established practice but also in many ways a more likely alternative than toleration. Locke by no means converted Proast through their public exchange of letters, but that may argue the seriousness of the commitments or "prejudices" in play, and reinforce the sense that such a conflict could only be resolved through conversion. Locke's letters nonetheless trace out a terrain of contestation, thereby registering a nascent form of secularism as the transformation of both religious and political sensibilities within a theological-political landscape. The letters would later be described as a turning point in the story of modern secularism as separation's birth from the wars of faith. But, in the first instance, they served to contest and transform the patterns of authority, sociability, and institutional power in both religious and political domains of late seventeenth-century life. This is registered most clearly in the rhetorical configuration of the letters, to which we shall now turn.

It would be difficult to reconstruct the sound of Locke's letters in the inner ears of their seventeenth- and eighteenth-century audiences, but it is nonetheless possible to uncover their key rhetorical gestures and to show how they both exceed the argument for separation and point toward a process of transformation. Some of the heated rhetorical quality of the *Letter* can be attributed to the conventions of time and place, some to the genre of the unsigned political pamphlet, and some was even introduced to the text by William Popple, who translated it into English from the original Latin. It is important, nonetheless, to note that this text played a part in renegotiating central aspects of both religious and political life, and that it did so in substantial measure through its rhetorical construction. Alongside its argument for government as an impartial arbiter of sectarian disputes, the letters imagined substantial changes in the parameters of English citizenship as well as Christian piety.

Reconfiguring these domains implied an engagement with the sensibilities that undergird judgments of religious and political propriety. Despite Locke's express statement that "all men know and acknowledge that God ought to be publicly worshipped," such an engagement even included the cultivation of suspicion toward *certain* public manifestations of religion.[22] Although the text announces a sharp distinction between religion and politics, it also acknowledges the practical intrication of these domains and works to shape the terrain on which they meet. Alongside the extraordinary analytic clarity with which civil government and religion, commonwealth and church, are separated and distinguished in the *Letter* lies an equally extraordinary rhetorical performance in which these terms are crystallized with one another.

The fields of religion and politics are in constant interrelation. Arguments leveled at the enforcement of certain "Christian principles" against dissenters, for example, are peppered with interpretations, invocations, and elaborations of those very same principles, and the *Letter* devotes a great deal of energy to elaborating the ethical-political principles of Christianity, whether it is (i) setting priorities for churches by arguing that curbing sin is more important than patrolling conformity, (ii) projecting a mode of charitable conduct proper for public life, or (iii) inflecting its argument in a number of other directions. Here are examples of these first two kinds of inflection:

(i) "For if it be out of a Principle of Charity, as they pretend, and Love to Mens Souls, that they deprive them of their estates, maim them with corporal Punishments, starve and torment them in noisom Prisons, and in the end even take away their Lives; I say, if all this be done meerly to make Men Christians, and procure their Salvation, Why then do they suffer *Whoredom, Fraud, Malice, and such like enormities*, which (according to the Apostle) manifestly relish of Heathenish Corruption, to predominate so much and abound amongst their Flocks and People? These, and such like things, are certainly more contrary to the Glory of God, to the Purity of the Church, and to the Salvation of Souls, than any conscientious Dissent from Ecclesiastical Decisions, or Separation from Publick Worship, whilst accompanied with Innocency of Life."[23]

(ii) "No Violence nor Injury is to be offered him, whether he be Christian or Pagan. Nay, we must not content our selves with the narrow Measures of bare Justice: Charity, Bounty, and Liberality must be added to it. This the Gospel enjoyns, this Reason directs, and this that natural Fellowship we are born into requires of us."[24]

---

[22] Locke, "A Second Letter Concerning Toleration," 38.
[23] Locke, *Letter*, 24.
[24] Locke, *Letter*, 31.

Despite its express injunction against "jumbling" heaven and earth, the text of the *Letter* does not seek to cleanly divide or exclude theology, theological foundations, religion, religious discourse, and scriptural hermeneutics from its arguments for toleration. On the contrary, it mixes them throughout. Nor does the claim that these parts of the argument are simply reducible to Protestant Christianity explain their import. As a transformative mode of secularism, Locke's arguments here renegotiate the connections between certain dimensions of politics, including the shape, tenor, and extension of a public sphere, and certain dimensions of religion, including the authority of the Anglican Church, but also the relative importance of ritual and doctrinal conformity, and the proper interpretation of scripture in its bearing on the conduct of public life.

These passages, and many others like them, extend the argument of the *Letter* between religion and politics such that the text makes neither a purely civil argument about the distinction between the commonwealth and the church, nor a purely theological argument about the necessary relation between individual souls and the worship of their creator. From the perspective of separation, such arguments do not qualify as secular, but from the perspective of transformation, their secularity inheres precisely in negotiating both legal-political and ethical-religious dimensions of social comportment as part of negotiating a new settlement between religion and politics. Secularity neither inheres in this instance in a purely civil form of judgment nor follows as a consequence of theological presuppositions about the soul, the conscience, or the various kingdoms of God. The secularity of the text inheres in its negotiation of patterns of sociability, including but not reducible to the establishment of new forms of the boundaries between religion and politics. The rhetorical force of the *Letter* at these points is bent toward shaping the socio-political regulation of religio-moral vices such as "Whoredom, Fraud and Malice" and toward the Christian-ethical inflection of public-political conduct through the interjection of "Charity, Bounty and Liberality." The concept of separation gives little or no purchase on how these inflections contour modern secular sensibilities, but a theory of secularism as conversion shows their central importance.

Locke produces a panoply of positions in his letters, and some of the tension between them can be reduced by noting how they are meant to construct a transformative edifice rather than to cohere in a single beam of argumentation. Insofar as a process of conversion grapples with deeply engrained dispositions and seeks to shift long-standing patterns of communal loyalty and affiliation, this makes sense of the letters' movements back and forth between positions, launching arguments from scripture against the application of scripture, and from the perspective of the "true" church in favor of toleration. They include arguments on behalf of Christianity as the world's mildest and most peaceable religion turned against the violence unleashed in Christianity's name. Although the letters aim to persuade their audience that dissenters should not be persecuted as a point of policy, they also press their audience in a broader movement toward adopting new stances on the public importance of Christianity, including the appropriate ways in which churches may intervene in matters of common significance, as well as standards according to which individuals (magistrates, clergy, laity, each) ought to comport themselves in public life. So while the letters address particular points of contention, they also address the qualitative nature of the communities structured by churches and the self-understanding and self-presentation of the individuals who populate these communities. These are neither matters of conversion between faiths nor of conversion to or from a certain faith but rather a conversion both of individual dispositions and of forms of community that shape and sustain these dispositions, in both religious and political domains. The secular moment here is not only a moment that separates public and private, or political and religious, but instead depends on their mutual transformation, which registers as a conversion of individuals toward a chastened and restrained mode of religiosity, as well as toward a more hesitant and circumspect mode of public comportment. The "purely civil or political perspective" that Locke articulates requires the recoding of attitudes toward both religion and politics, and although the *Letter* by no means accomplished that transformation, it participates in and serves as a register of this conversion process.

Viewed from within a modern secular imaginary that privileges the separation of religion and politics, the argument of the *Letter* is relatively straightforward. Locke recognized that great peril accompanies the crossing of religion into politics, and he argued plainly that it is necessary for the health of each to cleanly divide these domains. From the perspective of secularism as a process of transformation, however, the force of that argument is less significant than the complex negotiation between forms of religion and politics that cannot be separated, for better or for worse. The *Letter*, in such a view, works to redefine "religion" and "politics," and it becomes clear from this perspective that its apparently straightforward arguments about separation cannot even be stated without transgressing the boundaries between religious conviction and political judgment. Indeed, in the *Essay*, as we have seen herein, the problem is staged in these terms: political judgments are dangerous when they are tinged with an aura of the sacred, whereas religious conscience is dangerous when it is founded in worldly opinion; trouble emerges from the continuous, chiasmal, and crystalline interrelation of the fields of religion and politics. The *Letter* moves across the permeable boundary that separates religion and politics, and it shows how important parts of the terrain of public life are shaped by the rapid, tumultuous, and confusing transactions governed by the crystallized forms of religious and political power and authority.

The *Letter* suggests that Christianity can be conjoined with public life in beneficial ways, but it also presents the disastrous consequences of certain other conjunctions. The first two sentences of the *Letter* present these opposing faces:

> Honoured Sir, Since you are pleased to inquire what are my thoughts about the mutual toleration of Christians in their different professions of religion, I must needs answer you freely, that I esteem toleration to be the chief characteristical mark of the true church. For whatsoever some people boast of the antiquity of places and names, or of the pomp of their outward worship; others, of the reformation of their discipline; all, of the orthodoxy of their faith – for everyone is orthodox to himself – these things, and all others of this nature, are much rather marks of men striving for power and empire over one another than of the Church of Christ.[25]

This Janus-faced opening situates toleration in the warm embrace of "the true church" while it warns against the depredations of false churches. Having already pursued the first sentence's suggestion, we can turn now to follow that of the second. This sentence provides one basis for the text's argument for separation by naming a condition in which "everyone is orthodox to himself," but it also introduces a trope of "Pretence," which performs a critical rhetorical function in the *Letter*. Sometimes varied as "specious Coloration," pretense figures a dangerous type of entanglement of religion and politics. A politically neutral epistemological condition in which each is orthodox to himself becomes dangerous when populated by "men striving for power and empire" over one another. If the *Essay* impugns the status of certain (unspecified) religious and moral doctrines by imputing their origins to the "Superstition of a Nurse" and the "Authority of an old Woman," the *Letter* employs the figure of pretense systematically to produce doubt about religious motivations for public action. Where the *Essay* suggests that belief rests on superstition rather than a more solid foundation, the *Letter* drives this point further by figuring the churches' mobilizations of belief as maneuvers for worldly

---

[25] Locke, *Letter*, 23.

advantage, presenting public religion as a machinery actuated for purely political ends.

Through the deployment of the trope of pretense, the *Letter* strips religious commitment of its specifically religious nature, and it attributes political vices of "ambition" and "avarice" to religion. In the previously cited passage, for example, the *Letter* substitutes "antiquity of places and names," "pomp of their outward worship," "reformation of their discipline," and "orthodoxy of their faith" for what could be called longstanding tradition, holy sacrament, sincere devotion, and regard for scripture. And although the sources of political unrest are difficult to locate, religious zealotry – a "burning zeal for God, for the Church, and for the salvation of souls" – is portrayed as a potent catalyst of unrest.[26] The *Letter* binds such religious "Zealotry" to false "Pretence" such that religious zealotry in the *Letter* emerges as a function of political ambition. For this reason, the *Letter* could easily be mistaken as an argument that religion is dangerous in political life and thus as an argument for the separation of religion and politics, but the problem of religious zealotry in the *Letter* is more complicated than such an interpretation allows, for the figure of zealotry destabilizes the distinction between religion and politics.

The *Letter* does not argue for a direct connection between religious conviction and political violence, nor does it simply argue that religion is a dangerous matter to be separated from politics. Locke maintains instead that Christianity in itself is peaceable; upon entertaining the suggestion that Christians "are more inclinable to factions, tumults, and civil wars" than "Jews and Pagans," the *Letter* answers,

> If it be so, truly the Christian religion is the worst of all religions and ought neither to be embraced by any particular person, nor tolerated by any commonwealth... But far be it from us to say any such thing of that religion which carries the greatest opposition to covetousness, ambition, discord, contention, and all manner of inordinate desires, and is the most modest and peaceable religion that ever was.[27]

The *Letter* argues that intolerance is the root of discord, not religion per se, for "it is not the diversity of Opinions (which cannot be avoided), but the refusal of Toleration to those that are of different Opinions (which might have been granted), that has produced all the Bustles and Wars that have been in the Christian World upon account of Religion."[28] Religious

---

[26] Locke, *Letter*, 24.
[27] Locke, *Letter*, 54.
[28] Locke, *Letter*, 55.

zealotry, in the *Letter*, is neither the true root of discord nor is it even essentially religious. Rather than tying all the "Bustles and Wars" of the day to *Christian* intolerance, as might be expected from an argument for separation, through the trope of pretense, Locke's *Letter* ties them to the worldly desire of power, spoils, ambition, dominion, and tyranny inflected by covetousness and pride. Locke writes that "Bustles and Wars" will mark politics,

so long as those that ought to be the Preachers of Peace and Concord, shall continue, with all their Art and Strength, to excite men to Arms, and sound the Trumpet of War. But that Magistrates should thus suffer these Incendiaries, and Disturbers of the Publick Peace, might justly be wondred at; if it did not appear that they have been invited by them unto a Participation of the Spoil, and have therefore thought fit to make use of their Covetousness and Pride as means whereby to increase their own Power. For who does not see that *these Good Men* are indeed more Ministers of the Government, than Ministers of the Gospel; and that by flattering the Ambition, and favouring the Dominion of Princes and Men in Authority, they endeavour with all their might to promote that Tyranny in the Commonwealth, which otherwise they should not be able to establish in the Church.[29]

The *Letter* cannot make Christianity itself responsible for violence, and it shifts responsibility from religion proper to a form of religious zealotry. However, religious zealots are a nuisance, not for religion's sake but for the sake of ambition and avarice. Indeed, these zealots only masquerade as religious. Pretense figures a dangerous intersection of religion and politics, at which composite dispositions such as religious zealotry appear. Such dispositions are neither simply religious nor purely political, but they present serious threats to public life.

From the perspective of secularism as separation, it seems obvious that religion and politics must be distinguished exactly, their just bounds settled and sealed by a high wall. But, although the text of the *Letter* presents a number of arguments for such a clear distinction, it acknowledges the intersection of religion and politics as a distinctive site of contestation. The rhetorical thrust of the *Letter* in general, and of its engagement with the problems of pretense and zealotry in particular, is to say something like the following: A certain mode of aggressive, bellicose, and overweening political comportment on the part of certain magistrates and clergymen, associated with the high church and aligned with a theologically inflected drive to conformity, foments dangerous social tendencies.

---

[29] Locke, *Letter*, 55.

But a more measured, restrained, and circumspect ethos of political comportment with a different theological inflection toward, for example, the sanctity of individual conscience might support a series of less violent, turbulent, and socially disruptive tendencies. It is one thing to argue that religion and politics should be separate, but Locke's letters also show that it can be quite another thing to contest modes of public comportment that conjoin religion and politics in an aggressive and destructive fashion.

The *Letter* seeks to engage the theological-political commitments of its audience, and in this it reflects larger processes, associated both with the "protestantization" of Christianity and the "rationalization" of politics, which worked to convert early modern political sensibilities by altering self-understandings, reorienting relations to national and spiritual communities, and reformulating patterns of political engagement in both theological and political registers. These dimensions of the *Letter*, however, can be eclipsed by the arguments for separation. Although the principle of separation figures importantly in the development of modern secularism, it should be seen as one part of a transformative process, which, in part through these letters, would produce new ways of inhabiting the space in which religion and politics overlap. In the case of the *Letter*, the process of transformation appears as one that would temper theological-political zealotry, in part through the promulgation of positive duties of toleration such as the following: "Peace, Equity, and Friendship, are always mutually to be observed by particular Churches, in the same manner as by private Persons," Locke's text enjoins. Those who hold office in the church "ought industriously to exhort all men... to Charity, Meekness, and Toleration; and diligently endeavour to allay and temper all that Heat, and unreasonable averseness of mind, which either any mans fiery Zeal for his own Sect, or the Craft of others, has kindled against Dissenters." Furthermore, the *Letter* suggests, "Civil Magistrates growing more careful to conform their own Consciences to the Law of God, and less sollicitous about the binding of other mens Consciences by Humane Laws, may, like Fathers of their Country, direct all their Counsels and Endeavours to promote universally the Civil Welfare of all their Children."[30] The *Letter* deploys the tropes of pretense and zealotry to name and to criticize destructive theological-political dispositions, but it also presents theological-political resources that might be used to temper

---

[30] Locke, *Letter*, 31, 34, 56.

these dangerous dispositions and reformulate the patterns of sociability that sustain them.

An unqualified commitment to secularism as separation was not prevalent among the audience of the *Letter* in either the seventeenth or the eighteenth centuries, nor does it seem to have been congruent with Locke's own self-understanding and political intentions. It would seem rather that the argumentative gestures and rhetorical strategies of his letters worked to shift perceptions of politicized religion and religious politics, not merely to argue for their separation but also to contour sites at which they would continue to cross one another. Read in this way, they suggest how seventeenth-century conflicts over toleration, and later conflicts over secularism proper, are carried out at least in part as contests about patterns of sociability inscribed within political dispositions. While these letters articulate rational grounds for differentiating religion and politics, they must also work to cultivate specific types of religious and political comportment under conditions in which religion and politics overlap. At certain points, this involves heightening distrust of Christianity's role in politics, although at other points in the letters, and in Locke's oeuvre, Christianity is of foundational importance for civil society.

This engagement with theological-political sensibilities is part of the import of the *Letter*, although as Locke recognizes in his discussion of "prejudice," a single beam of argument may well prove insufficient to the task of shifting such sensibilities. The figures of pretense and zealotry support the letters' arguments by depicting the crystallization of religion and politics in dangerous formations and by urging the letters' audience to consider certain dimensions of the conjunction of religion and politics in a new light. In this view, the rhetoric of the *Letter* coincides with larger processes working to convert faith in the necessity of disseminating theological commitments through the medium of public life into a new faith conditioned by the necessity of withholding certain of these commitments from one's public life. To reduce this process to a principle of separation obscures the transformation of religious dispositions and patterns of sociability entailed by the new norms of restraint and circumspection.

The most emblematic sentence of the *Letter* as an argument for separation can now be reconsidered in the light of this interpretation. When this sentence was introduced at the outset of this chapter as part of the foundation for Jefferson's metaphoric wall of separation, it was quoted only in part. In full, it runs as follows:

But however, that some may not colour their Spirit of Persecution and unchristian Cruelty with a Pretence of Care of the Publick Weal, and Observation of the Laws; and that others, under Pretence of Religion, may not seek Impunity for their Libertinism and Licentiousness; in a word, that none may impose either upon himself or others, by the Pretences of Loyalty and Obedience to the Prince, or of Tenderness and Sincerity in Worship of God; I esteem it above all things necessary to distinguish exactly the Business of Civil Government from that of Religion, and to settle the just Bounds that lie between the one and the other.[31]

Locke's *Letter Concerning Toleration* argues the necessity of distinguishing between religion and civil government on a terrain in which these domains interpenetrate one another, and in which the constant exchange between them is often manifest as confusion between "Libertinism" and "Religion," between imposition and "Loyalty," and between political vice and religious virtue. The *Letter* attends to the power of a rhetoric that cloaks worldly concerns in religious garb, as well as the power of a rhetoric that hides particular interests beneath the ideal of civic virtue. But it moves in this terrain itself when it mobilizes the theological-political figure of zealotry to undercut both the sanctification of belief and the public deployment of partisan religious claims. Likewise, it mobilizes the theological-political resources of Christianity against excesses of the same zealotry. Although the *Letter* articulates a principle of separation, then, it sets this principle within the larger processes at work converting the theological-political sensibilities that informed public life in early modern Europe.

Conclusion

The separation of church and state at the root of a distinctly modern secular imaginary is under intense pressure in global political life, but part of my aim in this chapter has been to suggest that the formation of modern secularism should never have been reduced to this concept. If the foundational discourses of modern secularism represented by Locke's *Letter Concerning Toleration* articulate a clear principle of separation between government and religion, between tolerance and intolerance, they also bear the marks of larger processes in which that principle of separation is embedded. Locke's letters register a transformation of theological and political vocabularies and commitments, which reshaped modern citizens and communities, and which has been commemorated

---

[31] Locke, *Letter*, 26.

and consolidated within narratives that continue to contour debates about modern secularism. Although these narratives emphasize separation, and reinforce distinctions such as that between "the tolerant" and "the intolerant" and "the secular" and "the religious," secularism as such should not be reduced to the separation of religion from politics. Negotiating the parameters of secularism today demands, it would seem, a renewed engagement with ethical, theological, pragmatic, and political investments placed within the concept of separation.

Secularism is, of course, no one thing but rather a historically contingent composite of discourses, institutions, principles, practices, dispositions, narratives, and identifications. Despite this complexity, conversion narratives in which secularism emerges from a crisis in traditional religious life play prominent roles in negotiating the distinctions between Christianity and politics in Euro-America and between a secular-Christian Euro-America and the rest of the world. Beneath these stories of separation, there are long histories of interaction and co-implication in which religion and politics are jointly contested and reshaped. And although the principle of separation of church and state is a critical part of Euro-American secularism, this principle is enfolded within a larger process that transforms both religion and politics. This transformative process presents, I would argue, a more plausible starting point from which to theorize modern secularism. Insofar as it rests upon a specifically Christian concept of conversion, extending this framework of analysis to global contexts would be problematic and yet, as I will argue in the conclusion of this book, the crystalline concept of conversion lends itself to such a projection much more readily than the leading alternative.[32] And even if the projection of the concept of conversion remains problematic, the critique of the concept of separation developed here should be broadly applicable in multiple global sites.

A hard-won commitment to exclude religion from public discussion of important collective problems has grown up along with the commitment to secularism as separation, and yet Euro-American politics, to say nothing of global politics, is permeated by religion at all levels. A theory of secularism as a process of crystalline conversion helps to explain the persistence of religion in modern politics, for in this view, secularism has never been merely a matter of excluding religion from politics but rather has always been one of negotiating the contested terrain upon which

---

[32] Warner et al., *Varieties of Secularism in a Secular Age*; Jakobsen, *Secularisms*; Hurd, *The Politics of Secularism in International Relations*.

boundaries between religion and politics are drawn and redrawn. Figuring this transformation as conversion helps to explain both the persistent fact of religion's entanglement with politics and the insistence upon narratives of separation despite this fact. Alongside the injunction to pull theological-political formations apart implied by theories of secularism as separation, it is of critical importance to recognize that religion and politics are nevertheless interconnected, and that their intersection is a site of legitimate contestation where questions of power and authority are negotiated, that it is a site of critical importance to the practice of effective democratic citizenship. These latter points came no less naturally to Locke than the former. Recovering some of his facility in grappling with the connections between religion and politics on a terrain in which tolerance and intolerance overlap, and in which neither can be viewed as strictly religious or strictly political, may in fact be necessary to cultivate those practices of citizenship necessary to sustain democratic governance under conditions of deep pluralism in which there is no reason to think that the public importance of "religion" is receding.

Bibliography

Anidjar, Gil. "Secularism." *Critical Inquiry*, vol. 33, 2006: 52–77.
Asad, Talal. *Formations of the Secular: Christianity, Islam, Modernity*. Palo Alto, CA: Stanford University Press, 2003.
Asad, Talal. *Genealogies of Religion: Discipline and Reasons of Power in Christianity and Islam*. Baltimore, MD: Johns Hopkins University Press, 1993.
Augustine. *Confessions*. Oxford: Oxford University Press, 1998.
Blumenberg, Hans. *The Legitimacy of the Modern Age*. Cambridge, MA: MIT Press, 1983.
Brown, Peter. *Augustine of Hippo: A Biography*. Berkeley: University of California Press, 2000.
Connolly, William E. *Why I Am Not a Secularist*. Minneapolis: University of Minnesota Press, 2000.
Davis, Kathleen. *Periodization and Sovereignty: How Ideas of Feudalism and Secularization Govern the Politics of Time*. Philadelphia: University of Pennsylvania Press, 2008.
Dreisbach, Daniel. *Thomas Jefferson and the Wall of Separation between Church and State*. New York: New York University Press, 2002.
Fitzgerald, Timothy. *The Ideology of Religious Studies*. Oxford: Oxford University Press, 2003.
Foucault, Michel. *The Hermeneutics of the Subject: Lectures at the College de France 1981–82*. New York: Palgrave Macmillan, 2005.
Freccero, John. *Dante: The Poetics of Conversion*. Cambridge: Harvard University Press, 1986.

Fredriksen, Paula. "Paul and Augustine: Conversion Narratives, Orthodox Traditions, and the Retrospective Self." *Journal of Theological Studies*, vol. 37, 1986: 3–34.
Genette, Gerard. *Narrative Discourse: An Essay in Method*. Ithaca, NY: Cornell University Press, 1980.
Habermas, Jürgen. "Religion in the Public Sphere." *European Journal of Philosophy*, vol. 14, 2006: 1–25.
Hadot, Pierre. *What Is Ancient Philosophy?* Cambridge, MA: Belknap, 2004.
Hamburger, Philip. *Separation of Church and State*. Cambridge, MA: Harvard University Press, 2002.
Hastings, Adrian, et al. "Conversion," in *The Oxford Companion to Christian Thought*. Oxford: Oxford University Press, 2000: 135–6.
Herman, David. *The Cambridge Companion to Narrative*. Cambridge: Cambridge University Press, 2007.
Hunter, Ian. *Rival Enlightenments: Civil and Metaphysical Philosophy in Early Modern Germany*. New York: Cambridge University Press, 2001.
Huntington, Samuel. "The Clash of Civilizations." *Foreign Affairs*, vol. 72, no. 3, Summer 1993: 22–49.
Hurd, Elizabeth Shakman. *The Politics of Secularism in International Relations*. Princeton, NJ: Princeton University Press, 2007.
Jakobsen, Janet, et al. *Secularisms*. Durham, NC: Duke University Press, 2008.
Jefferson, Thomas. *The Papers of Thomas Jefferson*. Princeton, NJ: Princeton University Press, vol. 1, 1950.
Keane, Webb. *Christian Moderns: Freedom and Fetish in the Mission Encounter*. Berkeley: University of California Press, 2007.
Locke, John. *An Essay Concerning Human Understanding*. Oxford: Clarendon, 1975.
Locke, John. *A Letter Concerning Toleration*. ed. James Tully, Indianapolis, IN: Hackett, 1983.
Locke, John. "A Second Letter Concerning Toleration," in *The Works of John Locke. A New Edition, Corrected in Ten Volumes*. London: Printed for Thomas Tegg; W. Sharpe and Son; G. Offor; G. and J. Robinson; J. Evans and Co. vol. 6, 1823: 59–137.
Mahmood, Saba. "Secularism, Hermeneutics and Empire: The Politics of Islamic Reformation," *Public Culture*, vol. 18, no. 2, 2006: 323–47.
de Man, Paul. "The Rhetoric of Temporality," in *Blindness and Insight*. New York: Routledge, 1986: 187–228.
de Man, Paul. "The Epistemology of Metaphor," in *Aesthetic Ideology*. Minneapolis: University of Minnesota Press, 1996: 34–50.
Marshall, John. *John Locke, Toleration and Early Enlightenment Culture*. Cambridge: Cambridge University Press, 2006.
Masuzawa, Tomoko. *The Invention of World Religions: Or, How European Universalism Was Preserved in the Language of Pluralism*. Chicago: University of Chicago Press, 2005.
McClure, Kirstie. "Difference, Diversity, and the Limits of Toleration." *Political Theory*, vol. 18, no. 3, 1990: 363–91.

Morrison, Karl F. *Understanding Conversion*. Charlottesville: University of Virginia Press, 1992.
Proast, Jonas. "The Argument of the Letter Concerning Toleration, Briefly Consider'd and Answer'd." ed. Peter A. Schouls, New York: Garland, 1984.
Rawls, John. *Political Liberalism*. New York: Columbia University Press, 1993.
Ricoeur, Paul. *Time and Narrative*, Volume 1. Chicago: University of Chicago Press, 1984.
Said, Edward. *Orientalism*. New York: Vintage Books, 1978.
Schmitt, Carl. *Political Theology: Four Chapters on the Concept of Sovereignty*. Chicago: University of Chicago Press, 2006.
Stepan, Alfred. "Religion, Democracy, and the 'Twin Tolerations.'" *Journal of Democracy*, vol. 11, no. 4, 2000: 37–57.
Sullivan, Winnifred. *The Impossibility of Religious Freedom*. Princeton, NJ: Princeton University Press, 2007.
Taylor, Charles. *A Secular Age*. Cambridge, MA: Belknap, 2007.
Taylor, Charles. "Modes of Secularism." ed. Rajeev Bhargava, in *Secularism and Its Critics*. Delhi: Oxford University Press, 1998.
Tully, James. "Governing Conduct." Reprinted in *An Approach to Political Philosophy: Locke in Contexts*. New York: Cambridge University Press, 1993: 179–241.
Viswanathan, Gauri. *Outside the Fold: Conversion, Modernity and Belief*. Princeton, NJ: Princeton University Press, 1998.
Walker, William. *Locke, Literary Criticism, and Philosophy*. Cambridge: Cambridge University Press, 1994.
Warner, Michael, et al. *Varieties of Secularism in a Secular Age*. Cambridge, MA: Harvard University Press, 2010.
Weber, Max. *Economy and Society*. Berkeley: University of California Press, 1978.
Weber, Max. *The Protestant Ethic and the Spirit of Capitalism*. New York: Routledge, 2001.
Zerilli, Linda. "'Philosophy's Gaudy Dress': Rhetoric and Fantasy in the Lockean Social Contract." *European Journal of Political Theory*, vol. 4, no. 2, 2005: 146–63.

3

The Crystalline Structure of Conversion

Henri Bergson's Two Sources

Il y a aujourd'hui un philosophe dont partout sonne le nom, que les gens de métier – même s'ils le discutent et le contredisent – jugent comparable aux plus grands et qui, écrivain autant que penseur, renversant la convention des barriers techniques trouve le secret de se faire lire à la fois au dehors et au dedans des écoles.

(There is a philosopher whose name is spoken everywhere today, whom those in the profession – whether they accept or reject him – compare with its greatest figures, a writer and thinker who, by surmounting the usual technical barriers, knows the secret to making his work read outside of the academy as well as in.)

– There are at least three books about Henri Bergson that begin with this sentence.[1]

Even if it seems to enjoin on us, as more in harmony with itself, certain rules of conduct, there will be a wide gap between this assent of the intellect and a conversion of the will... Antecedent to the new morality, and also the new metaphysics, there is the emotion, which develops as an impetus in the realm of the will, and as an explicative representation in that of intelligence.

To many ears it brings only the echo of the past; but others already hear in it, as in a dream, the joyous song of the future.

– Henri Bergson[2]

---

[1] Eduoard Le Roy, *Une philosophie nouvelle. Henri Bergson*, is the first to publish this expression. Georges Politzer, *La Fin d'une parade philosophique: le bergsonisme*, repeats it in introducing his critique of Bergson. And Philippe Soulez, *Bergson Politique*, recalls both of these instances in his own recent work.

[2] Henri Bergson, *The Two Sources of Morality and Religion*, 48–9; 165. Bergson, "The Life and Work of Ravaisson," in *The Creative Mind*, 252.

In the most straightforward sense, Bergson's signature concepts of the vital impulse (*élan vital*) and duration (*durée*) are unparalleled resources with which to construct a figure of conversion that moves beyond the authorized image of a break from the past and/or a split within the subject. Whereas the text of Augustine's *Confessions* tacitly problematized the simple figure of a break, Bergson's philosophical writings expressly develop the basis for a theory of conversion in which the transformation of the self is continuously driven by the creative force of time and of *life* itself working across multiple, crystalline layers of being. The theory of conversion that I derive from Bergson's work, in turn, is critical to the task of reimagining secularism beyond the separation of church and state. If Bergson is the great theorist of the crystalline structures that are key to imaging secularism differently, his work provides even more than this. His last major work, *The Two Sources of Morality and Religion*, turns to the moral, spiritual, and political crises of European modernity, proposing "spiritual reform" and "mystic intuition" as antidotes to the progressive "industrialization" and "mechanization" that had come to threaten humanity and *life* itself on a global scale by the interwar period in which he wrote. Drawing on an archive of religion – mainly, but not exclusively, Christianity – *The Two Sources* articulates a new kind of political theology as a response to the shortcomings of political modernity and, specifically, of modern secularism.[3] Bergson crystallizes religion and politics in this work – and it is in this sense an exemplary exercise in reimagining modern secularism.

Bergson was the first international intellectual superstar of the twentieth century, rivaled in France before the first world war only by Émile Durkheim, but although it was once true that Bergson "is a philosopher whose name is spoken everywhere," he has by now fallen so far from fashion that his work requires a reintroduction, and reintroducing it may even require justification. This chapter turns to Bergson because *The Two Sources of Morality and Religion* draws from the archive of Christian spirituality to reframe the distinctions among morality, politics, and religion in ways that remain pertinent to the task of rethinking modern secularism as a process of crystalline conversion.[4] Despite a recent

---

[3] For extremely creative contemporary efforts at reinventing political theology, see John D. Caputo, *The Weakness of God*; Catherine Keller, *Face of the Deep*; and Philip Goodchild, *Theology of Money*.

[4] This chapter does not survey Bergson's work, locate it within a history of ideas, or seek to trace its reception in detail – such work has been admirably performed by other scholars. The landmarks of Bergson studies from which I take my bearings include: as

resurgence of interest in Bergson's work, *The Two Sources* has generally been neglected, and the majority of this chapter will mine that remarkable text, which serves both as a basis for theorizing the crystalline process of conversion and also, like Augustine's *Confessions*, as a register of the work of conversion in the course of its author's life.

Where Bergson's earlier work, *Matter and Memory*, produces the most sustained and rigorous examination of crystalline structures, it is only when this concept is translated to the context of social analyses in the *Two Sources* that its full importance becomes clear. Bergson is, once more, *the* philosopher of crystalline structures, and my reading of the *Two Sources* shows how this concept can form the basis for imaging an alternative to the dominant conception of secularism. Where the modern secular imaginary imposes a distinction between religion and politics, figured as a break between irreconcilable fields, Bergson suggests that religion, politics, and morality can be seen instead as distinct, but interlocking and necessarily interdependent layers of one single crystalline structure. Where the authorized image of conversion posits a stark choice and transition from old to new, from "religious" to "secular" for example, Bergson suggests that the new emerges continuously from the old, and that the old presses into and coexists within the new as the source of novelty, that the interaction between the distinct layers of a crystalline structure is more fundamental than their separation. Less abstractly, Bergson suggests that "religion" must continue to play a number of critical roles within modern ethical and political life, but that "religion" must also be continuously re-created to match the evolving needs of *life* itself. Conversion, in a Bergsonian perspective, is not necessarily the dramatic event suggested by the authorized image; it is instead a continuously renewed process that jostles and effectively adjusts the crystalline structure of identity.

---

representatives of his early reception, William James's *Pluralistic Universe*, A. O. Lovejoy's *Bergson and Romantic Evolutionism*, and Eduoard Le Roy's *The New Philosophy of Henri Bergson*; from the contemporary work on Bergson (all of which owes a debt to Gilles Deleuze's *Bergsonism*), Paola Marrati's *Gilles Deleuze: Cinema and Philosophy*, and Suzanne Guerlac's *Literary Polemics* and *Thinking in Time*, as well as Keith Ansell-Pearson's *Philosophy and the Adventure of the Virtual*, Elizabeth Grosz's *The Nick of Time*, John Mullarkey's *Bergson and Philosophy*, and William E. Connolly's *Pluralism*; on Bergson's life and milieu, *Bergson Politique* and *Bergson: Biographie* by Philippe Soulez and Frédéric Worms, provide excellent overviews (in French), as do R. C. Grogan's *The Bergsonian Controversy in France 1900–14*, Mark Antliff's *Inventing Bergson*, Donna V. Jones's *The Racial Discourses of Life Philosophy*, and Sanford Schwartz's *The Matrix of Modernism* (in English).

This chapter's study of Bergson, like the next chapter's study of Rawls, focuses on the supplementation of philosophical reason by elements of "the religious," more specifically on the role of conversion within public practices argumentation. Where I focus on the question of Rawls's fame in the next chapter, almost to the exclusion of the substance of his arguments, my approach in this chapter is nearly the opposite. In the case of Rawls, my claims are counterintuitive and, insofar as conversion plays a relatively muted, perhaps even obscured role in his life and work, the task of that study is largely to reveal its role. In the case of Bergson, who inspired a massive, devoted popular following based upon his avowedly "mystical" rejection of a narrowly "intellectualist" (i.e., secularist) conception of reason, the salience of conversion is more obvious, and the task instead is to explore in depth the central role of conversion in his life and work. The chapter is divided into four parts: an introduction to Bergson and his method, a definition of crystalline structure, an exploration of crystalline conversion in *The Two Sources*, and conclusions about the continuing significance of Bergson's crystalline theory.

Bergson and "Bergsonism"

Somewhat ironically, in contrast with Rawls, one of the last great American intellectuals of the twentieth-century, Bergson's fame was much greater and much more widespread, but it will in all likelihood also have been much less lasting than Rawls's. Despite the push in contemporary scholarship to reestablish Bergson as a key philosopher of life, time, and creativity, and as a pioneering process philosopher, "Bergsonism" will never recover the prominence it enjoyed at the outset of the twentieth century. Bergson himself might have appreciated the irony with which his work would become a fixture of the French philosophical establishment in the early twentieth century, only to be rejected by the next generation as a by-then classical and, by-implication, passé "Bergsonism" by mid-century. Ironically, Bergson himself might have predicted the eclipse of "Bergsonism" insofar as its apparent necessity follows from one of his central theses: the force of *life* itself, expressed in creation, produces a constant stream of novelty, on the condition that novel creations too become solid and static, that in time they die, and that they are ultimately superseded by new and unforeseen creations. Making is accompanied by unmaking, for Bergson, within *life* itself and within the crystalline process of conversion. At the same time, Bergson insists that the past is never lost and that layers of the past can be reactivated within the present; that observation informs my attempt to reactivate certain parts of Bergson's work today.

From his earliest published work, an introduction to Lucretius with an annotated translation of *De Rerum Natura*, Bergson evinced a concern for the ethical and political consequences of philosophical arguments – one that would persist throughout his career. It is worth remarking that Bergson's first work treats one of the Western tradition's great a-theistic texts, and Bergson argued that Lucretius' philosophical achievement lay not only in refuting the fear of death but also in recovering the poetic force of Democritus' and Epicurus' atomic conception of the universe. The fear of death cannot be defeated by argument alone in Bergson's view; it cannot be defeated without providing a poetic conception of the universe sufficient to convert one's life to independence of such fear. Bergson admired Lucretius' creation of the "most gripping pictures" that were "meant solely to make us understand some great philosophical principle," which in turn served the classical philosophical aim "to free the human soul" by showing "that everything in nature can be explained without recourse to the gods." Bergson suggests that Lucretius' genius derives in large part from the "indisputable fact . . . that the theory of atoms offers a poetic conception of the universe" of sufficient interest "to capture and enslave an imagination."[5] Philosophy here is a matter of poetry, which is in turn a matter of conversion, and the same can be said for "Bergsonism" itself.[6]

Like Lucretius, Bergson roots his major works in a poetic conception of the universe as the fount of novelty. Bergson set out to resist what he saw as the leading tendencies in Western metaphysics, the subordination of time to space, and of becoming to being. His two great concepts of duration and the vital impulse free time as becoming from subordination to spatialized being and articulate the primacy of *life* itself as a process of self-differentiation. These concepts, however, are inseparable from the poetic and literary practices through which Bergson gave them expression. Bergson often developed his arguments as a critique of the classical philosophical tradition, represented above all by Plato and Kant, arguing that this tradition is riddled with false alternatives, such as the choices between materialism and idealism, or determinism and free will, or efficient and final causality. According to Bergson, the tradition drastically

---

[5] Bergson, *The Philosophy of Poetry*, 13–4.
[6] For an argument about the intimate connection between poetry and conversion in a much different context, see Molly Murray, *The Poetics of Conversion in Early Modern English Literature*; and for a brief study of the poetics of Bergson's concept of the *élan vital*, see Sholom Kahn, "Henri Bergson's Method."

underestimates the complexity and creativity of thought, an appreciation for which Bergson seeks to restore by deconstructing and rearticulating these master disjunctions point by point.[7] Although Bergson writes with exceeding analytic clarity and conceptual lucidity, his style is punctuated with metaphoric expressions that both supplement the analyses and direct them effectively toward the reader's imagination. In *Creative Evolution*, for example, he elaborates an analytic distinction between the making and unmaking action of nature:

If I consider the world in which we live, I find that the automatic and strictly determined evolution of this well-knit whole is action which is unmaking itself, and that the unforeseen forms which life cuts out in it, forms capable of being themselves prolonged into unforeseen movements, represent the action that is making itself.

Bergson continues this analysis by reframing this distinction as a metaphor:

Now, if the same kind of action is going on everywhere, whether it is that which is unmaking itself or whether it is that which is striving to remake itself, I simply express this probable similitude when I speak of a centre from which worlds shoot out like rockets in a fire-works display – provided, however, that I do not present this centre as a *thing*, but as a continuity of shooting out.[8]

And he extends the metaphor further to encompass an image of god: "God thus defined, has nothing of the already made; He is unceasing life, action, freedom" etc. Although this conjunction is surprising in the text of *Creative Evolution*, it is strictly consistent with Bergson's metaphorical economy, and anticipates the closing metaphor of *The Two Sources*, in which he suggests that "the universe ... is a machine for the making of gods."[9] Punctuating the classical economy of philosophical analysis within Bergson's texts is a metaphoric economy that is no less consistent and important, and which is comparable to that of Lucretius in its imaginative force. Bergson's use of a poetic register of expression in which one thing comes to be seen as another begins to show both the significance

---

[7] On the complexity of thought, see especially Bergson, *Matter and Memory*, and Gilles Deleuze and Félix Guattari, "Conclusion: From Chaos to the Brain." For a sustained argument that Bergson practices "deconstruction *avant la lettre*," see Suzanne Guerlac, *Thinking in Time*, and for a somewhat different account of his method, see Deleuze, *Bergsonism*.
[8] Bergson, *Creative Evolution*, 248.
[9] Bergson, *Two Sources*, 317.

of conversion within his work and to explain the secret of his success "outside of the academy as well as within."

The Two Sources of Morality and Religion restores moral and religious practice to the wider social and biological contexts in which they are set. This gesture of expanding the compass of reflection in order to reframe a problem is familiar from Bergson's earlier works: *Creative Evolution* places human intelligence within the evolution of the species, *Matter and Memory* envelops the mind within a living body, and *Time and Free Will* locates moments of consciousness within the continuous duration of thought. Bergson's philosophical method could be summarized as restating classical problems so as to acknowledge the concrete reality of time as duration, qualitative multiplicity, self-differentiating tendency, and becoming. Not unlike the young Marx's remark that "the formulation of a problem is its solution," according to Bergson, "it is a question of *finding* the problem and consequently of *positing* it, even more than of solving it. For a speculative problem is solved as soon as it is properly stated."[10] Another way of stating his method would be to say that he makes new distinctions between the tendencies whose conjunction produce phenomena and then moves in two directions: first, following these tendencies back to their common source in a *virtual whole*; and second, delineating the complex relations these distinct tendencies maintain as one is actualized and the other remains virtual, thus forming a multilayered or crystalline structure. According to Bergson, solutions to classical philosophical problems only have value when these problems are reconstructed appropriately.

Reversing the Platonic precedence of being over becoming meant for Bergson that change is the primary datum, and that, in the famous dictum of *Creative Evolution*, insofar as it is possible to think of origins, it is necessary to resist the implication that "all is given" from the outset.[11] On the contrary, if it is anything, for Bergson, the future is open, conditioned but not determined by the past. Recollecting the passages analyzed previously:

> Now, if the same kind of action is going on everywhere, whether it is that which is unmaking itself or whether it is that which is striving to remake itself, I simply express this probable similitude when I speak of a centre from which worlds shoot out like rockets in a fire-works display – provided, however, that I do not present this centre as a *thing*, but as a continuity of shooting out. God thus defined, has nothing of the already made; He is unceasing life, action, freedom.

[10] Karl Marx, "On the Jewish Question"; Bergson, "Introduction Part II," 51.
[11] Bergson, *Creative Evolution*, 37, 39, 45, 51, 268.

Creation so conceived, is not a mystery; we experience it in ourselves when we act freely.[12]

According to Bergson, one of the most dangerous, albeit necessary, illusions within political life lies in the assertion of self-identity, stasis, solidity, and completion as well as the attachment of value to these states. Just as it would be once more for the so-called post-structuralist theorists at the close of the twentieth century – including Jacques Derrida, Michel Foucault, and Gilles Deleuze – one of Bergson's key motifs is the complication and reversal of identity's precedence over difference: identity, for Bergson, is constructed through a process of retrospective attribution, preceded by the qualitative multiplicity of the virtual and its continuous differentiation in the actual.[13] The constancy of identity is local and relative; it emerges from within the transformative movements of life and time: "On flows the current, running through human generations, subdividing itself into individuals... They are nothing else than the little rills into which the great river of life divides itself, flowing through the body of humanity."[14] Intuition (in a philosophical register) and mysticism (in a spiritual one) depend upon access to these deeper currents of transformation, and this is why Bergson would say that "true mystics simply open their souls to the oncoming wave" of becoming and the new. This philosophical framework provides a rigorous basis on which to develop a theory of conversion as a process of crystalline transformation.[15]

Crystalline Structures

The concept of crystalline structure is the key to the figure of conversion I derive from Bergson's work, and key as well to a reimagined secularism.[16] According to the *Oxford English Dictionary*, a crystal is "the standard type of clearness or transparency," as shown "in the phrase 'as clear as crystal.'" In one sense, then, a crystal is a figure for perfect transparency.

---

[12] Bergson, *Creative Evolution*, 248.
[13] Gilles Deleuze, *Difference and Repetition*; Jacques Derrida, *Writing and Difference*. For an extended argument that Bergson represents not only a forerunner of post-structuralism but also an important supplement to this tradition, see Guerlac, *Thinking in Time*.
[14] Bergson, *Creative Evolution*, 269–71.
[15] Bergson, *Creative Evolution*, 99.
[16] Bergson addresses what I call here the problem of "crystalline structure" under the heading of "circuits" at greatest length in chapters two and three of *Matter and Memory*. Chapters three and four of Gilles Deleuze's *Cinema 2* elaborate his interpretation of the Bergsonian crystal image.

Next to this figurative sense, the *OED* also notes that chemists define the crystal as "a form in which the molecules of many simple elements and their natural compounds regularly aggregate by the operation of molecular affinity: it has a definite internal structure, with the external form of a solid enclosed by a number of symmetrically arranged plane faces, and varying in simplicity from a cube to much more complex geometrical bodies." Like glass, a crystal is a homogeneous mass, but whereas the structure of glass is identical in all directions, the structure of a crystal is biased and distinctly stratified in a series of planes. Crystals are composed of layers that produce order and structure through the arrangement of planes and patterns within a homogeneous physical substance. A crystal is thus materially consistent but formally structured. Although they are not properly alive, crystals are nonetheless spontaneous, self-organizing structures – they exhibit in that sense some of the key characteristics of life. A crystal produces difference (strata) within a homogeneous substance (sodium chloride, or table salt, for example), within an ongoing process of (trans)formation.

For Bergson, individuals are "little rills into which the great river of life divides itself" through the accretion of coordinated ensembles of habit, layered within and connected to the larger structures that surround them, and a human being expresses new possibilities simply by enfolding new layers of habit. Human beings are not crystals, but the structure of human identity is crystalline. Following Bergson all the way down might lead one to say, with Deleuze, that these little rills of human being are nothing more than the solidification of habit, a temporary site of repetition and consistency within the larger flux and flow of impersonal life, of *life* itself. Although such a picture of the human is contentious, the picture of human agency that Bergson consistently develops from *Time and Free Will* to the *Two Sources* is somewhat less so. Whatever the human is or is not, agency according to Bergson emerges through a brief interval of indetermination, in which existing habits are suspended and in which new habits may come into being. In such moments, the crystalline structure of human being is disrupted, and its layers become susceptible to reconfiguration. Switching metaphors, Deleuze proposes a figure of "stammering" to capture the kind of creative indetermination in which Bergson locates human agency.

Stammering is an event within language that disrupts, inflects, and reroutes its course, but it is not itself reducible to an ordinary use of language. A stammer opens an interval of indetermination within speech, irreducible to a pattern of speech, but nonetheless giving "birth to a foreign language within language."[17] Stammering for Deleuze and indetermination for Bergson disrupt habitual responses to situations and therefore enable the emergence of new and unprecedented responses. When such new responses gain sufficient consistency, they solidify within a new regime of habit. In Augustine's *Confessions*, for example, beneath the authorized image of a sharp break and instantaneous transformation, the text registers a continuous process in which Augustine learns to speak the foreign language of the Christian scriptures within patterns of provincial Latin inflected by the movements of Ciceronian rhetoric, Neoplatonic philosophy, and Manichean spirituality. Even in his old age, Augustine would not erase the habits and language of his pagan youth, although his recitation of the *Psalms of David*, of the Gospels, and of Paul's *Letters*, which began as stammering interjections, would achieve sufficient solidity and regularity to constitute a reliable language of their own. He recurred to the wisdom of Plotinus to the very end, and his new regime of speech was punctuated by the fragments and cadences of earlier regimes throughout. Like Augustine's *Confessions*, Bergson's *Two Sources* both explicitly thematizes conversion and registers the process of conversion within the life of its author. *The Two Sources* registers a late stage in a process by which Christian mysticism would be enfolded within the crystalline patterns of Bergson's thought and writings.

Although Deleuze has famously argued that the method of Bergson's philosophy consists in analyzing the composite nature of experience into its pure elements, it is important to add that Bergson also continuously shows how disparate elements are contracted within the crystalline structures of actual experience. One of the best known and one of the most enigmatic examples of a crystalline composite is Bergson's conjunction of industrial mechanization and the creation of gods in the closing lines of *The Two Sources*:

Men do not sufficiently realize that their future is in their own hands. Theirs is the task of determining first of all whether they want to go on living or not. Theirs the responsibility, then, for deciding if they want merely to live, or intend to make just the extra effort required for fulfilling, even on their refractory planet, the essential function of the universe, which is a machine for the making of gods (*la fonction essentielle de l'univers, qui est une machine à faire des dieux*).[18]

The picture of the universe as a machine for the making of gods combines two series of thought – for example, modern, technical-scientific

[17] Gilles Deleuze, "He Stuttered," 112.
[18] Bergson, *Two Sources*, 317.

and primitive, mythic-religious – soldering them together in a single crystalline formation. There is no dialectic, no negation, no emergence of one term from the other: a modern secular age does not emerge from a break with the religious past. Rather, these "ages" coexist as distinct and interlocking planes within a single crystalline structure, so long, according to Bergson, as humans wish to go on with something more than mere life. Mankind not only fabricates its gods, it also places the stamp of divinity on reason: "We must add that there are, behind reason, the men who have made mankind divine, and who have thus stamped a divine character on reason, which is the essential attribute of man."[19] Bergson's work produces a cascading series of connections among time, the universe, machines, man, fabulation, and the divine – his writing produces an apparently endless stream of crystalline structures that assemble composites by contracting two or more series without reducing any one to the others. Ultimately, conversion and, therefore, also secularism depend for Bergson on the proliferation of crystalline structures.

Bergson recurs doggedly to the crystalline structures of experience: matter and memory fused in their duality; recollection, perception, and affection joined in experience; intellect and intuition accompanying each other in thought; the closing pressure of habit and the opening pull of aspiration conjoined in moral, political, and religious life. The analysis of the concept of justice in *The Two Sources* is another example of this structure. "All moral ideas interpenetrate each other," Bergson writes, "but none is more instructive than [justice] ... because here the two forms of obligation are seen to dovetail into each other."[20] One series combined in the image of justice is determined by substitution, exchange, equality, and reciprocity, all of which lead to the relative demand of "an eye for an eye" in retribution. The other series conjoined in this crystal is determined by the "justice of the 'rights of man', which no longer evokes ideas of relativity and proportion, but, on the contrary, of the incommensurable and the absolute."[21] Justice, therefore, demands "an eye for an eye" and the "absolute dignity" of each individual at the same time: one facet of the crystal reflects the perfect exchangeability of individuals, the other indicates that their singularity must be drawn "out to infinity."[22] This crystalline composite is reducible to neither facet: justice lies within and

---

[19] Bergson, *Two Sources*, 68.
[20] Bergson, *Two Sources*, 69.
[21] Bergson, *Two Sources*, 69–70; 74.
[22] Bergson, *Two Sources*, 74.

between these two series, neither the one nor the other, but both at once.²³

"Bergsonism" itself is a crystalline composite, which helps to explain its broad popular appeal. From his early essay on Lucretius to the late *Two Sources*, Bergson begins with a classical atheism; develops a philosophical analysis that extracts the concept of "free will" from its theological origins; moves onward to reconceptualize the problems of "spirit" and "teleology" by rethinking with striking originality the problems of time, memory, and evolution; and concludes by rearticulating all of these concepts within a Christian vocabulary of universal love. Once again, however, this development does not unfold as a dialectical process of discovery, emerge through a break, or constitute a simple reversal; rather, the literary, philosophical, scientific, and theological dimensions of Bergson's writings accrete as layers, which coexist and influence one another as distinct facets or planes of the single substance of "Bergsonism." Toward the end of *The Two Sources*, Bergson would write:

> No doubt we are here going beyond the conclusions we reached in *Creative Evolution*. We wanted then to keep as close as possible to the facts. We stated nothing that could not in time be confirmed by the tests of biology. Pending that confirmation, we had obtained results which the philosophic method, as we understand it, justified us in holding to be true. Here we are in the field of probabilities alone. But we cannot reiterate too often that philosophic certainty admits of degrees, that it calls for intuition as well as for reason, and that if intuition backed up by science, is to be extended, such extension can be made only by mystical intuition. In fact, the conclusions just set out complete naturally, though not necessarily, those of our former work.²⁴

Bergson argues delicately here, noting that his intuitions are only probable, that they are natural but not necessary consequences of his earlier work and thought. One might say that he layers his theories of religion, morality, intelligence, instinct, habit, emotion, repetition, difference, and creativity in a singular formation. Recalling the text of Augustine's *Confessions* and Deleuze's metaphor, it may be best to say that Bergson stammers toward a new way of thinking in *The Two Sources*. Therein

---

²³ As illustration of a crystal image, Deleuze favors the moment in Rosellini's *Europa 51* in which the heroine "sees certain features of the factory, and thinks she is seeing convicts: 'I thought I saw convicts...' (it should be noted that she does not evoke a simple recollection, the factory does not remind her of a prison, the heroine calls up a mental vision, almost an hallucination). She could have seized on other features, and had a different vision: the workers' entry, the call of the siren, I thought I saw condemned survivors, running towards dark shelters..." (*Cinema 2*, 46).

²⁴ Bergson, *Two Sources*, 256.

lies the heretofore unrecognized significance of this text: Bergson marks the distinction between a mode of reason that pertains to philosophy and the sciences (intelligence) and one that pertains to mystical experience (intuition) but he argues that both modes are essential to thought. *The Two Sources* will likewise distinguish among moral, political, and religious obligation, but it ultimately argues that these forms of obligation issue from the same source, from *life* itself – contemplated under two aspects, personal and impersonal, and thus conceived as two sources. The essential fact, in other words, according to Bergson, is not that of separation (of intelligence and intuition, religion and morality) but rather of a complex process of transformation through which these divided terms each touch and reroute the other.

Two Sources – No One Source: Bergson's Crystalline Conversion

For the purposes of rethinking the problem of modern secularism today, the achievement of Bergson's *Two Sources* is to suggest how morality, politics, and religion – those domains differentiated and cleanly separated within the modern secular imaginary – exist in a composite and crystalline relation. To put this another way, within the crystalline structure of *life* itself, morality, politics, and religion are stratified and divided in layers – the analogy is precise, for like the layers of a crystal, the multiple forms of obligation peculiar to morality, politics, and religion are distinct but nonetheless immanent to a single *life*. Bergson's title is thus misleading, for although he refers throughout the text to *Two Sources*, he ultimately argues that there is in truth only one source, *life* itself. And the title is misleading in another sense, for it may suggest that morality and religion follow from different sources, while again Bergson argues throughout that the source of morality and religion is one and the same. Religion and morality, pressure and aspiration, open and closed: all of Bergson's great disjunctions can, in principle, be traced to a single source – *life* itself – despite the fact that they appear within experience in different forms. This view represents a radical departure from the dialectical relation – in which the secular emerges from the religious – that is ordinarily posited between these terms and a departure from the strong image of separation that ordinarily figures their relation.

If the moral, political, and religious, in Bergson's view, coexist as distinct layers within a single social formation, which is an immanent function of *life* itself – all three domains are traversed by conversion, and conversion itself appears as the key to figuring the modes of obligation that characterize these three domains. In Bergson's view, the distinctions between domains are real but inessential. Despite their differences, analysis of these three domains reveals two kinds of force at work: "pressure" and "aspiration." Life creates through division, according to Bergson, and thus does pressure contribute to the closure of personal being, whereas aspiration allows the opening of impersonal becoming. These two forces are, however, only different expressions of a single, creative process, namely *life* itself. They compose facets within life's crystalline structure, which can be powerfully figured by conversion, for conversion is perhaps the most precise figure for the processes that close an individual off, securing a new personal identity, and also those processes that tear open old identities by carrying an individual through the passage of depersonalization. Conversion, in Bergson's view, is a proper name for the transformation of those habits in which moral, political, and religious obligations are expressed. In Bergson's view, furthermore, one and the same logic of conversion applies to an individual and a society; to speak of secularism as a process of conversion, therefore, is not to make an analogy but rather to analyze one and the same set of processes expressed at different scales.

Both advocates and detractors have always agreed that "Bergsonism" depends upon a critique of intellectualism, and it is therefore not surprising that in Bergson's view, conversion is not reducible to a shift on the plane of the intellect. It is in this sense decisively unlinked from an image of conversion as exchanging one creed (propositional form of belief) for another, an image that Bergson would fault as intellectualist. As a significant change in the habits that form the self and shape its relation to others, conversion is neither motivated by nor reducible to intellectual calculations, nor as it pertains to the will, can it be motivated by the intellect. And yet, like purely intellectual operations, conversion unfolds on a plane that is suspended between what Bergson calls the "infra-intellectual," repetitive force of habit, and the "supra-intellectual," innovative force of "intuition," "mysticism," and "creative emotions." It is possible to say that conversion fires across the plane of the intellect, allowing the aspirational force of mystical emotions to touch and intervene in the compulsive force of habit. Conversion requires the deactivation of the old habits that sustain judgment and identity and the production of new ones, but it must make recourse to something beyond both habit and the intellect as part of this process – this something is, according to Bergson, nothing more or less mysterious than the impersonal force of *life* itself as an impulse to continuous, creative change. The simplicity of this framework is deceptive, for its analysis is powerful and its implications are far-reaching.

The Two Sources was Bergson's last book-length study, but it represents his first extended work in social theory, more precisely in the study of morality, politics, and religion. This work develops an argument about the repetitive pressure of habit and the aspirational pull of creative emotions, based implicitly on the concepts familiar from Bergson's earlier works, such as the coloration of experience by affect, the contingent and subtractive nature of perception, and the unpredictable but continuous insertion of memory into each moment of experience, and of course the grand concepts of duration and the vital impulse. Although the entire machinery of Bergson's philosophy is implicitly mobilized within the argument, the text of *The Two Sources* is remarkably accessible; in other words, it stretches a smooth surface of elegant argumentation over the complexities developed over the course of Bergson's philosophical career. The text is divided into four long chapters: "Moral Obligation," "Static Religion," "Dynamic Religion," and "Final Remarks: Mechanics and Mysticism." The last chapter serves to recapitulate and intensify themes and arguments introduced earlier in the text and to focus them on the industrialized (or "mechanized") conditions of interwar Europe. The second and third chapters deal with the two functions of religion corresponding to the two forms of society: static religion and the closed society; dynamic religion and the open society. But it is the first chapter that grounds the work and most clearly delineates its two critical crystalline structures: first, the open/closed society and, second, the morality/religion/politics composite.

In this first chapter, Bergson traces the pressure of obligation, which holds a closed society together, and the drive of aspiration, which opens a society outward and expands its boundaries. One of the title's two sources corresponds to aspiration and opening, the other corresponds to pressure and closing; but again, the text's major disjunction between aspiration and pressure, between the open and the closed, produces a crystalline composite, for both sources emerge from the creative force of *life* itself. They form two facets of a crystalline structure: *life* itself is divided between a closed and conservative tendency (captured by Spinoza, for example, as the *conatus*, and more generally in modern philosophy as the drive to self-preservation understood as the drive to persist), and an open and transformative tendency, best understood as a contrary tendency of depersonalization and the drive to change. Here, conversion appears at the intersection of aspiration and pressure, opening and closing, depersonalization and self-identification, unmaking and making. An experience of conversion, for Bergson, registers the disruption of an individual life as the disruption of less-than-human habits through the intervention of more-than-human creative emotions.

Conversion, then, represents the intersection of the divided tendencies of conservation and innovation inherent within *life* itself, at both an individual and a social level. It is clearly a religious experience, but it is not only that, for whereas "religion" has been the site for a number of significant innovations related to "mystical" experience, according to Bergson, religious "mysticism" is not essentially different from philosophical "intuition." Mysticism and intuition are two names for one-and-the-same process of depersonalization through which an individual makes contact with the creative force of *life* itself. Religion and morality in their closed forms are both rooted in structurally identical regimes of habit (they rest within the disciplinary practices and institutions that form ethical subjects in particular ways), and they are both periodically reshaped in their opening moments by structurally identical affective interventions (they are reformulated, in other words, when existing orders are disrupted and undone by complex new affects). Consider Bergson's movement among moral, political, and religious aspiration articulated at some length here:

> Today, when in imagination we call to life these great moral leaders, when we listen to their words and see them at work, we feel that they communicate to us something of their fervor, and draw us in their wake; this is no longer a more or less attenuated compulsion, it is a more or less irresistible attraction. But neither does this second force, any more than the first, call for an explanation. For you cannot reject these two data: a compulsion, or something like it, exerted by habits, which correspond, in man, to what you call instinct in animals, and, beside this, a certain stirring up of the soul, which you call emotion; in the one case you have primal obligation, in the other, something which becomes an extension of it; but in both cases you are confronted by forces which are not strictly and exclusively moral, and whose origin, therefore, it is no special duty of the moralist to trace... Reinstate the duality of origin, and the difficulties vanish. Nay, the duality itself merges into a unity, for "social pressure" and "impetus of love" are but two complementary manifestations of life, normally intent on preserving generally the social form which was characteristic of the human species from the beginning, but, exceptionally, capable of transfiguring it, thanks to the individuals who each represent, as the appearance of a new species would have represented, an effort of creative evolution.[25]

In other words, Bergson acknowledges the modern tendency to separate religion from politics, acknowledges that religious and political

---

[25] Bergson, *Two Sources*, 96–7.

practices are in fact quite different, but argues that the key tendencies that shape religion, politics, and morality issue from the same sources. The creative force of *life* itself, in other words, cuts across the divisions among religion, politics, and morality as it periodically intervenes to transform them. A modern secular imaginary, premised on the separation of religion, morality, and politics, traces surface distinctions at the cost of obscuring the deeper transformational processes that set these distinctions in any particular crystalline formation.

The Two Sources' opening paragraph announces the central conceptual themes of memory, obligation, and command, layering the philosophical and scientific research that culminated in *Creative Evolution* with the moral, political, and mystical dimensions of Christian spirituality. Obligation, justice, moral law – either as the moral law dictated by reason in the Kantian tradition, or the personal command of God and responsibility in the Abrahamic tradition – Bergson works in all of these registers, attentive to the multiple layers of obligation. "The remembrance of forbidden fruit is the earliest thing in the memory of each of us, as it is in that of mankind," Bergson begins, alluding to the story of the fall in *Genesis* and associating this story with layers of collective memory and the structure of the individual capacity for memory.[26] However, this originary memory is obscured by ordinary experience, and Bergson moves on to consider the natural experience of obligation: "What a childhood we should have had if only we had been left to do as we pleased!... But all of a sudden an obstacle arose, neither visible nor tangible: a prohibition. Why did we obey? *The question hardly occurred to us*. We had formed the habit of deferring to our parents and teachers."[27] The argument takes two decisive steps here: first, the facts of obedience and authority are naturalized, requiring no recurrence to a mystical origin or fictive contract, leaving no need for a sense of justice; second, experience establishes the illusion that obligation inheres in an authority that lies beyond experience.

Already, this habit of obedience, itself only just visible, seems to derive from something more than mere habit: "We did not fully realize this, but behind our parents and our teachers we had an inkling of some enormous, or rather some shadowy, thing that exerted pressure on us through them. Later we would say it was society."[28] However, this appearance derives from a poorly framed, retrospective analysis of the composite form of experience. And if we were moved to speculate further about the relation

---

[26] Bergson, *Two Sources*, 9.
[27] Bergson, *Two Sources*, 9.
[28] Bergson, *Two Sources*, 9.

between the individual and the social forces that loom beyond it, "we should compare it to an organism whose cells, united by imperceptible links, fall into their respective places in a highly developed hierarchy."[29] Bergson recurs to this organismic image continuously in what follows; it is a tempting and useful illusion: "Everything, yet again, conspires to make social order an imitation of the order observed in nature."[30] The first page, then, outlines the crystalline structure of religion, myth, childhood, obedience, nature, habit, law, command, pressure, society, and biology produced within Western moral and political thought. This is not yet a theory but rather a matrix, or image, of the mixed state of experience, not as yet properly resolved into its parts.

If the illusion of obligation as such hovers above individuals, and above society, buried within them is a more primordial and primary aspect of obligation, the regime of habit, and in this view, social life as a whole "appears to us a system of more or less deeply rooted habits, corresponding to the needs of the community."[31] Habits regiment the smallest gestures and expressions, and they also pattern the largest social institutions, so that, for Bergson, "the individual and society thus condition each other, circle-wise."[32] For humans, and human societies, habit and intelligence fulfill the roles instinct plays for other animals – they are virtual instincts. Although subject to evolution in the longer duration of a species, instinct is invariant with respect to individuals. In contrast, *virtual* instincts can change: according to Bergson, the difference between human societies and beehives lies primarily in this fact. Human intelligence is differentiated from the animal intelligence by its extraordinary inventiveness and, in particular, by its facility in inventing new tools: nature "endowed man with a tool-making intelligence. Instead of supplying him with tools, as she did for a considerable number of the animal species, she preferred that he should make them himself."[33] Other animals are born with their tools – organic tools, their bodies. Human intelligence is technical and inventive: it produces inorganic tools that are grafted on to the body to extend its capacities and increase its functions as a compensation for a less elaborate set of organic tools. Habits and institutions no less than concrete artifacts are technical productions of the human intelligence. "Let us go further still. If our organs are natural instruments, our instruments

[29] Bergson, *Two Sources*, 8 (emphasis added).
[30] Bergson, *Two Sources*, 14.
[31] Bergson, *Two Sources*, 9.
[32] Bergson, *Two Sources*, 199.
[33] Bergson, *Two Sources*, 284.

must then be artificial organs. The workman's tool is the continuation of his arm, the tool-equipment of humanity is therefore a continuation of its body."[34] Habit and intelligence are nature's consolation for having attenuated in humans what is a more fully expressed range of instinct in other animals: "If ants exchange signs, which seems probable, those signs are provided by the very instinct that makes the ants communicate with one another. On the contrary, our languages are the product of custom. Nothing in the vocabulary, or even in the syntax, comes from nature."[35] What differentiates humanity according to Bergson is the development of this second nature, this virtual reality, wherein humans extend themselves through habit and intelligence.

Every habit pertains, in a sense, to obedience and contributes to a generalized sense of obligation: "each of these habits of obedience exerts a pressure on our will. We can evade it, but then we are attracted towards it, drawn back to it, like a pendulum which has swung away from the vertical. A certain order of things has been upset, it *must be* restored. In a word, as with all habits, we feel a sense of obligation."[36] According to Bergson, however, this root of obligation is projected from the experiences of everyday habit/obligation, such that the everyday conditions and even produces the image of a transcendent source. "We have any number of particular obligations, each calling for a separate explanation. It is natural, or, more strictly speaking, it is a matter of habit to obey them all."[37] None of these particular obligations derive their force from a single source; rather, they are bound to discrete habits and assigned determinate territories. It becomes natural to think that they are each particular instances of a more general obligation:

Each of these habits, which may be called "moral," would be incidental. But the aggregate of them, I mean the habit of contracting these habits, being at the very basis of societies and a necessary condition of their existence, would have a force comparable to that of instinct in respect of both intensity and regularity. This is exactly what we have called the "totality of obligation."[38]

The totality of obligation is not determined, as instinct, but rather is the mere and essential fact of a habit of contracting habits. The root of obligation is not super-obligation – conceived either as a categorical

---

[34] Bergson, *Two Sources*, 309.
[35] Bergson, *Two Sources*, 28.
[36] Bergson, *Two Sources*, 9.
[37] Bergson, *Two Sources*, 21.
[38] Bergson, *Two Sources*, 26–7.

imperative, a commandment, or any other particular kind of duty or responsibility – but rather the abstract and natural need for contracting individual, limited habits. One is obliged only to acquire obligations. So, for Bergson, it is true both that the only general obligation is that of having obligations, and the only necessary habit, that of acquiring habits. One is obliged to contract habits, and habits produce obligation.

Although each single habit is contingent, "everything conspires to make us believe that this regularity is comparable with that of nature."[39] *The Two Sources* opens by mapping the crystalline structure of obligation and law: habit, nature, society, morality, theology. Isolating the components of the crystal image formed in the concept of "lawful regularity" shows how networks of exchange are constituted within operative images of causality and law. In this case, meaning is transferred in both directions between positive law and natural regularity: what repeats with regularity in nature is assumed to obey the command of a law, and laws are taken to command the regular repetition of behaviors. Therefore, the image of "lawful regularity" installs law as the basis for natural necessity and installs natural necessity as the basis for positive law. And the more perfectly the gap between a contingent regularity and a natural necessity is closed, the more perfectly human *habit* approximates animal *instinct*: thus are we "being perpetually brought back to the same comparison," wherein the "members of a civic community hold together like the cells of an organism."[40] Images of God, nature, and man conspire to obscure a machinery of habit that is open in principle to variation, for "we should make a great mistake if we tried to ascribe any particular obligation, whatever it might be, to instinct. What we must perpetually recall is that, no one obligation being instinctive, obligation as a whole *would have been* instinct if human societies were not, so to speak, ballasted with variability and intelligence. It is a virtual instinct, like that which lies behind the habit of speech."[41] Once again, as Bergson says, "everything conspires" to produce crystalline images of law, necessity, obligation, and instinct that reproduce a closed, circular repetition of social order. The conspiracy to promote the placid face of obligation, however, is constantly accompanied by the disruptive virtual machinery of variability.

If the *Two Sources* refers to the grand distinction between the closed society and the open society, and between the static and dynamic forms

---

[39] Bergson, *Two Sources*, 10.
[40] Bergson, *Two Sources*, 10.
[41] Bergson, *Two Sources*, 28.

of religion and morality, the closed society might be figured as a circle, a structure that reproduces itself through obligation and habitual repetition, law-like, static, natural, calculable. The closed society – and the closed individual – are sustained through the pressure of habit to repeat the same. The intellect, according to Bergson, operates between the open and the closed, but the experience of conversion cuts across this distinction. In Bergson's argument, conversion is a central moral, political, and religious phenomenon but also a perfectly natural function of the creative force of *life* itself. Conversion takes place at the intersection of opening and closing tendencies: it is the point at which old obligations give way to the new, at which an individual is unmade and remade again, at which a life is altered by the currents of *life* itself running through it. In the classical Christian view – consider Augustine's tears and Paul's blindness – this experience is registered as a crisis, just as the moment of declining or resisting obligations registers as a crisis in the modern Kantian image of moral obligation.[42] However, Bergson suggests that the figure of crisis presents only a partial picture of the range of possible conversion experiences and, in the modern case, that the figure of conversion as crisis is too tightly governed by the presuppositions of Kantian moral theory. Bergson's rebuke to Kant is decisive on this point: in the first instance, the ordinary condition of human action is not well described as action in accordance with maxims formulated by an intellectual faculty; on the contrary, "habit is enough, and in most cases we have only to leave well enough alone in order to accord to society what it expects from us." Obligation and obedience ordinarily function smoothly, following the circuitry of habitual behavior set in place to enable, speed, and simplify action by constructing responses that approximate instinct. Myriad social relations mediate the individual's experience of obligation, for "society has made matters very much easier for us by interpolating intermediaries between itself and us: we have a family; we follow a trade or a profession; we belong to our parish, to our district, to our country."[43] Social roles mediate the impersonal fact of social obligation and any individual's personal obligations so that when a virtual obligation "has become fully concrete, it coincides with a tendency, so habitual that we find it natural, to play in society the part which our station assigns to us."[44] And, therefore, "duty, in this sense, is almost always done automatically; and obedience to duty, if we restrict ourselves to the most usual case, might

---

[42] Bergson, *Two Sources*, 17.
[43] Bergson, *Two Sources*, 18.
[44] Bergson, *Two Sources*, 19.

be defined as a form of non-exertion, passive acquiescence."[45] Actions in accordance with duty are thus essentially habitual; far from an ideal case or limit condition as in the Kantian scheme, they are the very substance of everyday life.

The actualization of duty is not taxing; rather, it results in the pleasant feeling of reconciling one's individual and social selves by actualizing the virtual pressure of contracted habit. Bergson's account is closely attuned to the speed of human thought and action, to the automation of human action, thought, and speech: the rapid machinery of habit supports the placid appearance of obligation. Although human intelligence constantly accompanies, modifies, challenges, and supports obligation, it generally falls in line with the micro-regimentation of habit that underlies it. Obligation is a crystalline composite of nature, law, theology, and morality, but it does not derive from intelligence – radically reformulating the language of Kantian moral theory, Bergson argues that:

> In a word, an absolutely categorical imperative is instinctive or somnambulistic, enacted as such in a normal state... [I]s it not evident that, in a reasonable being, an imperative will tend to become categorical in proportion as the activity brought into play, although intelligent, will tend to become instinctive? But an activity which, starting as intelligent, progresses towards an imitation of instinct is exactly what we call, in man, a habit. And the most powerful habit, the habit whose strength is made up of the accumulated force of all the elementary social habits, is necessarily the one which best imitates instinct.[46]

Bergson does not deny the pertinence of the intellect to moral, political, and religious obligation, but he argues that we tend to misunderstand its role and overestimate its importance. Although obligation is a strict function of habit, its habits are often the sedimentation or efflorescence of the intellect; part of the distinction between habit and instinct lies in the intellect's capacity to reform habit. Intelligence is capable of initiating the process of forming new habits, but it does not master this process and often cannot anticipate its conclusion. The imperatives of the intellect are transformed as they solidify into the organic tools of habit. When habits conflict, they produce moments of indetermination, and the intellect may be engaged to resolve the conflict. The vast majority of moral conduct, however, occurs below or before the intervention of the intellect: below are what Bergson calls the infra-intellectual pressures of habit and above is the supra-intellectual draw of aspiration.

---

[45] Bergson, *Two Sources*, 19.
[46] Bergson, *Two Sources*, 26.

The articulation of life's needs in the form of institutional habit constitutes the biological basis for what Bergson calls closed societies and accounts for their tendency to move in circular repetition and to incorporate their constituents within the regularity of the whole. These societies are closed in the sense of self-sufficient containment but also in the sense that "their essential characteristic is... to include at any moment a certain number of individuals, and exclude others."[47] The social logic of inclusion under which they operate requires exclusion, and this is dramatized by the limit condition of war: "Our social duties aim at social cohesion; whether we will or no they compose for us an attitude which is that of discipline in the face of the enemy."[48] This is the form of

> a society which aims only at self-preservation; the circular movement in which it carries round with it individuals, as it revolves on the same spot, is a vague imitation, through the medium of habit, of the immobility of instinct. The feeling which would characterize the consciousness of these pure obligations, assuming they were all fulfilled, would be a state of individual and social well-being similar to that which accompanies the normal working of life. It would resemble pleasure rather than joy.[49]

The pleasure offered by the closed society is that of vital health, regularity, smooth function, predictability, and fit – this structure consolidates and defends a particular form of life.

Bergson's conception of life, however, is not exhausted by the life of a single individual, for individuals are traversed at all points by the larger, pre-personal force of *life* itself. This argument is first presented in *Creative Evolution* where Bergson writes that:

> we must no longer speak of *life in general* as an abstraction, or as a mere heading under which all living beings are inscribed... Regarded from this point of view, *life is like a current passing from germ to germ through the medium of a developed organism*. It is as if the organism itself were only an excrescence, a bud caused to sprout by the former germ endeavoring to continue itself in a new germ. The essential thing is the *continuous progress* indefinitely pursued, an invisible progress, on which each visible organism rides during the short interval of time given it to live.[50]

Habit, intelligence, instinct, and sociability are immanent to life, but *life* itself transcends the individual organism, such that it is not merely a

---

[47] Bergson, *Two Sources*, 30.
[48] Bergson, *Two Sources*, 31.
[49] Bergson, *Two Sources*, 51.
[50] Bergson, *Creative Evolution*, 26–7 (emphasis in the original).

property or attribute of any given organism. A life is on the one hand riddled with the nonliving, and on the other a mere efflorescence or local accretion within a larger movement. It is the condition of an individual life that it take a particular form, for precisely the same reason that an individual is obliged to acquire obligations, and individuals strive to persist within the forms they have adopted. This, Bergson argues, is the nature of a life. But the nature of *life* itself also exceeds the individual, opening the movement of depersonalization as another natural process. Conversion, for Bergson, means entering precisely such a process of depersonalization that follows from an intuitive or mystical connection with the larger, impersonal movement of *life* itself.

The inorganic and impersonal bases of life – the current of *life* itself – suggest a second form of society, the open society, which differs in kind from the closed society. For the gesture of universality, the movement of a society opening beyond family, friend, and neighbor to include all of humanity, even to include all of the living as such, is different in kind from the movement of closed, habitual obligation: "We must, in a single bound," Bergson writes, "be carried far beyond it [our humanity], and, without having made it our goal, reach it by outstripping it. Besides, whether we speak the language of religion or the language of philosophy, whether it be a question of love or respect, a different morality, another kind of obligation supervenes, above and beyond the social pressure."[51] This other kind of obligation constitutes the aspirational gesture of the open society by supervening to open habits to disruption and transformation. Whereas sedimentation, consolidation, and maintenance of order describe one facet of the crystalline structure of conversion, another facet can be brought forth that displays disruption, variation, and transformation. What Bergson calls "creative emotions" are the catalyst for this second form of conversion.

The feelings Bergson catalogs as examples of creative emotions are capable of every shade of subtlety, and they may be subtle or overwhelming. As was the case with obligation, creative emotions traverse the crystalline structures interacting with and being refracted by the other layers. The intellect too is brought into motion by creative emotions, but it only ever catches up to developments already underway in such cases – it is neither the source nor the regulator of creative emotions. The play of creative emotions, according to Bergson, is like "what occurs in musical emotion, for example. We feel, while we listen, as though we could

[51] Bergson, *Two Sources*, 33.

not desire anything else but what the music is suggesting to us."⁵² In an early argument for the autonomy of affect, Bergson presses the musical analogy further to suggest that creative emotions are structures that exist independent of the individuals who experience them, so that "in point of fact it does not introduce these feelings into us; it introduces us into them, as passers-by are forced into a street dance. Thus do pioneers in morality proceed. Life holds for them unsuspected tones of feeling like those of some new symphony, and they draw us after them into this music that we may express it in action."⁵³ Just as Bergson insists that the life of habits unfolds in an "infra-intellectual" range of experience, the life of emotions unfolds in a "supra-intellectual" range of experience. These creative emotions may become fixed as what Deleuze and Guattari would come to call "monuments of sensation" – detached blocs of percept and affect.

Creative emotions drive thought from its familiar course and may jar individuals into stammering. "A work of genius which is at first disconcerting may create, little by little," Bergson notes, "a conception of art and an artistic atmosphere which bring it within our comprehension; it will then become in retrospect a work of genius; otherwise it would have remained what it was at the beginning, merely disconcerting."⁵⁴ Although the crisis or failure of shared criteria is one way to mark the moment of conversion, it is important also to notice the creative elements of thought that not only bring intellectual crises about but also contribute to their resolution. In such moments of potential conversion, one is called upon to produce new habits sufficient to express the demand of new needs, desires, and emotions.

Creative emotions can be stamped with a date and name, catalogued and categorized, for they are "real" human "inventions" just as much as inorganic tools or complete works of art are. Next to the circulation of words, Bergson designates emotions as another "coin" of sociability and human exchange. The artist harkens back to a feeling he or she

---

⁵² Bergson, *Two Sources*, 40.
⁵³ Bergson, *Two Sources*, 40. For contemporary engagements with "affect theory" that span a number of fields and perspectives, see Sara Ahmed, *The Cultural Politics of Emotion*; Melissa Gregg and Gregory Seigworth, eds., *The Affect Theory Reader*; Brian Massumi, *Parables of the Virtual*; William E. Connolly, *Neuropolitics*; Kathleen Stewart, *Ordinary Affects*; Davide Panagia, *The Political Life of Sensation*; Sharon Krause, *Civil Passions*; Martha Nussbaum, *Upheavals of Thought*; Hasana Sharp, *Spinoza and the Politics of Naturalization*; and Paul Gilroy, *Darker than Blue*. Much of this work owes a debt to Gilles Deleuze – see in particular Deleuze and Guattari's *A Thousand Plateaus* – and to Baruch Spinoza's *Ethics*.
⁵⁴ Bergson, *Two Sources*, 75.

seeks to express in creating an artwork, and seeks to render this feeling exchangeable, but "There are [also] emotions which beget thought; and invention, though it belongs to the category of the intellect, may partake of sensibility in its substance."[55] Emotions, then, accompany both "artistic" and "intellectual" activities:

> It is the emotion which drives the intelligence forward in spite of obstacles. It is the emotion above all which vivifies, or rather vitalizes, the intellectual elements with which it is destined to unite, constantly collecting everything that can be worked in with them and finally compelling the enunciation of the problem to expand into its solution. And what about literature and art? A work of genius is in most cases the outcome of an emotion, unique of its kind, which seemed to baffle expression, and yet which *had* to express itself. But is not this so of all work, however imperfect, into which there enters some degree of creativeness?[56]

The emotions manifest a vital impetus that sustains human activity. The same impetus also incites, directs, and drives action to its conclusion. As the totality of habits forms the pressure that closes social institutions on themselves, creative emotions aspire to open these institutions to the outside, and therefore, to transform them.

In treating this creative emotion, "we are dealing with an emotion capable of crystallizing into representations and even into an ethical doctrine."[57] It is in this sense that emotion is important for considering "the genesis of the moral disposition."[58] Creative emotions can govern conduct as surely as habit: "if the atmosphere of the emotion is there, if I have breathed it in, if it has entered my being, I shall act in accordance with it, uplifted by it; not from constraint or necessity, but by virtue of an inclination which I should not want to resist," although the force they exert is of a different kind.[59] Each habit, no less than each creative emotion, engenders action without resistance. The distinction Bergson posits between habitual and creative action is one of tone: habitual action terminates in pleasure; creative action, which follows "an inclination which I should not want to resist," terminates in joy.

Bergson suggests that social institutions emerge at the intersection of opening and closing tendencies: each regime of habit, individual and collective, crystallizes centripetal, circular conservation and centrifugal lines of flight. Habit is the past's bearing on the present: it determines the self's consistency, contracting past and present. The intellect is too

---

[55] Bergson, *Two Sources*, 43.
[56] Bergson, *Two Sources*, 46.
[57] Bergson, *Two Sources*, 47.
[58] Bergson, *Two Sources*, 47.
[59] Bergson, *Two Sources*, 48.

The Crystalline Structure of Conversion

slow and mechanical to affect this consistency, and instead it refines and economizes the logic of habit, settling questions of priority when conflict arises, but failing to master the paradox of founding identified by Rousseau.[60] And yet, amid this regime of circular contraction, there are openings and new proposals. In Bergson's terms:

> Would intelligence recognize the superiority of the proposed morality, since it can appreciate differences of value only by comparing them with a rule or an ideal, and this ideal and this rule are perforce supplied by the morality which is already in occupation? On the other hand, how could a new conception of the universal order of things be anything but yet another philosophy to set alongside of those we know? Even if our intelligence is won over, we shall never see in it anything but an explanation, theoretically preferable to the others. Even if it seems to enjoin on us, as more in harmony with itself certain rules of conduct, there will be a wide gap between this assent of the intellect and a conversion of the will. But the truth is that the doctrine cannot, as a purely intellectual representation, ensure the adoption and, above all, the practice of the corresponding morality, any more than the particular morality, considered by intelligence as a system of rules of conduct, can render the doctrine intellectually preferable.[61]

It is the creative force of *life* itself in combination with chance events that impel a change of form: "Antecedent to the new morality, and also the new metaphysics, there is the emotion, which develops as an impetus in the realm of the will, and as an explicative representation in that of intelligence."[62] From one and the same source, according to Bergson, emerges moral, political, and religious innovation: creative emotions, he argues, issue from *life* itself and carry us back to our responsibility for life, precisely by tearing apart existing and partial regimes of habit. The importance of conversion here lies in its capacity, as a depersonalizing transformation, to allow passage to a better form of life. Obligation, according to Bergson, traverses morality, politics, and religion but so to does the refusal and rearticulation of our obligations. It follows that conversion might be understood not as a transformation in which "all is given" at the outset but precisely as a transformation that leads into an unknown future.

Conclusions: "A Machine for the Making of Gods"

"The intellect," according to Bergson, "is characterized by a natural inability to comprehend life," but he strives nonetheless to articulate a faith in the human power to produce genuinely new possibilities for

---

[60] For a discussion of Rousseau's paradox, see Chapter Four.
[61] Bergson, *Two Sources*, 49.
[62] Bergson, *Two Sources*, 49.

life.⁶³ He is attuned to the materiality of thought, and he recognizes the importance and naturalness of human interaction with the inorganic world: technology both enhances and threatens the possibilities of thought and of *life* itself. Bergson is a "vital materialist" in the terms outlined by Jane Bennett, and as Gilles Deleuze, Paola Marrati, Elizabeth Grosz, and Keith Ansell-Pearson have already shown, his work might at many turns remain an important resource on which to draw in navigating the changing material conditions of human culture – biotechnology, information technology, the invention of cinema, and related visual media included.⁶⁴ Bergson's work, however, is equally insightful with respect to the problem of modern secularism – it is this connection that has been largely overlooked.⁶⁵

The beehive and the anthill constantly recur in Bergson's writing, and they often do so as a warning sign, against the limitations of an Aristotelean teleology, also against the organicism of modern nationalism, and against the interpretation of life and of nature as merely conservative.⁶⁶ Each colony pictures a society that functions as a collective organism governed perfectly by the natural laws of instinct, capable of assimilating all new experience within the confines of instinctive repetition. Hive and hill perfect the tendencies of closed societies: they reproduce themselves by continuously enacting the demands of habitual action without deviation. As such, they form one surface of the crystal image that represents human societies. The second surface reflects creative figures – mystics and artists – who fold new gestures, intuitions, emotions, and ideas into the medium of old habits and thereby contract a new series of habit. In the language that Cavell will articulate, these creative figures stand in constant danger of losing the world they share with others by outstripping it, but taking this risk is necessary to sustain the life of the shared world. Each time these figures project themselves beyond the world of shared criteria, they open the possibility that others will follow them into a new world. Bergson's crystalline figure of conversion suggests the importance of difference, plurality, and creativity for such a possibility.

---

⁶³ Bergson, *Two Sources*, 165.
⁶⁴ Jane Bennett, *Vibrant Matter*.
⁶⁵ Although Derrida's "Faith and Knowledge: The Two Sources of 'Religion' at the Limits of Mere Reason" is unusual in its allusion to Bergson's text, this text does not contain a sustained engagement with Bergson, and *The Two Sources* is, as a rule, more often avoided than engaged.
⁶⁶ On nationalism and the organic metaphor, see Pheng Cheah's *Spectral Nationality*, or my review of it, "Spectral Nationality," in *Modern Language Notes*.

Bergson writes that "a philosopher worthy of the name has never said more than a single thing: and even then it is something he has tried to say, rather than actually said."[67] In his view, a philosopher devotes his or her works to crafting a conceptual language capable of rendering visible a single, concrete intuition that demands expression. It is "something simple, infinitely simple" that "follows him like his shadow through the ins and outs of his thought." And, "the truth is that above the word and above the sentence there is something much more simple than a sentence or even a word: the meaning, which is less a thing thought than a movement of thought, less a movement than a direction."[68] Like a great work of art, it is something absolutely new and unprecedented. Bergson's thought evolved over time, but it nonetheless traced the contours of a single intuition: that life is equivalent to duration, which is equivalent to a tendency of continuous change, which is equivalent to creativity. Where *Creative Evolution* names this tendency the vital impetus (*élan vital*), *The Two Sources* calls it God: "In our eyes, the ultimate end of mysticism is the establishment of a contact, consequently of a partial coincidence, with the creative effort which *life* itself manifests. This effort is of God, if it is not God himself."[69] One might speculate that Bergson began to call the *élan vital* by the name of God to integrate his by-then old philosophical conclusions with the dictates of a religious faith that would emerge for him late in life, but he insists that this change does not disrupt the integrity of his earlier conclusions. He sees no need, in other words, to reject the old or to distance himself from it.

If at bottom, *life* itself is continuous change, the self is only self-identical in a secondary or illusory sense – self-identity in this view appears as a snapshot or cross-section of time, for "what is real is the continual *change of* form: *form is only a snapshot view of a transition.*"[70] Individuals, in Bergson's view, strive to persist as they are, aided in part by the repetitive and circular force of habit, but in the end – and at the beginning – change is a more rudimentary condition than identity, and the possibility of significant change, what is known as conversion, is therefore a standing possibility within individual lives that express the creative tendency of *life* itself. If the contraction of habit establishes a closed, circular mode of time, the more profound truth of time is that of becoming, figured

---

[67] Bergson, "Philosophical Intuition," 112.
[68] Bergson, "Philosophical Intuition," 109.
[69] Bergson, *Two Sources*, 220.
[70] Bergson, *Creative Evolution*, 302.

as the eternal return of difference within repetition, which suggests that habits resist time's drive to produce change, but only locally and provisionally, for habits also respond to the pressure of difference as they resist the change it imposes. Opening one's soul to the oncoming wave might begin by loosening one's habitual resistance to the fact that one's self and one's surroundings are constantly changing. In this frame of reference, one would have to recognize the contribution of minor conversion experiences – discovery, insight, failure, mood, thought, loss, decision, avoidance, reversal – to the pattern of daily experience. The suggestion is not that these will all carry substantial political significance but instead that it will be difficult to say in advance which will and which will not.

Bergson drew sustenance from the great mystics (*les grands mystiques*) of the Christian tradition. "Just think of what was accomplished in the field of action by a St. Paul, a St. Teresa, a St. Catherine of Siena, a St. Francis, a Joan of Arc, and how many others besides! Nearly all this superabundant activity was devoted to spreading the Christian faith."[71] But he admired these saints for their "superabundant activity" more than their spiritual insight or moral exemplarity: his great saints initiate the creation or transformation of institutions. Read with Bergson, it is not surprising to find that so many of Paul's, Augustine's, and Luther's writings are less concerned with an abstract and cognitive relation to God than they are with the establishment of practices and communities. Bergson's concern with the mystical tradition, therefore, pivots on his account of how institutions are infused with the creative energies of individuals, in which,

> there is an exceptional, deep-rooted mental healthiness, which is readily recognizable. It is expressed in the bent for action, the faculty of adapting and re-adapting oneself to circumstances, in firmness combined with suppleness, in the prophetic discernment of what is possible and what is not, in the spirit of simplicity which triumphs over complications, in a word, supreme good sense.[72]

Bergson saw a need for building the institutions and habits needed to reconfigure the patterns of social organization established within a modern world unraveling around him. *Mental health expresses itself in adapting and re-adapting oneself to circumstances.* In Bergson's view, the great

---

[71] Bergson, *Two Sources*, 228.
[72] Bergson, *Two Sources*, 228.

saints – better, the great mystics – are those who change social institutions without distinction among morality, politics, or religion.

When Deleuze expressed his admiration for Jean-Luc Godard's ability to intervene in social life by inventing new cultural forms, he noticed that "it's as though, in a way, he's always stammering... it's this creative stammering... which makes Godard a force."[73] Associating Godard's work with the opening chapter of Bergson's *Matter and Memory*, Deleuze would note, "That's not to say that Godard's a Bergsonian. It's more the other way around; Godard's not even reviving Bergson, but finding bits of Bergson along his way as he revivifies television."[74] And, in particular, Deleuze focused on Godard's ability to create new crystalline images by contracting series of individuals, objects, and events in film. It is the production of new crystalline images, the proliferation of crystals as such that makes the difference:

The convict *and* his wife. The mother *and* child. But also images *and* sounds. And the clockmaker's movements when he's in his clockmaking sequence *and* when he's at his editing table: an imperceptible border separates them, belonging to neither but carrying both forward in their disparate development, in a flight or in a flow where we no longer know which is the guiding thread, nor where it's going.[75]

Enlarging perception to encompass both this *and* that together increases the possibilities of thought and action by producing new sites of indetermination: Deleuze calls this "stammering" but, following Bergson, one could also call this an appeal to the crystalline nature of experience, subjectivity, and *life* itself. The concept of crystalline structure allows Bergson and Deleuze to generalize and expand what is often understood as the work of metaphor. If a metaphor is a figure of language that substitutes and therefore effects an equivalence between nonidentical terms, a figure that enfolds difference within identity, crystals are natural structures that conjoin layers of difference without linguistic mediation. Disengaging the regular function of habit by entering creative encounters serves as the basis for the possibility of conversion. Such encounters and conjunctions open small doorways across imperceptible borders. As Augustine's life and work suggest, the marquee experience described within conversion

---

[73] Gilles Deleuze, "Three Questions on *Six Times Two*," 37–8.
[74] Deleuze, "Three Questions on *Six Times Two*," 43.
[75] Deleuze, "Three Questions on *Six Times Two*," 45.

narratives emerges from, and is folded back within, the crystalline structure of a process of conversion.

Because individuals and institutions are crystalline structures composed of layers of inter-involved circuits of habit, crossing these imperceptible borders can yield unexpectedly dramatic results when new circuits of habit take form. Moving away from the standard image of conversion as separation dictated by the narrative convention of a strong and decisive break toward a crystalline image of conversion as stammering allows for the production of more supple accounts of social transformations: the concept of a crystalline structure complicates the figure of conversion and opens the figure of conversion onto the problematic of a deep and multidimensional pluralism. The concept of a crystalline structure emphasizes that conversion may also be partial, that it may affect some layers of being while leaving others in place, that it may engage multiple and irreconcilable sources at the same time. These new engagements are facilitated by a heightened sensitivity to the compulsions of habit, the work done to fabricate ("to fabulate" as Bergson would say) a stable self-identity, and techniques of contracting new elements within one's existing ensemble of habits.

As the processes of globalization continue to connect and contract the world, producing ever more deeply pluralistic nation-states, in which ongoing politics of recognition foreground this pluralism ever more prominently, this sheer proximity and unavoidable interdependence place increasing levels of transformative pressure on existing religious and political institutions, as well as upon individual dispositions, sensibilities, and identities. One strong tendency, under such conditions, is to retrench identity – reasserting, for example, the essential place of a certain language, lineage, religion, race, ethnicity, culture, or tradition to national identity and imposing a reconversion to a state of lost purity. Bergson suggests the possibility of pursuing another trajectory, by embracing the transformation of identity through its intersection with difference. Against the closing tendency of reconversion to an already authorized past, to the same, he sets the opening tendency of conversion to an uncertain, crystalline future.

The following are well-known facts about Bergson's life: over a long course of time, he underwent a conversion from Judaism to Roman Catholicism, but this conversion was never made official. His will requested that a Catholic priest officiate at his funeral, but it added that a rabbi should be asked to officiate in the event that his first choice would not be sanctioned by the church. In spite of official offers of exemption made on account of his fame, as an old man, he stood in line to register with the authorities of German-occupied France as a Jew. He contracted the illness that would ultimately lead to his death in doing so. He said that he had not officially and publicly converted to Roman Catholicism in view of the rising tide of European anti-Semitism: he wished instead to stand with a Jewish minority in the face of persecution.

The distance between Augustine and Bergson is immense, as is the distance between *Confessions* and *The Two Sources*, as is the distance between the former's authorized image of conversion and the latter's more complex, crystalline figure. In connection with the problem of modern secularism, Bergson's figure suggests that the moral, the political, and the religious – that past, present, and future – can never be cleanly severed, that their separation is only ever an appearance, masking a deeper truth of the past's active conservation in the present, and the present's continual differentiation within the future. Conversion, and thus also secularism, according to Bergson, depend upon opening oneself – whatever the cost and danger – to the unknown, to the necessity, that is, of change, and the possibility of arriving at humanity by outstripping it.

Bibliography

Ahmed, Sara. *The Cultural Politics of Emotion*. New York: Routledge, 2004.

Ansell-Pearson, Keith. *Philosophy and the Adventure of the Virtual: Bergson and the Time of Life*. New York: Routledge, 2002.

Antliff, Mark. *Inventing Bergson: Cultural Politics and the Parisian Avant-Garde*. Princeton, NJ: Princeton University Press, 1993.

Bennett, Jane. *Vibrant Matter: A Political Ecology of Things*. Durham, NC: Duke University Press, 2010.

Bergson, Henri. *Creative Evolution*. Mineola, NY: Dover, 1998.

Bergson, Henri. "Introduction Part II," in *The Creative Mind: An Introduction to Metaphysics*. New York: Citadel Press, 1946: 18–72.

Bergson, Henri. "The Life and Work of Ravaisson," in *The Creative Mind: An Introduction to Metaphysics*. New York: Citadel Press, 1946: 187–216.

Bergson, Henri. *Matter and Memory*. New York: Zone Books, 1991.

Bergson, Henri. "Philosophical Intuition," in *The Creative Mind: An Introduction to Metaphysics*. New York: Citadel Press, 1946: 87–106.

Bergson, Henri. *The Philosophy of Poetry: The Genius of Lucretius*. New York: Philosophical Library, 1959.

Bergson, Henri. *The Two Sources of Morality and Religion*. Notre Dame, IN: University of Notre Dame, 1977.

Caputo, John D. *The Weakness of God: A Theology of the Event*. Bloomington: Indiana University Press, 2006.

Cheah, Pheng. *Spectral Nationality: Passages of Freedom from Kant to Postcolonial Literatures*. New York: Columbia University Press, 2003.

Connolly, William E. *Neuropolitics: Thinking, Culture, Speed*. Minneapolis: University of Minnesota Press, 2002.
Connolly, William E. *Pluralism*. Durham, NC: Duke University Press, 2005.
Derrida, Jacques. "Faith and Knowledge: The Two Sources of 'Religion' at the Limits of Mere Reason," in Derrida and Vattimo, eds., *Religion*. Palo Alto, CA: Stanford University Press, 1998: 1–78.
Deleuze, Gilles. *Bergsonism*. New York: Zone Books, 1988.
Deleuze, Gilles, and Félix Guattari. "Conclusion: From Chaos to the Brain," in *What is Philosophy?* New York: Columbia University Press, 1994: 201–18.
Deleuze, Gilles. *Cinema 2*. Minneapolis: University of Minnesota Press, 1989.
Deleuze, Gilles. *Difference and Repetition*. New York: Columbia University Press, 1994.
Deleuze, Gilles. "He Stuttered," in *Essays Critical and Clinical*. Minneapolis: University of Minnesota Press, 1997: 107–114.
Deleuze, Gilles. "Three Questions on *Six Times Two*," in *Negotiations 1972–90*. New York: Columbia University Press, 1997: 37–45.
Deleuze, Gilles, and Felix Guattari. *A Thousand Plateaus: Capitalism and Schizophrenia*. Minneapolis: University of Minnesota Press, 1987.
Derrida, Jacques. *Writing and Difference*. Chicago: University of Chicago Press, 1978.
Gilroy, Paul. *Darker than Blue: On the Moral Economies of Black Atlantic Culture*. Cambridge, MA: Harvard University Press, 2010.
Goodchild, Philip. *Theology of Money*. Durham, NC: Duke University Press, 2009.
Gregg, Melissa, and Gregory Seigworth, eds., *The Affect Theory Reader*. Durham, NC: Duke University Press, 2010.
Grogin, R. C. *The Bergsonian Controversy in France 1900–14*. Calgary: University of Calgary Press, 1988.
Grosz, Elizabeth. *The Nick of Time: Politics, Evolution, and the Untimely*. Durham, NC: Duke University Press, 2004.
Guerlac, Suzanne. *Literary Polemics: Bataille, Sartre, Valéry, Breton*. Palo Alto, CA: Stanford University Press, 1997.
Guerlac, Suzanne, *Thinking in Time: An Introduction to Henri Bergson*. Ithaca, NY: Cornell University Press, 2006.
James, William. *A Pluralistic Universe*. Cambridge, MA: Harvard University Press, 1977.
Jones, Donna V. *The Racial Discourses of Life Philosophy: Negritude, Vitalism, and Modernity*. New York: Columbia University Press, 2010.
Kahn, Sholom J. "Henri Bergson's Method." *Antioch Review*, vol. 5, no. 3, Autumn 1945: 440–51.
Keller; Catherine. *Face of the Deep: A Theology of Becoming*. New York: Routledge, 2003.
Krause, Sharon. *Civil Passions: Moral Sentiment and Democratic Deliberation*. Princeton, NJ: Princeton University Press, 2008.
Le Roy, Eduoard. *Une philosophie nouvelle: Henri Bergson*. Paris: Alcan, 1913.
Lovejoy, A. O. *Bergson and Romantic Evolutionism*. Berkeley: University of California Press, 1914.

Marrati, Paola. *Gilles Deleuze: Cinema and Philosophy*. Baltimore, MD: Johns Hopkins University Press, 2008.
Marx, Karl. "On the Jewish Question," in *The Marx-Engels Reader*. New York: Norton, 1978: 26–52.
Massumi, Brian. *Parables for the Virtual: Movement, Affect, Sensation*. Durham, NC: Duke University Press, 2002.
Mullarkey, John. *Bergson and Philosophy*. Notre Dame, IN: University of Notre Dame Press, 2000.
Murray, Molly. *The Poetics of Conversion in Early Modern English Literature: Verse and Change from Donne to Dryden*. Cambridge: Cambridge University Press, 2011.
Nussbaum, Martha. *Upheavals of Thought: The Intelligence of Emotions*. Cambridge: Cambridge University Press, 2001.
Panagia, Davide. *The Political Life of Sensation*. Durham, NC: Duke University Press, 2009.
Politzer, Georges. *La Fin d'une parade philosophique: Le bergsonisme*. Paris: J. J. Pauvert, 1967.
Scherer, Matthew. "Review of Spectral Nationality: Passages of Freedom from Kant to Postcolonial Literatures." *Modern Language Notes*, vol. 20, no. 5, December 2005: 1239–44.
Schwartz, Sanford. *The Matrix of Modernism: Pound, Eliot, and Early Twentieth-Century Thought*. Princeton, NJ: Princeton University Press, 1985.
Sharp, Hasana. *Spinoza and the Politics of Naturalization*. Chicago: University of Chicago Press, 2011.
Soulez, Philippe. *Bergson Politique*. Paris: Presses universitaires de France, 1989.
Soulez, Philippe, and Frédéric Worms. *Bergson: Biographie*. Paris: Flammarion, 1997.
Spinoza, Baruch. *Ethics*. Indianapolis: Hackett, 1991.
Stewart, Kathleen. *Ordinary Affects*. Durham, NC: Duke University Press, 2007.

4

Saint John (Rawls)

The Miracle of Secular Reason

> Let us not then merely assert that reason, present in each of us, compels our respect and commands our obedience by virtue of its paramount value. We must add that there are, behind reason, the men who have made mankind divine, and who have thus stamped a divine character on reason, which is the essential attribute of man.
> – Henri Bergson[1]

> An ounce of the Bible is worth a pound (possibly a ton) of Aristotle.
> – John Rawls[2]

John Rawls is a Saint. In the words of Amy Gutmann, who remarked, when delivering his eulogy, that she felt "privileged to have lived in his time," Rawls was "saintly as well as wise."[3] Within certain communities of political theorists, within a much wider intellectual public as well, a similar devotion was evident in the expressions of personal admiration that followed in the wake of Rawls's death. Expressions of admiration and devotion, of love and loss, are perfectly natural in modern Western cultures of mourning but, at the same time, this kind of response may have embarrassed a highly private person, who by all accounts went to great lengths to avoid celebrity, let alone sainthood. It certainly presents a series of problems to consider for proponents of secular liberalism who share in these feelings of reverence and for students of modern secularism more generally: How is it that after all these centuries, and

---

[1] Henri Bergson, *Two Sources of Morality and Religion*, 68.
[2] John Rawls, "A Brief Inquiry into the Meaning of Sin and Faith," preface.
[3] Amy Gutmann, "A Tribute to John Rawls 1921–2002."

in the face of all its protestations to the contrary, even an avowedly secular, liberal, democratic politics still needs a saint? If it is clear that the figure of separation is insufficient to account for the complexities of modern secularism, what can Rawls's position as the patron saint of this formation tell us about the relation between religion and politics inscribed within it?

Although it may only have been offhand, Gutmann's remark prompts serious questions about the persistence of a disavowed political-theological moment within the discourse of secularism, for it would be somewhat scandalous to find that the paradigmatic theoretical discourse of secular, liberal, democratic politics is intimately bound up with and permeated by religion.[4] To put this another way, the arguments of Rawls's major works, *A Theory of Justice* and *Political Liberalism*, are intended to be secular in the precise sense that they are to be independent of all metaphysical traditions, including of course all religious traditions. Such a post-metaphysical theory cannot depend on the saintliness of its author, but the history of this work's reception and its author's biography hint that even this self-consciously post-metaphysical discourse depends on traces of religion and, in particular, on the saintly persona of its author. This chapter will show how forms of modern secularism, such as that developed by Rawls, work to produce the very distinction between religion and politics while violating the boundary they establish between these fields, for modern secularism works in a double movement, transforming social worlds while obscuring the traces of this process. I would like to argue that secular discourses' attempts to sever themselves cleanly from the domain of the religious, consigning certain dimensions of human experience to one or the other domain and defining each domain against the other, obscure important dimensions of both "secular" and "religious" conduct, and obstruct the important task of continuing to rethink the possibilities of modern secularism itself.

---

[4] I use the contraction "political-theological" here to indicate the dynamic relation between religion and politics characteristic of modern secularism. This usage refers to a rich modern tradition that theorizes this conjunction, although it is not reducible to these ways of crystallizing the problem. See, e.g., Carl Schmitt's *Political Theology* on the notion of "political theology"; Baruch Spinoza's *Theological-Political Treatise* on the notion of the "theologico-political"; Leo Strauss's *Spinoza's Critique of Religion* on the notion of the "theologico-political problem"; and Émile Durkheim's *Elementary Forms of Religious Life* on the notion of the "religio-political." I use the term "scandal" here in its traditional theological sense of a "stumbling block," or something that stands as a barrier to faith – here, faith in contemporary secular, liberal democratic theory.

Faith in a particular image of reason, inherited from Kant, exemplified in the argumentation of *A Theory of Justice*, and thematized in *Political Liberalism*, informs Rawls's project. Despite the mundane forms reason takes in duties of civility and principles of reciprocity, for example, above everything else, Rawls expresses a faith in reason as the transcendent power that secures constitutional orders and, along with them, the possibility of human dignity and social justice. In his own words, "political philosophy assumes the role Kant gave to philosophy generally: the defense of reasonable faith... in our case this becomes the defense of reasonable faith in the possibility of a just constitutional regime."[5] Or as Joshua Cohen and Thomas Nagel put it,

> those who have studied Rawls's work, and even more, those who knew him personally, are aware of a deeply religious temperament that informed his life and writings, whatever may have been his beliefs. He says, for example, that political philosophy aims at a defense of reasonable faith... and kindred reflections express an aspiration to a comprehensive outlook on the world, which is an element of what we mean by a religious temperament."[6]

But faith in Rawlsian secularism, which functioned in many parts of the academy with the inevitability of common sense for roughly a generation, appears now in retrospect as a fragile and tenuous formation. It is this formation – more precisely, the texture of affect and identity that sustains faith in modern secular liberalism in Rawls's mold – that forms the focus of this chapter. I will argue that Rawls exemplifies secular conversion as a tendency of closure in Bergson's terms, as a movement toward safety and certainty, which conforms to the authorized image of conversion identified in Augustine's *Confessions*.

The work of secularism as a process of transformation can be rendered visible by tracing the problem of conversion through Rawls's work and life and, more specifically, by following the construction of the smooth, authorized surface of contemporary secular discourse in *A Theory of Justice* and *Political Liberalism*. According to Rawls, the arguments in these texts are at once freestanding in the sense that they require no metaphysical commitments but are also the natural fruit of European historical experience, and the logical consequence of a Euro-American intellectual tradition, whose acceptance requires no transformational moment of

---

[5] Rawls, *Political Liberalism*, 172.
[6] Thomas Nagel and Joshua Cohen, "Introduction" to *A Brief Inquiry into the Meaning of Faith and Sin*, 5.

political founding. In Rawls's presentation, contemporary political institutions overlay a largely realized process of secularization, such that the distinction between religion and politics is already complete, and such that the adoption of political liberalism requires no interference between or conversion of interests. The smooth surface of this presentation projects the moment of conversion into a distant past and yet, familiarity with the experience of Rawlsianism over the past fifty years and the sense of novelty associated with it, as well as familiarity with Rawls's biography, complicate that surface by reinstating a much more recent moment of discontinuity and by revealing the rougher texture of conversion that surrounds it.

To pick up the first point, one need only notice that Rawlsianism is commonly said to have originated a new departure for political philosophy by resurrecting it from a "moribund state."[7] It is a central feature of the reception of Rawls's work, accepted by critics and adherents alike, that it marks an unanticipated and seemingly inexplicable point of discontinuity in the recent tradition of political thought. Just as Rawls himself has been elected for sainthood, *A Theory of Justice* has been canonized among the great books of the tradition, a fact that has contributed to a studiously dispassionate text's being received with genuine passion – gratitude and affirmation in some places, indignation and denunciation in others – on either side of what Sheldon Wolin refers to as the "Liberal/Democratic Divide" pressed open by this work.[8] Although Rawls disclaims originality, his work continues to be received along with a mythic aura as a special body of work, a body of particular importance.

The public face of secular, liberal democracy – the emergence of which is generally taken to be coextensive with Western modernity – seeks to exclude theology from government, both when it underwrites political authority and when it makes claims upon the deep currents of faith that flow within individual conscience. That exclusion may, in fact, be the most economical way of stating the official stakes of modern secularism: continuing a gesture exemplified by Spinoza's *Theological-Political Treatise*, secularism forecloses the discourse of miracles and closes pathways to the domain of individual belief involved in such discourse. There is a tension within this public presentation, however, insofar as Rawls stands

---

[7] Peter Laslett had put this claim quite directly, writing: "For the moment, anyway, political philosophy is dead," in his *Politics, Philosophy and History* (vii).
[8] Sheldon Wolin, "The Liberal/Democratic Divide."

at the pinnacle of a modern, secular, liberal discourse and yet, Rawlsianism enfolds theological tropes formally excluded from this discourse, including the saintly nature of Rawls himself and the miraculous appearance of his work. This tension is not limited to Rawlsianism: indeed, one could write a history of the entwined formations of secular liberalism by tracing their subtle and unavowed reincorporations of the theological, despite its formal exclusion.[9] If Rawlsian secularism, like Locke's arguments for toleration, articulates a new relation between religious and political experience rather than simply excluding religious motifs, the figure of conversion once again sheds light on this process. That is to say that the figure of conversion helps to trace the convergence of "the religious" and "the political" within Rawlsian secularism by focusing attention on the ways in which this doctrine takes root and the particular dimensions of human experience to which it appeals and upon which it depends. Adequately addressing Rawlsian liberalism requires taking seriously the nature of the claims it makes on its audience, which is to say, taking seriously the ways in which it engages in a multilayered, crystalline process of conversion.

Approaches to Rawls generally eschew the kinds of rhetorical analyses that depend upon the machinery of literary theory and, more specifically, they ignore the relations established between text and reader. The existing critical responses to Rawls can be divided into two general categories. On the one hand, there is an internal criticism that scrutinizes the order of liberties, the enumeration of basic goods, the propriety of assuming a greater or lesser risk aversion on the part of rational actors, and the like but shows little interest in situating these matters within the larger historical, political, and intellectual framework of secular liberalism, let alone problematizing that framework. Critics internal to the project of formulating a theory of justice tend to produce highly technical and strictly analytical inquiries concerning the coherence, clarity, and consistency of the project. On the other hand, there is an external criticism focused precisely upon the larger context and framework of secular liberalism, which in turn shows little appetite for engaging with the questions particular to Rawlsianism that exercise the first group of critics. Sadly, this division of labor tracks two major pathways of avoidance: one either quibbles with Rawls or denies that he is worth quibbling with. One either assumes that the theory

---

[9] For a venerable version of this argument, see Claude Lefort, "The Permanence of the Theologico-Political?"; for one of its most recent iterations, see Giorgio Agamben, *The Kingdom and the Glory*.

of justice elaborated in the text has no purchase on the political situation of the reader, in which case it is at best a distraction, or one assumes that the reader's own situation is superfluous to the purposes of articulating a philosophical theory, because this situation can only introduce empirical confusion into what should be an endeavor of a priori knowledge. Both assumptions preclude the questions that will be posed here: How does the text draw a reader into a process of conversion? And what kind of conversion does the text invite? Although most commentators acknowledge that many theorists and philosophers have come to care about Rawls, nobody asks how they come to care, with the assumption being that the answer is either self-evident or evidence of nothing worth noting: either Rawlsians are predisposed to find this work meaningful – perhaps because, in the course of their education, they absorbed the conventions of a community that endorses such work – or Rawls's work is seen to carry its own seal of meaningfulness, perhaps because, as Kant would have it, the moral law inspires awe in its beholders as do the starry heavens above.[10]

One could say, however, that for one to be convinced of the importance of a theory of justice, one must first be convinced that people act out of a sense of justice; and to be convinced that people act out of a sense of justice, one must first be convinced of the importance of a theory of justice. Accepting that, according to a commonplace historical reconstruction, the mid-century Anglo-American world of political thought was marked by an absence of concern both for the sense of justice and for the principles of justice, then it would seem that there is, indeed, an air of the miraculous in the success of Rawls's work. As Bergson suggests, there are two tendencies at work within this complex process of conversion: the opening movement in which Rawls's work comes to seem credible to those working within its parameters, and the closing movement in which the variant of liberalism elaborated by Rawls in terms of the kind of thought, sorts of interest, and fields of sense opened by the project is consolidated and becomes final.

If one takes seriously the suggestion that *A Theory of Justice* and *Political Liberalism* should be placed in the company of Plato's *Republic* and other great books of the tradition, one should recognize that approaching Rawls's texts requires attention to their literary qualities, and if one takes seriously the comparison with Rousseau's *On the Social Contract*, the performative aspects must also be brought into focus. More directly, like Locke's letters, Rawls's texts should be read as political interventions that

---

[10] Immanuel Kant, *Critique of Practical Reason*, 133 [ak 5:161].

enact specific practices of democratic politics as they engage in deliberative as well as persuasive dialogue, seek to impart conviction, and work to convert individuals and institutions. This is neither to justify the terms of the conversation Rawls conducts nor the reverse; rather, it is to ask: How is it that his voice has been such a powerful force both in stirring and in conducting this conversation? In other words, might taking Rawls as a saint help to reveal how certain elements of belief, passion, myth, yearning, and suffering are incorporated in the circulation of his doctrine? If there is neither sufficient reason for this conversation nor adequate compulsion to engage in it, how do we account for its occurrence? One could call this an investigation into the politics of the liberal everyday, as a politics of conversion, or research into the crystalline structure established between a society's articulation of its experience and the institutions of a society's basic structure that condition this experience.

In what follows, I will first, articulate the problem of miraculous events and place Rawls's theory of justice in connection with the social-contract tradition as articulated by Rousseau, to indicate how a moment of political paradox originally dissolved by the hands of God finds resolution in the miraculous works of a saint; second, holding to the criterion that saintly or miraculous works inspire wonder, explore the captivating power of Rawls's saintly persona; and finally, adducing a second criterion of saintliness, I will suggest how certain semi-private dimensions of Rawls's biography hold a key to his work's rhetorical appeal and to the kind of conversion this work involves.

Miracles Wrought by God's Hand and by the Touch of a Saint

Owing in great measure to their central importance in the lives of Christian churches, miracles, saints, and conversion have been the subject of intense disputation within the various traditions of theological, political, and philosophical discourses throughout the history of Western Christianity. It will not be possible to provide a historical account of the shifting relations between these terms here, given the overwhelming complexity of the topic, but it will be possible to indicate their barest traditional sense in order to show how they work in my argument.[11] Miracles appear as disruptions of the natural order that defy explanation in accord with the canons of human reason. An interest in miracles derives in no small

---

[11] For a discussion of the figure of the miracle spanning its ancient origins and contemporary invocations, see Hent de Vries, *Of Miracles and Special Effects*, forthcoming.

measure from their relation to revelation, which is to say, from their power to testify to the presence of the divine: miracles are "events inexplicable by the operation of natural forces and therefore regarded as manifestations of special divine activity."[12] But it is also in the nature of the miraculous to be subject to contestation. Philosophical engagements, from Spinoza's and Hume's on, have centered on the necessarily dubious quality of any *evidence* that can be offered for the occurrence of miracles. Political engagements, such as Hobbes's and Locke's, have centered on the problem of sovereign *authority* that is motivated by the necessity of deciding on such dubious evidence. The Christian gospels themselves countenance the problem of distinguishing true from false miracles, motivated by nothing less than the problem of distinguishing true and false messiahs. The Greek employs a range of terms for events that we now gather under the Latinate term "miracle" – such as *erga* (works), *semia* (signs), *dunameis* (powers), and *terata* (wonders) – and this may be seen as a relic of the variability and uncertainty of the terrain they demarcate.[13] Miracles, in short, stand at the center of a complex relation between faith and reason: on the one hand, the recognition of a miracle depends upon faith, because the evidence offered for it must appear contrary to all reason; on the other hand, the occurrence of a miracle functions as evidence for one's faith in the truth of any revelation. It is at this intersection that miracles take on their most political valence: as Hobbes recognized, deciding upon the truth or falsity of a miraculous event is a function of authority, on the one side, but, on the other, as can be seen in the cases of prophets, apostles, and saints, miracles themselves produce authority, serving as warrants for the legitimacy of the figures who perform them. The significance of our other two terms can be laid out much more quickly: saints are those who, above all else, work miracles, the wonder of which, in turn, is capable of effecting conversion.

That Rawls has produced works is beyond dispute: he has written a great deal that has been read widely with deep appreciation for some time. To recapture the sense of a miracle, paradox, or scandal here, it should be noted that it is not entirely clear why these works should

---

[12] "Miracles," in *A Dictionary of Religion and Ethics*.
[13] For a comparison of the Biblical instances of these terms, see "Miracles," in *Encyclopedia of Religion and Ethics*. For arguments concerning miracles, see Baruch Spinoza, *Theological-Political Treatise*, chap. 6; David Hume, An *Enquiry concerning Human Understanding*, chap. 10; Thomas Hobbes, *Leviathan*, chap. 37; and John Locke, "A Discourse of Miracles," in *Reasonableness of Christianity and a Discourse of Miracles*.

have been attended by wonder – why, that is, anybody has cared, continues to care, or should come to care so deeply about Rawls's work. Rawls's oeuvre comprises a first major statement, *A Theory of Justice* (1971), around which revolves all of his subsequent work; the revision of his *Theory* in *Political Liberalism* (1993); its extension to international relations in *The Law of Peoples* (1999); its working notes in his *Collected Papers* (1999); and the teaching that went on concurrently with its formulation in *Lectures on the History of Moral Philosophy* (2000) and in the forthcoming *Lectures on Social and Political Thought*; and its final restatement in *Justice as Fairness* (2001). These texts comprise some two thousand to three thousand printed pages, and yet they are devoted exclusively to what had been and, in some quarters, continues to be the dubious topic of justice. It is certainly remarkable that by one recent estimate, *A Theory of Justice* alone has sold somewhat better than a quarter of a million copies in English and has been translated into two dozen languages since its initial publication.[14] To this one might add some three thousand or more academic publications generated in response to Rawls; countless more citations made of his work in the work of others; conferences convened and institutions established, funded, and secured under his name; as well as the students he has instructed personally or by proxy, his work long having served as a staple of undergraduate and graduation education.[15]

A measure of his work's more concrete political impact could be based upon its circulation among and influence upon policy makers, public institutions, and, perhaps above all, judges and other legal practitioners, although these are more difficult to trace. Although the animus expressed in the piece, not to mention the forum in which it is published, renders it suspect, there is probably some truth in Alan Ryan's claim in the *Washington Times* that "through the invisible medium of Supreme Court clerks and the more visible medium of the Harvard, Yale, Stanford, Chicago, etc. law reviews, Mr. Rawls's ideas have crept into the law of the land."[16] Although it circulates only on the level of hearsay, a somewhat

---

[14] Thomas Pogge, "Memorial for John Rawls" and "A Brief Sketch of Rawls's Life."
[15] According to Anthony Simon Laden, "three thousand articles that discuss the work of John Rawls have been published in journals of philosophy, law, economics, political science, and related fields" ("The House that Jack Built"). Consider, as well, Amy Gutmann's observation that "Many students read Rawls in their philosophically formative years and grew up, as it were, with strong Rawlsian sympathies" ("The Central Role of Rawls's Theory").
[16] Alan Ryan, "How Liberalism, Politics Come to Terms."

more credible, common narrative attributes to Rawls not only responsibility for having shifted analytical philosophy away from its concern with "small-scale problems" to return to the care for public problems exemplified by John Dewey but also for having shifted a philosophical discourse of governance regulated by the utilitarian principles championed by John Stuart Mill toward a discourse that accords a central place to individual rights.[17]

But to say that Rawls's influence has been widespread is not to attest to the sense of wonder it has created: the latter claim requires a different kind of justification. The most direct measure of an individual's status within a given discipline is the extent to which other members of that discipline feel an obligation to engage with his or her work and formulate an opinion about it: everyone working in the field of political theory or political philosophy, it seems, has an opinion about Rawls. What is noteworthy in surveying these opinions is not their general approval of or admiration for what Rawls has done but rather the collective sense that his work has effected a shift in the pathways of disciplinary interest. Stuart Hampshire is about as guarded on this point as anyone but, in the *New York Review of Books*, he writes of *A Theory of Justice*, "I think that this book is the most substantial and interesting contribution to moral philosophy since the war."[18] More forcefully, Sheldon Wolin, writing in *Political Theory*, maintains that "Insofar as it is possible to attribute to one man and one book the principal responsibility for both developments, [namely, the intellectual superiority of liberalism over its critics and the return of analytic philosophy to the subject of politics] John Rawls incontestably would be that man and his *A Theory of Justice* would be that book. His accomplishment is nothing less than to have set the terms of liberal discourse in the English-speaking countries."[19] Likewise, according to a piece written for *Dissent* by Amy Gutmann, "Political thinking in the academy has changed since the 1950s and early 1960s in at least three significant ways... All three of these changes are attributable to the influence of *A Theory of Justice*."[20] And in introducing a series of lectures addressed to the American Philosophical Association, Stanley Cavell concurs that "John Rawls's *A Theory of Justice*... has, more than any other book of the past two decades, established the horizon of

---

[17] For the former development, see Alexander Nehamas, "Recent Trends in American Philosophy," and for the latter, Amy Gutmann, "The Central Role of Rawls's Theory."
[18] Stuart Hampshire, "A New Philosophy of the Just Society."
[19] Wolin, "The Liberal/Democratic Divide," 97.
[20] Gutmann, "The Central Role of Rawls's Theory."

moral philosophy for the Anglo-American version or tradition of philosophy (at least)."[21] In a more personal register, H. L. A. Hart notes in the *University of Chicago Law Review*, "No book of political philosophy since I read the great classics of the subject has stirred my thoughts as deeply as John Rawls' *A Theory of Justice*."[22] Michael Sandel, having built his career debating Rawls, aptly notes in the *Harvard Law Review*, "rare is the work of political philosophy that provokes sustained debate. It is a measure of its greatness that John Rawls's *A Theory of Justice* inspired not one debate, but three."[23] And in more popular publications such as the *New York Times Book Review*, the *Times Literary Supplement*, *The Economist*, the *Listener*, the *Nation*, the *New Republic*, the *New Statesman*, the *Spectator*, the *Observer*, the *Washington Post*, and so forth – all of which, remarkably, published reviews – the "broad critical acclaim, even fame" of *A Theory of Justice* has been even more pronounced.[24] However they determine its influence and assess its substance, these sources agree that Rawls's project has decisively influenced the direction of political thought. They all mark Rawls's intervention as a turning point.

Despite its recognition of this fact, critical reception of Rawls has not attended to the significance of his project's success as an event in the life of political thought. Apart from my summary in the preceding paragraph, no theorist or philosopher, to my knowledge, has undertaken to address, in a serious and sustained fashion, the basic fact of this importance or to attend to the logic of its miraculous appearance. Instead, commentators note that Rawls has "set the terms" or "established the horizons" of philosophical discourse, and then proceed to rebut, critique, or repudiate his position as they would rebut, critique, or repudiate any other. Rawlsian discourse has yet to encounter a form of criticism that seeking neither to discern whether it truthfully represents something else, namely, our current political condition, nor whether it provides a serviceable tool with which to intervene in this condition, seeks rather to discern and describe what its particularity and appeal consist in. The concern that has been lacking, then, is to articulate and diagnose Rawls's work in terms of its capacity to claim and hold one's interest, in other words, in terms of its miraculous capacity to fascinate, to incite wonder, and to effect conversion.

---

[21] Stanley Cavell, *Conditions Handsome and Unhandsome*, 3.
[22] H. L. A. Hart, "Rawls on Liberty and its Priority."
[23] Michael Sandel, "Political Liberalism."
[24] Daniels, *Reading Rawls*, xi.

Placing his work in closer connection with the social-contract tradition from which it departs will help to demonstrate how the claim for the miraculous nature of Rawls's works and for his own saintly status can be made serious. A recent survey of the critical literature, undertaken by one of Rawls's former students, indicates that the question of what Rawls's project was remains open even for critics working within its tradition.[25] One might begin to examine Rawls's place in social-contract theory by recalling that the key moments of this tradition are Hobbes, Locke, Rousseau, and Kant.[26] It can reasonably be said that these authors are concerned with two points: (i) addressing the concrete historical conditions of the emergence and consolidation of nation-states and the extension of suffrage, as well as the congruent civic turmoil, revolution, war, and conquest; and (ii) addressing the ideational condition of a failure of traditional religious worldviews and the emergence of scientific and philosophical thought oriented toward and governed by the threat of skepticism (namely, the threat that our words cannot enable us to reach the world, each other, or our own selves). This moment in political thought has been treated either as coextensive with a new departure given by the age of Enlightenment or, more darkly, as Nietzsche has given it to us, as the culmination, although still unwitting, of the long good-bye European culture pays to its dead God and, as Carl Schmitt has given it to us, as the latest installment in a long line of sociological reinscriptions of the theological tradition.[27] Whatever precise determinations one settles upon,

---

[25] Laden identifies the persistence of two divergent "blueprints" guiding most of the critical literature on Rawls: "The standard blueprint of the structure of Rawls's work includes four related elements: (1) Rawls is engaged in a grand philosophical project; (2) in particular, he is developing a theory in the traditional sense of that word; (3) that theory is Hobbesian in that it starts from an account of human rationality; and (4) it aims to show the rationality of justice via its centerpiece, the argument from the original position in favor of the choice of the two principles of justice," whereas, according to "an alternative blueprint... (1) Rawls's projects are focused and narrower than is generally thought; (2) he is engaged in philosophy as defense rather than philosophical theorizing; (3) his arguments are meant to serve as public justifications rather than as deductions from premises about human nature or rationality; and (4) the central idea and high point of his achievement is the idea of public reason and its accompanying picture of political deliberation" ("The House That Jack Built," 371, 379).

[26] Rawls writes, "My aim is to present a conception of justice which generalizes and carries to a higher level of abstraction the familiar theory of the social contract as found, say, in Locke, Rousseau, and Kant." Viewing Hobbes as a difficult case, Rawls declines to associate himself with that part of the tradition, noting only that "for all of its greatness, Hobbes's *Leviathan* raises special problems" (Rawls, *A Theory of Justice*, 11 n. 4).

[27] For a paradigmatic statement of this standard interpretation of the Enlightenment, see Immanuel Kant, "An Answer to the Question: 'What Is Enlightenment?'"; for a concise

and no historian would be satisfied to settle upon any single one, both the concrete and ideational tendencies can safely be said to have pressed political theory to articulate afresh its own foundations, thus giving birth to the theory of the social contract. However the relation is stated, the emergence of new forms of state power in need of justification, together with the need to secure the certainty of human knowledge and meaning as they slipped free of tradition, conditioned modernity and the articulation of contract theory.

But to say that Rawls's politics responds to the pressures of the modern condition and that this modern condition is marked by a theological order waning in the face of an ascendant secular power says too much and too little at once. The relation between theological and secular orders of authority has been the object of continuous, delicate, and varied treatment starting with one of the contract tradition's early modern formulations in the work of Hobbes. Indeed, as recent scholarship asserts: this delicate treatment has been central to these theories.[28] It has been clear from the outset that Rawls is most directly indebted to Kant: he and his critics have undertaken what, by now, must be considered an exhaustive exploration of this debt. Tracing the lineage back a step further to Rousseau will shed more light on the theological problematic, however, as well as the peculiar political reinscription of this problematic performed by Rawls's work. What is to be shown, then, is how Rawls is continuous with Rousseau, how he inherits what is known in contemporary political theory as the Rousseauean "paradox of politics," and how his mode of negotiating this paradox is no less original than Rousseau's, no less forceful, and no less with which to be contended.[29] It is worth noting that the contract tradition has never been silent about this paradox, and one remarkable feature of Rawls's work is that, far from neglecting this political moment, he has *performed* a solution of the paradox that has elsewhere only been indicated at a formal or theoretical level. One might call this the theologico-political moment of Rawlsian secular liberalism.

statement of this theme, which runs throughout Nietzsche's works, see, e.g., *The Gay Science*, especially 279–80 (section 343); for a concise statement of Schmitt's argument, see his *Political Theology*, 36.

[28] Talal Asad's work is exemplary here. See especially "What Might an Anthropology of Secularism Look Like?" in his *Formations of the Secular*.

[29] This was treated by Paul Ricoeur in his "The Political Paradox," in *Legitimacy and the State* and by Connolly himself in both *Political Theory and Modernity* and *The Ethos of Pluralization*.

In *The Social Contract*, Rousseau faces the problem of founding a just and enduring polity given man's imperfect (whether innocent or corrupt) political, cultural, and moral state. This is Rousseau's way of introducing his project: "I want to inquire whether there can be a legitimate and reliable rule of administration in the civil order, taking men as they are and laws as they can be," where *taking men as they are* acknowledges that while "man is born free...everywhere he is in chains."[30] From the hands of God, man comes well formed; by virtue of life in this world, he is corrupt: only by establishing the proper order of political association can this perfection be reclaimed. In this sense, Rousseau translates part of the classical Christian problematic of conversion or, at least, the Augustinian form of this problematic as we are given it in *Confessions*, into a modern idiom. Rousseau departs from Augustine in imagining that the necessary conversion will turn man toward the life of republican, or civic, virtue rather than toward God. He continues his introduction by asking, "How did this change [i.e., man's enslavement in his fallen state] occur?" and answers, "I do not know," because the modern condition to which he is responding is largely determined by the recognition that men are incapable of comprehending the laws of heaven. But concerning the question, "What can make it legitimate?," what can serve as an *earthly* resolution of the problem, he maintains, "I believe I can answer this question," and his answer is that a good-enough redemption of the situation consists in approximating the proper form of the social contract and establishing the agency of the general will, by which the split in man's nature between private and public interest, between inclination and reason, can be resolved. In its more famous form, the solution is one in which man is forced to be free and made desirous of his own bondage to the law through his reconciliation with his society.[31]

But this account omits stating clearly the conditions of the paradox. Elsewhere, Rousseau puts the central problem as follows: "How will a blind multitude, which often does not know what it wants because it rarely knows what is good for it, carry out by itself an undertaking as vast and as difficult as a system of legislation?"[32] It is helpful to recall the force of the *Two Discourses*: for Rousseau, man is irresolvably split – even in the rightly constituted order he remains, necessarily, divided, or "doubly engaged," as citizen and subject, private and public being – and in his

---

[30] Jean-Jacques Rousseau, *On the Social Contract*, 46.
[31] Rousseau, *On the Social Contract*, 46.
[32] Rousseau, *On the Social Contract*, 67.

current condition, moreover, both his will and his reason are corrupt. This is at once a theological and a sociological assessment: human nature and human society mirror one another in their corruption. But if Rousseau's doctrine is controlled by a distinct understanding of man's condition as a fallen being and his culture as marked by a corruption of nature, it is equally governed by a concern to hold out the hope of, indeed to formulate a plan for, the redemption of his soul and of his society. Having placed man in the world, Rousseau's God is not Hobbes's God, retreating on high, nor is he Spinoza's God, retreating into nature, but rather, he personally touches upon the social contract at two significant points, both of which determine and authorize the precise form of Rousseau's democratic hope.

The figure of God is evident in all of the books of the *Social Contract*, but it is in the second and fourth that God's presence is most significant. There, in the chapters "On the Legislator" and "On Civil Religion," God can be seen supervening upon the contract in its founding moment and subtending its continuation in time. When Rousseau notes that "Gods would be needed to give laws to men," this is not only because a patient, disinterested, and dispassionate knowledge of man's good exceeds his capacity for comprehension.[33] It is not only a problem of limited knowledge or insufficient reason. Rather, the problem is that nothing in man's nature guarantees his acceptance of the law, even when it is given its proper formulation. This is one critical point at which Kant and Rousseau part ways. Were demonstration of the proper form of the social contract, and steady reflection upon this form, sufficient to establish it, Rousseau's having drafted *The Social Contract* would have been sufficient to solve the problem, or paradox, of politics. But, according to Rousseau, there is nothing in man's original nature to stir in him reverence for the law, and we have no right to hope, as Kant does at the conclusion to the *Critique of Practical Reason*, that "Two things fill the mind with ever new and increasing wonder and awe, the oftener and the more steadily we reflect on them: the starry heavens above me and the moral law within me."[34] Where right, for Kant, inspires reverence of its own accord; and right, for Hobbes, inspires reverence only when it comes bearing a sword or threatening war; and right, for Locke, requires only the tacit consent granted it by virtue of one's mere presence in society; Rousseau has nothing to guarantee the needed reverence for the law, save for the grace of God or,

---

[33] Rousseau, *On the Social Contract*, 68.
[34] Immanuel Kant, *Critique of Practical Reason*, 133 [ak 5:161].

what amounts to the same, the proper education of man's social spirit. In the *Social Contract*, the agent of this education alternately takes the form of the profession of civil religion, which ensures one's continued compliance with the law, and the figure of the wise legislator, who gives the law, and whose "great soul is the true miracle that should prove his mission."[35]

The problem of our condition, and this is what makes it a paradox calling for miraculous resolution, is double: man's reason is benighted and his will is corrupt. Were one intact, it could suffice to correct the other, but because neither is in order, to establish and maintain a just order, God must touch twice, once through the legislator upon reason and again through the doctrines of civil religion upon the mass of man's habits, mores, and moral sentiments. Here is the classical formulation of the paradox: "In order for an emerging people to appreciate the healthy maxims of politics, and follow the fundamental rules of statecraft, the effect would have to become the cause; the social spirit, which should be the result of the institution, would have to preside over the founding of the institution itself; and men would have to be prior to laws what they ought to become by means of laws."[36] Without the "social spirit," which men lack because they have been raised in an unjust society, the "rules," which could alone serve to order a society just enough to conjure this spirit, cannot be formulated. Likewise, without the "fundamental rules of statecraft," which are nowhere written and which would be necessary to constitute the kind of society that could produce men able to "appreciate" its maxims, the "social spirit," which alone could guide the formulation of such rules, cannot be conjured.

Rousseau continues, in a less-often quoted sentence: "Since the legislator is therefore unable to use either force or reasoning, he must necessarily have recourse to another order of authority, which can win over without violence and persuade without convincing."[37] Here, because a political wisdom that uses its "own language, rather than that of the common people" fails to persuade in the absence of a social spirit that would animate conviction, and because force, in the form of another's violent dominion, fails to win one over by failing to accord with the dictates of one's own reasoning, the legislator must have recourse to something other than

---

[35] Rousseau, *On the Social Contract*, 70.
[36] Rousseau, *On the Social Contract*, 69.
[37] Rousseau, *On the Social Contract*, 69.

reason or force.³⁸ In short, to effect the conversion needed for a legitimate social order, what is called for is nothing less than the revealed authority of the miraculous event.

Therefore, Rousseau concludes: "This [paradox] is what has always forced the fathers of nations to have recourse to the intervention of heaven and to attribute their own wisdom to the Gods; so that the people, subjected to the laws of the State as to those of nature, and recognizing the same power in the formation of man and of the City, might obey and bear with docility the yoke of public felicity."³⁹ Only through the appeal to heaven, then, can spirit and reason come to obey what is made to appear as a law of nature, just as it is only through a "purely civil profession of faith" that "the sentiments of sociability without which it is impossible to be a good citizen or a faithful subject" can be maintained.⁴⁰ Rousseau reasserts, then, the centrality of myth and miracle to the problem of political founding: specifically, he affirms the necessity of a discourse that exceeds reason and law – that appeals to powers beyond the scope of these faculties, beyond the proper functions of reason and law.

Where God's place has been so elegantly suppressed in Kant's critical system that contemporary Kantian liberals can proceed as though he were never there, God strides unavoidably to the foreground in Rousseau's work. The theological basis of the civil order, figured as the need for conversion, which is so clear in Rousseau's *Social Contract*, is renegotiated but preserved throughout Rawls's work. Whatever else changes between *A Theory of Justice* and *Political Liberalism*, the negotiation of Rousseau's paradox persists in the procedure of *reflective equilibrium*, where an adequate "sense of justice" must be present in advance for an individual to adopt the "principles of justice," as well as in the procedure of Kantian, or constitutional, *construction* as it is undertaken by a society in *Political Liberalism*. What has gone unnoticed is the persistence not only of the paradox but of its theological negotiation as well: rather than placing his "wisdom" in the mouth of gods, through an array of textual procedures, and through the agency of those who have been drawn to follow him and enshrine him as such, Rawls is made to accede to the position of a "saintly as well as wise" interlocutor capable of stirring the needed conviction without express recourse to gods.

---

³⁸ Rousseau, *On the Social Contract*, 69.
³⁹ Rousseau, *On the Social Contract*, 69.
⁴⁰ Rousseau, *On the Social Contract*, 130.

In its new form, the problem goes something like this: On the one hand, Rawls's logical demonstrations are not sufficient to compel a reader to change his or her principles, certainly not if he or she does not accept the norms operative in the demonstration. As Rawls himself might have put it, "principles of justice" cannot direct one's conduct if the corresponding "sense of justice" is not in place, or, perhaps more directly, much as there may be no way to tolerate the intolerant, there is no way of reasoning with the unreasonable. On the other hand, it certainly cannot be maintained that Rawls has – or, at least, when he launched his project, that he *had* – at his disposal an institutional apparatus sufficient to inculcate such a sense of justice through disciplinary practices alone. In other words, although it is not satisfying to say that he has made his point through propositional reasoning, it is not satisfying, either, to say that he has had his way through literal force. As Rousseau so carefully put the point, what is required is an appeal to "another order of authority." In what follows, I will call this, alternately, the saintly measure, the rhetorical form, and the micropolitical circulation of his doctrine. The better part of Rawls's saintly wisdom depends upon the powerful circulation of unacknowledged appeals to registers of thought and feeling that in turn act as another order of authority. It has been a source of frustration for his interpreters from early on that Rawls's arguments do not adhere to the norms of pure game theory, or to the confines of Kantian philosophy, or to any other single level of argumentation. In the literature, this eclecticism is generally seen as a lamentable eccentricity and a regrettable lapse of rigor, but much of the authority wielded by Rawls's arguments within each level of argumentation derives precisely from the crystallization of these levels of discourse, conjoining a specific micropolitics and rhetoric in a saintly measure.

The Fascination of Saints

Paul Ricoeur has suggested something like a concern for the mode of fascination in which readers are held in thrall to Rawls's texts: "I propose to say that justice as fairness... attempts to solve the difficulty of Rousseau's famous paradoxical legislator... [so that] justice as fairness may be understood as the *earthly* solution to this paradox" and, more to the point, switching from the register of philosophical logic to that of the philosopher's lived experience, "the awesome magnitude of the attempt to devise such a solution may explain the fascination Rawls' book has exerted for nearly 20 years over friends and adversaries alike."[41] Accounting for the fascination that Ricoeur notes, I would suggest, requires accounting for the experience of confronting the text not as a collection of abstract arguments but as a rhetorically sophisticated, affectively nuanced, and saintly performance directed toward readers susceptible to conversion. If the problematic of political theology is classically concerned with God's sovereign relation to man – Who are God's agents among men?, What are his instruments of power and retribution?, What duties does man owe?, Is God bound like man by contract?, and so forth – I would like to suggest that theologico-political moments inhabit modern secularism in more subtle registers as well. A theologico-political moment persists here in a minor key as the requirement of conversion that hovers somewhere between coercion and consent, between force and reason – effects that Rousseau observed without naming them as such – and which I will argue are enabled by the saintly persona produced within Rawls's texts.

Although it is not uncommon to hear complaints about the prosaic qualities of Rawls's texts, there is in fact a great deal of style to the exposition. Among his reviewers, Stuart Hampshire has come closest to recognizing this, writing that *A Theory of Justice* "is a very persuasive book, being very well argued and carefully composed, with possible objections and counterarguments fairly weighed and considered: at the same time it conveys a moral vision and a ruling idea, and a strongly marked personal attitude to experience."[42] A good part of understanding the general "fascination" with Rawls noted by Ricoeur involves understanding the textual operations that contribute so forcefully to producing it.

The triad of *ethos*, *pathos*, and *logos* provides an apt framework within which to begin investigating Rawls's procedure. Aristotle's *Rhetoric* describes this classical arrangement of persuasive devices as follows:

> Of the modes of persuasion furnished by the spoken word there are three kinds. The first kind depends on the personal character of the speaker; the second on putting the audience into a certain frame of mind; the third on the proof, or apparent proof, provided by the words of the speech itself. Persuasion is achieved by the speaker's personal character [*ethos*] when the speech is so spoken as to make us think him credible. We believe good men more fully and more readily than others... his character may almost be called the most effective means of persuasion he possesses. Secondly, persuasion may come through the hearers, when the speech stirs their emotions [*pathos*]... It is towards producing these

---

[41] Paul Ricoeur, "On John Rawls' *A Theory of Justice*."
[42] Hampshire, "A New Philosophy of the Just Society."

effects, as we maintain, that present-day writers on rhetoric direct the whole of their efforts... Thirdly, persuasion is effected through the speech itself when we have proved a truth or an apparent truth by means of the persuasive arguments suitable to the case in question [*logos*].[43]

Commentaries on Rawls's work have consistently avoided the first two modes of persuasion identified by Aristotle, *ethos* and *pathos*, taking his work to be purely argumentative and focusing exclusively on the third mode, *logos*. This is hardly surprising: what constitutes the remarkable power of the character Rawls projects and the emotional appeal he makes is also what renders these dimensions virtually invisible. That character and those emotions are perfectly congruent with the arguments made: in other words, the proponent of a politics based in reasonable conduct inflects his arguments with the force of his own exemplary reasonableness so as to induce in his audience the desired form of reasonable response. In the form of the prose, one finds projected what William James calls the philosopher's "essential personal flavor" or "philosophical temperament," or what Stanley Cavell designates the achievement of a distinctive "personal voice." A large part of Rawls's saintly measure inheres in the force of his personal character and the power of his emotional appeals to inspire conviction in a reader who would otherwise be unprepared for it, thus producing a conversion of interest that cannot be explained with reference to argumentative force alone. In what follows, we will consider in turn examples of the appeal of character and the appeal of emotion.

To begin with, the essential outlines of Rawls's philosophical character can be specified rather easily. The foremost quality of his writing is to establish Rawls as a judicious speaker with eminent goodwill and abundant common sense: (i) he constantly calls to attention, explains, and duly weighs what he considers to be the most salient of opposing viewpoints; (ii) he is punctilious almost to the point of fault in crediting others for their corrections of his errors and contributions to his understandings; and (iii) he is painstaking in giving the reader his own arguments and ideas in thoroughly analyzed form, couching them in brief sentences and short subsections that can be immediately grasped and easily digested. This mixture of judiciousness, goodwill, and common sense is tempered by a pronounced humility. Rawls even goes so far as to disavow any claim for originality in his work, preferring that we see him only to be setting in order and clarifying certain prominent elements of a shared tradition.

---

[43] Aristotle, *Rhetoric* (1356a).

"Indeed," he writes in a striking moment of self-effacement, "I must disclaim any originality for the views I put forward. The leading ideas are classical and well known. My intention has been to organize them into a general framework by using certain simplifying devices so that their full force can be appreciated."[44] In the place of bold assertion, apt metaphor, piercing depth of vision, or fine discernment, we find in Rawls's prose the passive voice, demonstrative sentences, myriad simple formulations, and careful arrangement of subsections. Abjuring the fine, rare, challenging, creative, and counterintuitive in language (and concept), such prose has the cumulative effect of accentuating the propriety of its author's conclusions, which, the author insists, carry "their full force" in themselves and whose force depends only upon the author's "simplifying devices" to clear the obscurity that might impede it. Rawls claims for his prose, then, what Aristotle identified as the power of the best "arguments suitable to the case," and he disavows both the role his character plays in shading these arguments and the role the emotional responses produced in the reader condition the reader's reactions to the argument. It is the very lack of apparent audacity in his argumentation, however, that allows these disavowed modes of persuasion to find their way into a reading of his text, contributing to its subtle and distinctive powers of fascination.

The manner in which Rawls disqualifies moral perfectionism from playing a role in his own theory provides an excellent example of how his character functions to produce conviction. In Rawls's taxonomy, perfectionism is a subclass of the larger group of teleological doctrines, which include utilitarianisms and communitarianisms (of Aristotelian or other stripe), against which Rawls distinguishes deontological theories, including his own. Rawls argues against perfectionism at the point where he distinguishes theories of the right from theories of the good and declares the primacy of the former. This argument has touched off decades of intramural controversy among Anglo-American political theorists: it is of paramount importance, then, for Rawls to establish that the capacity for a "sense of justice," or one's "liability" to suffer guilt in the face of principles, conceived as an inherently human capacity, is a more appropriate basis for moral worth than any of the excellences that a doctrine of perfectionism asks one to achieve. The position Rawls takes is not striking in itself: it is merely a modest reformulation of the argument, familiar from Kantian moral philosophy, that one's rational nature constitutes one as a

---

[44] Rawls, *A Theory of Justice*, viii.

moral agent and qualifies one for moral consideration. What is interesting is how he takes this position.

Although there are well-tried arguments for taking the capacity to reason to be the sole basis for moral consideration, when Rawls works his way down to brass tacks, the character conjured by his prose carries more weight than his arguments strictly conceived. At a decisive moment in "The Sense of Justice," Rawls demurs on the level of propositional argument, writing that he "cannot discuss here the propriety of this [competing, perfectionist] assumption" and offering in the place of such a discussion his assessment that "it suffices to say" what he needs to say.[45] Rawls tends to refer potential points of contention to arguments developed elsewhere, allowing the larger edifice's coherence to bear the burden of proof for its individual points. At this moment in "The Sense of Justice," however, rather than being referred to a larger project, an argument for selecting the capacity for reason over the contending bases for moral consideration is deferred indefinitely. How is this gesture made plausible?

Rawls does present summary accounts of what utilitarian and perfectionist theories hold to be competing bases for moral consideration. These bases represent potential alternatives to the capacity for having "a [rational] sense of justice" that Rawls will ultimately hold to be "necessary and sufficient for the duty of justice to be owed to a person."[46] For utilitarianism, the capacities in question are those "for pleasure and pain, for joy and sorrow." Rawls dismisses this variant of moral naturalism with the estimable argument that it is insufficient to account for the moral indignation we do, in fact, feel at the sight of injustices perpetrated upon others. It has never been hard to argue against utilitarianism. On the more difficult question of perfectionism, Rawls proceeds as follows:

Such an aristocratic doctrine can only be maintained, I think, if one assumes a specific obligation on the parties in the original position: namely the obligation to develop human persons of a certain style and aesthetic grace, or the obligation to the pursuit of knowledge and the cultivation of the arts, or both. *I cannot discuss here the propriety of this assumption*, or whether if it were accepted it would justify the inequalities commonly associated with aristocracy. *It suffices to say* that in the analytic construction no such obligation is assumed. The sole constraints imposed are those expressed in the formal elements of the concept of morality, and the only circumstances assumed are those exhibiting the conflicts of claims which give rise to questions of justice. *The natural consequence of this*

---

[45] John Rawls, "The Sense of Justice."
[46] Rawls, "The Sense of Justice," 304–5.

construction is that the capacity for the sense of justice is the fundamental aspect of moral personality in the theory of justice.[47]

That is as far as justification reaches. The point is not to catch Rawls in a dogmatic preference for a moral universe fueled by one's susceptibility to guilt, resentment, and indignation about transgressions of right over an associational universe driven by feelings such as shame and pride concerning failure or achievement of the good. In fact, Rawls is more supple on this point than is commonly recognized: he maintains that "a complete moral doctrine includes both" motivation from shame and motivation from guilt.[48] But this claim is decisively argued neither here nor elsewhere in his texts; rather, it is continuously deferred. Having excluded the possibility of a purely Kantian appeal to the "fact of Reason" as the foundation for morality, Rawls employs a rhetorical strategy that invites us to accept this position on his authority without reason but clearly without force.

The argument against perfection is, moreover, layered with nuanced shades of feeling, and these shades of feeling ultimately bear much of the weight of the argument proper. Rawls's commonsensical manner establishes an implicitly antipathetic disposition toward an "aristocratic ethic which takes as necessary certain attributes and capacities such as strength, beauty, and superior intelligence" precisely by abjuring the qualities of "imagination and wit, beauty and grace" that serve as standard criteria of perfectionist virtue.[49] There is a direct relationship between the propositional content of Rawls's argument, namely, that the human capacity for reason is the basis for moral consideration, and the force of his rhetorical ethos, more precisely, the implication that Rawls's procedure is more direct, natural, and trustworthy than his contenders'. The exclusion of "imagination and wit, beauty and grace" from the discussion at a rhetorical level functions as a micropolitical device of persuasion – ultimately, of conversion – and a reader senses the inadequacy of perfectionism before coming to know what it is. The reasonable – indeed, the saintly – character that Rawls projects solicits the respect owed to reason itself.

Another example will draw out some of the ways in which Rawls mobilizes his readers' emotional responses to bolster his arguments. In the preface to *Political Liberalism*, Rawls writes, "I try to preserve, perhaps unsuccessfully, a certain conversational style," and this "conversational"

---

[47] Rawls, "The Sense of Justice," 305 (emphasis added).
[48] Rawls, *A Theory of Justice*, 485.
[49] Rawls, "The Sense of Justice," 305; *A Theory of Justice*, 443.

style invites the reader to embrace the very receptiveness to reasoning, in the sense of hearing, weighing, and selecting the best available argument, congruent with Rawls's moral and political program.[50] Consider the opening lines of *Political Liberalism* and the tone they set for the text. Rawls says, "Perhaps I should, then, begin with a definition of political liberalism and explain why I call it 'political.' But no definition would be useful at the outset. *Instead I begin with a first fundamental question* about political justice in a democratic society."[51] Rawls introduces his *Theory of Justice* with a similar gesture. There he begins, "I sketch some of the main ideas.... The exposition is informal and intended to prepare the way for the more detailed arguments that follow."[52] Were Rawls not so closely identified with the tradition of analytical philosophy, his embarkation upon these projects of rigorous philosophical argumentation by beginning a "conversation" with his audience and posing a question or a sketch rather than offering a definition would not be remarkable. But he is correctly identified with that tradition, and thus it is pertinent to see what he derives from departing from its norms. That Rawls begins with a question or a sketch signals his intent, present throughout *Political Liberalism* and *A Theory of Justice*, to elicit the reader's active involvement in the work at hand.

Although the conversation that takes place in what Rawls has called the "original position" has been criticized as no real conversation at all, the conversation opened by *Political Liberalism* is of another order. There, to pose a question to the reader is to imply that it is to be answered – it is to level a challenge and, perhaps, to open an engagement. Rawls is not in the least naïve on this count: he knows that the conversational form implied by the back-and-forth rhythm of question and answer tends to elicit a certain range of normative considerations. The demands of attentiveness, responsiveness, politeness, and so forth come to mind. It may well be that the more powerfully the norms of conversation are installed in the text, the less apt the reader will be inclined to radically dissent from the conclusions of the theory. It is not inconceivable, either, that he or she should become less likely to turn away from the discussion altogether. Or, to borrow the language of Rawls's own moral psychology, a reader may feel worthy only if he or she does not shirk the obligation to give and take reasons that all parties to the conversation could accept when

[50] John Rawls, *Political Liberalism*, xv.
[51] Rawls, *Political Liberalism*, 3.
[52] Rawls, *A Theory of Justice*, 3.

these obligations have been so diligently, carefully, judiciously, sensibly, and painstakingly observed by Rawls himself – and this thought may be accompanied by a feeling of shame at perhaps not being worthy. Alternatively, the thought may arise that one ought not to make "unreasonable" rebukes to a decent and "reasonable" interlocutor such as Rawls – a thought accompanied, perhaps, by a feeling of guilt by any reader tempted in this direction. Although the conversational style of *Political Liberalism*, in particular, should be kept distinct from what one imagines the parties to the original position to be doing in their conversation, and Rawls's remarks on moral psychology should be kept distinct from either of these conversations, Rawls violates these distinctions rhetorically as much as he defends them argumentatively, and these are strategic violations, not errors. Keen-sighted analytical philosophers such as Bernard Williams have long noticed slippage between levels of argumentation, but, because they have not been concerned with the rhetorical functions of Rawls's texts, they responded to such maneuvers only by crying foul or faulting them as mistakes and lapses in rigor rather than acknowledging them as part of an efficacious technique.[53] This technique, moreover, engages the whole person of the reader – it is not addressed to a disembodied, disembedded, or disinterested intelligence.

Recall the three levels of deliberation announced in *Political Liberalism*: carried on (i) by the representative figures imagined in the original

---

[53] Williams observes the translation of argumentative force from one conversation to the next with great precision: Considering a point made in Rawls's argument from the original position, he notes, "this comes perilously close to a requirement on the original choice, that it be of a system which *will be just* – which of course would be to moralise the original itself, and to put in at the beginning what we are supposed to get out at the end." Considering the unacknowledged force of a Kantian outlook on Rawls's argument for the strong preference for liberty, he notes, "the strong preference for liberty is part of the outlook in which men are in general seen as essentially autonomous beings, and Rawls is disposed to explicate it in terms of a Kantian view of human relations. This view is not supposed to be that of his contracting parties, but the choice they are pictured as making seems – to put it mildly – to make most sense when they are understood as already possessing this view of themselves." Concerning the unacknowledged influence of altruistic, hence moralized, assumptions, he notes, "the contracting parties were indeed introduced as fathers of families, with a natural concern for one generation ahead, but the way in which Rawls speaks of their commitment to not taking risks implies a heavier, and surely already moralised, onus of responsibility towards posterity"; and, in general, he notes that Rawls's conclusions "must rest both on a rather saintly view of things on the part of the contracting parties, and a quite unreasonable belief that they would retain such a saintly view if they were top dogs in [...] society," but he concludes only that Rawls has made a rather bad argument. (Bernard Williams, "Rawls and Pascal's Wager," 95, 96, 97, 99.)

position; (ii) by the ideal citizens of the theoretically constructed, well-ordered society; and (iii) by us, that is, John Rawls, you, and me, citizens of the world as we know it, who on the occasion of confronting a text such as *Political Liberalism* are meant to be engaged in a discussion about the proper conception of political justice.[54] Where these distinctions cross is precisely where Rawls's argument gains its force, when it does. Everything, for Rawls, depends upon one's willingness to be reasonable, and to be reasonable in a particular sense of the word, meaning primarily to make judgments in accordance with the criterion of reciprocity, that is, to propose and accept only principles that strike oneself and one's interlocutors as fair. I would claim that the rhetorical genius of Rawls's conversational prose is to incline *our* discussion, which takes place at the third level, to proceed in "reasonable" terms, where "reasonable" is understood in the sense given within the first two levels of deliberation, and to do so without our yet having explicitly accepted these terms. To explicitly accept these terms, we must already be reasonably inclined, and being reasonably inclined consists precisely in expressly accepting these terms as the ones that best describe this inclination. This, of course, recalls the condition of Rousseau's paradox of politics, and the measure of Rawls's saintliness is the extent to which he has, by mobilizing disavowed and largely unrecognized rhetorical modes, managed to negotiate this paradox. Put in other terms, the miracle of Rawlsianism lies in its subtle powers of conversion.

Although, Rawls says, philosophy and logic cannot coerce us, he admits that they might leave us "feeling coerced." This is a fantastic distinction to make. Here is Rawls's precise formulation: "Political philosophy cannot coerce our considered convictions any more than the principles of logic can. If we feel coerced, it may be because, when we reflect on the matter at hand, values, principles, and standards are so formulated and arranged that they are freely recognized as ones we do, or should, accept.... Our feeling coerced is perhaps our being surprised at the consequences of those principles and standards, at the implications of our free recognition."[55] Or perhaps it is the result of a powerful circuit of resonant thought and feeling being established among various

---

[54] As Rawls puts it, in order to avoid misinterpretation, "it is important to distinguish three points of view: that of the parties in the original position, that of citizens in a well-ordered society, and finally, that of ourselves – of you and me who are elaborating justice as fairness and examining it as a political conception of justice" (*Political Liberalism*, 28).

[55] Rawls, *Political Liberalism*, 45.

values, principles, standards, images, emotions, identifications, aspirations, and arguments Rawls crystallizes. All the while, Rawls is arguing for a moral and political order based upon the normative force of reason, a force derived from the individual feelings of guilt and shame one feels on account of one's actions in the face of this reason; he relies on putting something like this force into play to make his argument, or to make one listen long enough for him to make his argument, while his readers are held captive on pain of inchoate feelings that may only later come to be called guilt or shame. Indeed, he seems to assume that the disposition to have those feelings is already in place, working on and through the reader before the principles that would give them their name, their moral form, and their political authorization. In short, the reader is drawn to accept the very terms under discussion by the circulation of thought among multiple layers of the discussion itself, by way of a discourse that touches argument, feelings, and norms of conversational propriety at once, carefully disposing them in a crystalline order.

At his most provocative, Rawls is engaged in a sophisticated and rhetorically nuanced effort to foster the conditions of agreement needed to carry the convictions that his arguments are supposed to support. For Rawls's argument, everything depends upon his reader being *inclined* just so. And for a rhetorical analysis of this argument, everything depends on coming to understand how a reader is encouraged to become so inclined. Although it can be forcefully argued that Rawls's project fails as a diagnosis of our political condition and that it amounts to an unappealing account of what our politics should be, neither of these descriptions captures what Rawls is doing most effectively. And neither claim engages the modalities through which faith in the Rawlsian ideal of public reason is established and maintained. On the contrary, such critiques of Rawls, in arguing that he displaces politics or otherwise denies its importance, glide over the immense and, to judge from the broad, sympathetic reception of his work, effective effort he makes to convert his readers: such critiques take his strong performance to be a weak description, denying the simple fact that for so many, Rawls was and is a saint.

The Meaning of Suffering, Sin, and Sainthood

I would like to conclude by suggesting a second, related basis for the claim that Rawls was a saint. Along with the production of miraculous works, another central criterion of sainthood is that the story of a saint's life teaches something that cannot be taught in any other way. As one standard reference work puts the matter, "the designation of a man or a woman as a 'saint' is the judgment by the Christian community of the day, both in its local and universal form, as to the desired qualities of the exemplary Christian Life."⁵⁶ Hagiography functions to preserve the saint's example, which is seen as worthy of preservation because his or her life will have *instantiated* values whose viability and desirability cannot be suggested by reason or historical precedent alone. Saints, then, serve as sources of inspiration: they are exemplary figures who make possible what, but for their example, would be inconceivable; one recalls that this was the source of Bergson's fascination with saints. They embody human possibilities that call for identification and imitation. And, as is suggested by the shifts in character from the saints who attended the church's origins in a marginal community to those chosen after its ascent to an institutionalized state religion, the shifting values and political circumstances of a community are reflected in the lives of those it chooses to designate as saints.⁵⁷ Although I have sought to trace the significance of secular liberalism's having a saint, I will ask here why it might have this saint in particular. Having argued that much of Rawls's appeal lies in the authoritative style of his personal voice and its capacity to imbue discussion of political arrangements with the qualities of judiciousness, goodwill, and common sense, I will claim that the example of Rawls's life makes clear one source of the impulse to moral philosophy, philosophical justification in general, and the current imagination of what secular liberal political life entails, embodied in his *Theory of Justice* and *Political Liberalism*.

Following William James's contention that a philosopher's "temperament" or "essential personal flavor" determines the course and outcome of his or her work, as well as the extent of its effect upon its audience, allows us to see in another way the pertinence of biography, or hagiography, to political thought. On this point, James writes: "The books of all the great philosophers are like so many men. Our sense of an essential personal flavor in each one of them, typical but indescribable, is the finest fruit of our own accomplished philosophic education. What the system pretends to be is a picture of the great universe of God. What it is, – and

---

⁵⁶ "Saints," in *The Oxford Companion to Christian Thought*, 639.
⁵⁷ The *Oxford Companion to Christian Thought* points out that "Saints from different periods... stand in sharp contrast to each other," taking as an example that "Seventeenth-century philanthropic saints such as Vincent de Paul represent a very different model of holiness from that of the founding fathers of great 12th-century monastic orders, such as Bernard of Clairvaux or Norbert of Xanten."

oh so flagrantly! – is the revelation of how intensely odd the personal flavor of some fellow creature is."[58] James is far from lamenting this personalization of philosophical argument; he maintains, on the contrary, that "the one thing that has *counted* so far in philosophy is that a man should *see* things, see them straight in his own peculiar way, and be dissatisfied with any opposite way of seeing them."[59] Philosophical voices worth listening to, James tells us, will be distinctly inflected, and grasping the nature of these inflections is the highest measure of philosophical education. Rawls's rhetoric is not just a collection of various devices but also a collection of devices used to present his own distinctive character and to inspire the reader to adopt that character by participating in conversation with it. What is the nature of this inflection of character and, thus, of its appeal?

Insofar as Rawls was famous, personally famous, it was in part for his intensely private life and for his largely successful attempt to avoid celebrity.[60] Throughout his career, he gave very few interviews, and these never on personal topics. Toward the end of his life, however, Rawls did consent to undertake some form of autobiography. He authorized Thomas Pogge – first a student, later a friend – to publish a biographical sketch based on a series of conversations. Two vignettes from this text suggest that the story of Rawls's life is pertinent to the theory of justice he would develop:

John (Jack) Bordley Rawls was born on February 21, 1921, in Baltimore as the second of five sons of William Lee and Anna Abell Rawls. The most important events in Jack's childhood were the losses of two younger brothers, who died of diseases contracted from Jack. The first of these incidents occurred in 1928, when Jack fell gravely ill. Although [his younger brother] Robert Lee (Bobby) had been sternly told not to enter Jack's room, he did so anyway a few times to keep Jack company. Soon both children were lying in bed with high fever. The correct diagnosis and antitoxin came too late to save Bobby. His death was a severe shock to Jack and may have (as their mother thought) triggered his stammer, which has been a serious, though gradually receding, handicap for him ever since that time. Jack recovered from the diptheria, but the very next winter caught a severe pneumonia, which soon infected his brother Thomas Hamilton (Tommy). The tragedy of the previous year repeated itself. While Jack was recovering slowly, his little brother died in February of 1929.

---

[58] William James, "The Present Dilemma in Philosophy," 374.
[59] James, "The Present Dilemma in Philosophy," 364.
[60] This point has been suggested by Sheldon Wolin, who notes that "Rawls is truly the virtuous philosopher whose great personal achievement is to have rejected celebrity status" ("The Liberal/Democratic Divide," 97).

Saint John (Rawls)   161

Rawls proceeded to teach in the Harvard Philosophy Department from 1962 until his retirement in 1991. Rawls was an unusual person among the self-confident divinities of the Harvard Philosophy Department. With his caring interactions with students and visitors, his modesty, his insecurity and conciliatory attitude in discussions, one could have taken him for a visiting professor from the countryside next to his famous and overwhelmingly brilliant colleagues Quine, Goodman, Putnam, Nozick, Dreben, and Cavell. Rawls has always found it difficult to function in larger groups, especially with strangers, and even more so when he himself is the center of attention. On such occasions he may seem shy or ill at ease and is sometimes still bothered by his stammer.[61]

This is delicate ground, ground that some will want to avoid, much as, after his death, Ludwig Wittgenstein's friends and followers sought to avoid questions about his apparent homosexuality for fear that discussion of what was then seen as an acutely embarrassing subject could only diminish the importance, and impede the proper reception, of his work.[62] But if we take seriously the idea that the force of Rawls's project is constituted largely by its capacity to bring the desire for justice into circulation by rhetorical appeals to its readers, and the idea that political argument more generally is continuously informed by similar circuits of thought and feeling, the very real grounds of personal fault, regret, guilt, shame, and resentment are ones it would be best not to avoid.

The most remarkable feature of Pogge's biographical sketch, which takes up a mere fourteen printed pages, is the power with which it conjures a range of feelings. The scenes sketched herein are compounded by further thematic threads: Rawls's recounting of his childhood exposure to the racist and classist dispositions of his parents and those of his own privileged, or "lucky," social milieu; his recollection of following behind an older brother who excelled in sports and distinguished himself in war, two areas in which Rawls was not distinguished; and his humiliation by an influential undergraduate instructor in philosophy, Norman Malcolm, who in an "unpleasant" early encounter subjected "a philosophical essay which he [Rawls] himself thought rather good" to "very severe criticism," refusing to accept it and demanding its rewriting – remarkably enough, Rawls remembers this event as having led to "a gradual deepening of ... [his] interest in philosophy."[63] These accounts can sharpen focus on how forms of social suffering – from guilt, shame, resentment,

---

[61] Thomas Pogge, "A Brief Sketch of Rawls's Life," 2–3; "Memorial for John Rawls," 153.
[62] See Ray Monk, *Ludwig Wittgenstein*.
[63] Pogge, "A Brief Sketch of Rawls's Life," 4–6.

humiliation, and so forth – accompany both appeals to a notion of justice and attachments to such a concept. I mean to suggest that far from impoverishing a discussion of Rawlsian secularism by claiming that it can be reduced to the personal experience of its author, attention to the affective registers it engages and the everyday circumstances of the still "lucky," if less so of late, political experience of contemporary Western liberal democracies can enrich that discussion. If a secular mode of public reason is a less certain and more fragile achievement for this current generation than it was for the last, it demands all the more careful attention to what enables and sustains it, to what opens one to its possibilities.

An openness to the possibilities of public reason is but one side of the process of conversion at work here, and the other side is a closure to what lies beyond the limits of any current instantiation of public reason. Tracing this second tendency, Stanley Cavell has suggested that a threat of callousness or, worse, moral blindness inheres in *A Theory of Justice*'s promise to allow privileged citizens to accede to positions "above reproach," for this is in part to rise above the claims of injury entered by their less-privileged fellows (this point is pursued in Chapter Five).[64] On this basis, Cavell argues that *A Theory of Justice* should be supplemented by what he calls Emersonian Perfectionism, such that justice remains open to ever new demands. That is an important intervention, but it by no means exhausts the point it presses in Rawls's text. Here is the pertinent passage of *A Theory of Justice* quoted at greater length:

> If our information is accurate and our understanding of the consequences complete in relevant respects, we do not regret following a rational plan, even if it is not a good one judged absolutely... We may, of course, regret something else, for example, that we have to live under such unfortunate circumstances that a happy life is impossible. Conceivably we may wish that we had never been born. But we do not regret that, having been born, we followed the best plan as bad as it may be when judged by some ideal standard. A rational person may regret his pursuing a subjectively rational plan, but not because he thinks his choice is in any way open to criticism. For he does what seems best at the time, and if his beliefs later prove to be mistaken with untoward results, it is through no fault of his own. There is no cause for self-reproach. There was no way of knowing which was the best or even a better plan. // Putting these reflections together, we have the guiding principle that a rational individual is always to act so that he

---

[64] See Stanley Cavell, *Conditions Handsome and Unhandsome*, and *Cities of Words*, 82–101, 119–44, 164–89.

need never blame himself no matter how his plans finally work out... he can say that at each moment of his life he has done what the balance of reasons required, or at least permitted. Therefore any risks he assumes must be worthwhile, so that should the worst happen that he had any reason to foresee, he can still affirm that what he did was above criticism. He does not regret his choice, at least not in the sense that he later believes that at the time it would have been more rational to have done otherwise. This principle will not certainly prevent us from taking steps that lead to misadventure. Nothing can protect us from the ambiguities and limitations of our knowledge, or guarantee that we find the best alternative open to us. Acting with deliberative rationality can only insure that our conduct is above reproach.[65]

Cavell argues that when citizens accede to positions that are "above reproach," they may be closing their society to criticism, which may in turn help to make specific injustices sustainable. Juxtaposing this passage with certain painful episodes of Rawls's own life suggests, however, that acceding to a position that is "above reproach" might refer more directly to closing oneself – one's self – from criticism and therefore from the potential for radical change. Moving beyond reproach might in this sense mean that one has moved beyond the possibility of conversion, either preempting or completing such a process. Indeed, the section of *A Theory of Justice* in which this passage is couched deals with the problem of "deliberative rationality" in the context of choosing a complete "plan of life," and it depends upon the capacity to view oneself as "one enduring individual" and to acknowledge that "we are responsible to ourselves as one person over time."[66] It precludes quite precisely, the most easily recognizable image of conversion, as an event that disrupts the course of life, splitting a life and a person in two.

These scenes from Rawls's life help make plausible the extent to which his work's affirmation of a theory of justice, its commitments more generally to giving justifications for what we do, and its attachments to a form of secular liberalism that depends on precisely delimited legal protection from social injury are connected with cycles of reproach, guilt, and shame recurrent in political life. Although they find acute expression in his own memoirs, such experiences are not at all peculiar to Rawls. Part of confronting the basis of social suffering in Rawlsian secular liberalism entails recognizing more generally that liberal appeals to rights – in particular, the right to draw boundaries that allow one to refrain from certain conversations – serve the function of assuaging persistent modes

---

[65] Rawls, *A Theory of Justice*, 422.
[66] Rawls, *A Theory of Justice*, 416–24.

of suffering. It is a commonplace that religion relieves suffering, but such relief may also be central to the appeal of secular liberalism.[67] This may provide a key to the persistence of attachments to the promises of secular liberalism, a sense of the "religiosity" of secularism.

Surely one is not bound by one's early life, is not held to it – surely a clear line divides youth from maturity, as it does the new man from the old . . . or does it? Consider for a moment another connection between *A Theory of Justice*'s disclaimers about originality, explored earlier, and these remarks from another of Rawls's texts:

> Although our argument may seem to be drawn out at certain times, the main theme is extremely simple, and can be grasped at a glance. We intend to state nothing new, startling or original. What follows is a rehash of what everybody knows. But because everybody knows it, we are liable to forget it.

These lines are drawn from an undergraduate honors thesis written by the twenty-one-year-old Rawls.[68] And although the last sentence carries a lilt of ordinary language philosophy that will disappear from Rawls's mature voice, this is an unmistakable draft of the very disclaimer he will make in *A Theory of Justice*.

I began this chapter by noticing that Rawls has been called a saint and have attempted to give this claim a serious basis by demonstrating that where, in Rousseau's classical articulation, a persistent political-theological paradox of founding through recourse to gods has been dispensed with, the same paradox has been eased in Rawls's work by way of nuanced rhetorical appeals to its readers' sensibilities that attempt both to mobilize and to inflect these sensibilities in new directions. The measure of Rawls's saintliness lies in his skill at deploying these rhetorical means to

---

[67] On the question of suffering, see in particular chapter two of Talal Asad, *Formations of the Secular*; William E. Connolly, *Why I Am Not a Secularist*; and the exchange among Scherer, Hirschkind, Connolly, and Asad in *Cultural Anthropology*.

[68] The title of this essay is "A Brief Inquiry into the Meaning of Sin and Faith: An Interpretation Based on the Concept of Community"; it is an exercise in theology explicitly premised on the assumption that "there is a being which Christians call God and who has revealed Himself in Christ Jesus." At the same time, as the title advertises, the essay explicates the concepts of sin and faith within a framework determined by the concepts of personality and community. Once again, I leave the pertinence of these details as an open question. In writing this chapter, I consulted a facsimile copy of Rawls's undergraduate thesis provided by Princeton's Firestone Library. Since the time of this chapter's original publication, the thesis has been published as a book and is now widely available; see Rawls, *A Brief Inquiry into the Meaning of Sin and Faith*. For a thoughtful discussion of the significance of the early Rawls's positions, see Stephen K. White, "Fullness and Dearth."

the miraculous end of inspiring convictions that would otherwise remain unavailable. Insofar as political life contains a moral dimension – that is, insofar as an expansive concept of justice is somehow applicable to political life – the dimension of morality, justice, or social spirit that this further dimension represents stands in need of something like a miracle for its inception. Failing this, the arguments for morality lack sense, just as, in the absence of a sense of justice, the principles of justice lack lived significance. The extent to which these otherwise admirable appeals to justice deny the forms of suffering that ground them, and contribute to the denial of the suffering of others, in large part by denying the pertinence of conversion to democratic life, is a serious question that will be pursued in the next chapter. But it appears, in conclusion here, that even an avowedly secular, liberal democratic politics remains in deep need of its saints.

Bibliography

Agamben, Giorgio. *The Kingdom and the Glory: For a Theological Genealogy of Economy and Government*. Palo Alto, CA: Stanford University Press, 2011.

Aristotle. "Rhetoric," in *The Complete Works of Aristotle*. Vol. 2. ed. Jonathan Barnes. Princeton, NJ: Princeton University Press, 1984: 2152–269.

Asad, Talal. "What Might an Anthropology of Secularism Look Like?," in *Formations of the Secular: Christianity, Islam, Modernity*. Palo Alto, CA: Stanford University Press, 2003: 21–66.

Bergson, Henri. *The Two Sources of Morality and Religion*. Notre Dame, IN: University of Notre Dame, 2002.

Cavell, Stanley. *Cities of Words: Pedagogical Letters on a Register of the Moral Life*. Cambridge, MA: Belknap Press, 2004.

Cavell, Stanley. *Conditions Handsome and Unhandsome*. Chicago: University of Chicago Press, 1990: 3.

Connolly, William E. *Political Theory and Modernity*. Ithaca, NY: Cornell University Press, 1993.

Connolly, William E. *The Ethos of Pluralization*. Minneapolis: University of Minnesota Press, 1995.

Daniels, Norman. *Reading Rawls: Critical Studies on Rawls' A Theory of Justice*. Palo Alto, CA: Stanford University Press, 1989.

de Vries, Hent. "Of Miracles and Special Effects." *International Journal for Philosophy of Religion*, vol. 50, 2001: 41–56.

Durkheim, Emile. *Elementary Forms of Religious Life*. Oxford: Oxford University Press, 2001.

Gutmann, Amy. "A Tribute to John Rawls 1921–2002." Harvard University Center for Ethics and the Professions Web site at http://www.ethics.harvard.edu/memoriam_rawls.php.

Gutmann, Amy. "The Central Role of Rawls's Theory." *Dissent*, 1989: 338.

Hampshire, Stuart. "A New Philosophy of the Just Society." *New York Review of Books*, vol. 18, no. 3, 1972: 34–39.
Hart, H. L. A. "Rawls on Liberty and its Priority," in *Reading Rawls*. ed. Norman Daniels. Palo Alto, CA: Stanford University Press, 1989: 230–252.
Hobbes, Thomas. *Leviathan*. Indianapolis, IN: Hackett, 1994.
Hume, David. *An Enquiry Concerning Human Understanding and Other Writings*. New York: Cambridge University Press, 2007.
James, William. "The Present Dilemma in Philosophy," in *The Writings of William James: A Comprehensive Edition*. ed. John J. Mcdermott. Chicago: University of Chicago Press, 1977: 362–75.
Kant, Immanuel. "An Answer to the Question: 'What Is Enlightenment?'," in *Kant: Political Writings*. Cambridge: Cambridge University Press, 1991: 54–60.
Kant, Immanuel. *Critique of Practical Reason*. Cambridge: Cambridge University Press, 1996.
Laden, Anthony Simon. "The House that Jack Built: Thirty Years of Reading Rawls." *Ethics*, vol. 113, 2003: 367–90.
Laslett, Peter. *Politics, Philosophy and History*. Oxford: Basil Blackwell, 1970.
Lefort, Claude. "The Permanence of the Theologico-Political?," in *Democracy and Political Theory*. Cambridge: Polity Press, 1988.
Locke, John. *The Reasonableness of Christianity; with a Discourse of Miracles; and, part of a Third Letter Concerning Toleration*. Palo Alto, CA: Stanford University Press, 1958.
"Miracles." *A Dictionary of Religion and Ethics*. eds. Shailer Matthews and Gerald Birney Smith. New York: Macmillan, 1921: 285–6.
"Miracles." *Encyclopedia of Religion and Ethics*. ed. James Hastings. New York: Charles Scribner's Sons, 1970.
Monk, Ray. *Ludwig Wittgenstein: The Duty of Genius*. New York: Macmillan, 1990.
Nagel, Thomas, and Joshua Cohen. "Introduction" to *A Brief Inquiry into the Meaning of Faith and Sin*. Cambridge, MA: Harvard University Press, 2009: 1–23.
Nehamas, Alexander. "Trends in Recent American Philosophy." *Daedalus*. vol. 126, 1997: 209–23.
Nietzsche, Friedrich Wilhelm. *The Gay Science with a Prelude in Rhymes and an Appendix of Songs*. trans. Walter Arnold Kaufmann. New York: Vintage Books, 2010.
Pogge, Thomas. "Memorial for John Rawls: The Magic of the Green Book." *Kantian Review*, vol. 8, 2004: 153–5.
Pogge, Thomas. "A Brief Sketch of Rawls's Life," in *The Philosophy of Rawls*. vol. 1. eds. Henry S. Richardson and Paul J. Weithman. New York: Garland, 1999: 1–15.
Rawls, John. *A Brief Inquiry into the Meaning of Sin and Faith: With "On My Religion."* Cambridge, MA: Harvard University Press, 2010.
Rawls, John. "A Brief Inquiry into the Meaning of Sin and Faith: An Interpretation Based on the Concept of Community." Senior Thesis Submitted to the Department of Philosophy at Princeton University, 1942.

Rawls, John. *A Theory of Justice.* Cambridge, MA: Harvard University Press, 1971.
Rawls, John. *Political Liberalism.* New York: Columbia University Press, 1993.
Rawls, John. "The Sense of Justice." *Philosophical Review*, vol. 72, no. 3, 1963: 281–305.
Ricoeur, Paul. "On John Rawls' *A Theory of Justice*: Is a Pure Procedural Theory of Justice Possible?," *International Social Science Journal.* Paris: Unesco, 1990.
Ricoeur, Paul. "The Political Paradox," in *Legitimacy and the State*, ed. William E. Connolly. New York: New York University Press, 1984: 250–72.
Rousseau, Jean-Jacques. *On The Social Contract.* trans. Judith R. Masters. New York: St. Martin's, 1978.
Ryan, Allan. "How Liberalism, Politics Come to Terms," *The Washington Times.* 1993.
"Saints." *The Oxford Companion to Christian Thought.* eds. Adrian Hastings et al. Oxford: Oxford University Press, 2000: 639.
Sandel, Michael. "Political Liberalism." *Harvard Law Review*, vol. 107, no. 7, 1994: 1765–94.
Schmitt, Carl. *Political Theology: Four Chapters on the Concept of Sovereignty.* Cambridge, MA: MIT Press, 1985.
Spinoza, Baruch. *Theological-Political Treatise.* Indianapolis, IN: Hackett, 2001.
White, Stephen K. "Fullness and Dearth: Depth Experience and Democratic Life." *American Political Science Review*, vol. 104, 2010: 800–16.
Williams, Bernard. "Rawls and Pascal's Wager," in *Moral Luck.* Cambridge: Cambridge University Press, 1981: 94–100.
Wolin, Sheldon. "The Liberal/Democratic Divide." *Political Theory*, vol. 24, no. 1, 1996: 97–119.

5

The Wish for a Better Life

Stanley Cavell's Critique of the Social Contract

That it [ordinary language philosophy] is not a direct criticism makes it, to my mind, far more interesting than it would be if it were. Because the reasons it is not direct criticism can show us, if we can articulate them, something more interesting than particular mistakes a thinker has committed. It can show how coherent and tenacious a point of view can be, how much is at stake in maintaining it, and therefore show how complex the difficulties any serious criticism of it will exact – one meant seriously enough, I mean, to wish to change the mind which harbors the point of view, or else to be changed by it.

Like any conversion experience – any turning, however small, of a cheek, of a mood – the effect is apt to seem out of proportion to anything you might think to call its cause. Conversion (or as Emerson says it, aversion) is of its nature hard to explain, to others as to oneself.

– And why should the mind be less dense and empty and mazed and pocked and clotted – and why less a whole – than the world is?
– Stanley Cavell[1]

It is difficult and dangerous to generalize about conversion, for the experiences and possibilities named by this term are so various, particular, and context-bound, yet I will hazard that all – nearly all – forms of conversion have this in common: *they express the wish for a better life*. It is plain to see how such a wish might be pertinent to ethics, to aesthetics, to religion – this chapter will argue the political pertinence of the wish for a better life that is central to conversion and try to show its pertinence to a

---

[1] Stanley Cavell, *The Claim of Reason*, 166; *A Pitch of Philosophy*, 59; *Must We Mean What We Say?*, 266.

possible politics of secularism. The problem of translating the wish for a better life into philosophical, moral, and political registers rather precisely characterizes the trajectory of Stanley Cavell's philosophical writings. And I will argue that these writings also translate what Karl Marx understood as a revolutionary practice of critique – what he famously alluded to in an early letter as the "ruthless critique of everything existing" – to the everyday life of a possible democratic practice.[2] The reception of Cavell's work is ongoing, and I will argue the importance of its potential contributions to a series of standing problems in contemporary politics: how to sustain and even enact the wish for a better life in a "post-political" landscape; how to do so in the face of the shrinking political possibilities that attend globalization and neoliberalization; and in view of impending ecological catastrophe, how in the most general sense to recover the promise of revolution in an antirevolutionary world. Those are tall orders that extend far beyond the task of reimagining secularism proposed by this book but, as I suggested at the outset, establishing the more deeply, genuinely democratic practices that would be needed to fill these orders may require that we first reimagine secularism.

Particularly in his early writings, Marx understood the task of political critique to follow closely on the heels of the critique of religion, and Cavell's work translates this problematic as well, with the important amendment that political criticism neither proceeds after the critique of religion nor on the same bases as the critique of religion but instead unfolds in the very terms of the classical religious critiques of the Hebrew Bible, namely as "prophecy," and with the aim of conversion or transformation of self and community. It cements in uniquely insightful and far-reaching connection the problems of critique and conversion to suggest a possible way of rethinking secularism as an openness to the absence of community and the necessity of pursuing community despite its persistent failure. It is true that Marx is conspicuously absent from Cavell's texts – a particularly striking example of which is his all-but-complete omission from *Cities of Words*, Cavell's "textbook" on moral and political philosophy, which canvasses Emerson, Locke, Mill, Kant, Rawls, Nietzsche, Ibsen, Freud, Plato, Aristotle, Henry James, G. B. Shaw, and Shakespeare. Despite this, readers familiar with Cavell's interpretation of Wittgenstein's *Philosophical Investigations* will find the analogies with Marx's early injunctions immediate and precise, particularly where Marx writes that:

---

[2] The *"rücksichtlose Kritik alles Bestehenden"* of the *Deutsch-Franzozische Jahrbücher*.

The reform of consciousness consists *only* in enabling the world to clarify its consciousness, in waking it from its dream about itself, in *explaining* to it the meaning of its own actions. Our whole task can consist only in putting religious and political questions into self-conscious human form – as is also the case in Feuerbach's criticism of religion. // Our motto must therefore be: Reform of consciousness not through dogmas, but through analyzing the mystical consciousness, the consciousness which is unclear to itself, whether it appears in religious or political form. Then it will transpire that the world has long been dreaming of something that it can acquire if only it becomes conscious of it. It will transpire that it is not a matter of drawing a great dividing line between past and future [*einen grossen Gedankenstrich zwischen Vergangenheit und Zukunft*], but of carrying out the thoughts of the past. And finally, it will transpire that mankind begins no *new* work, but consciously accomplishes its old work.[3]

What Marx would come to understand as revolution is here figured as waking from a dream, anticipating the kind of response Wittgenstein would try to elicit to his (and our) captivity within the metaphysical fantasies of the philosophical tradition, and anticipating the kind of response Cavell himself proposes to the problem of modern skepticism. It seems possible that Cavell refuses the connection with Marx because it is too close. It is a short step, or a mere change of aspect, from any of these figures of awakening to the figure of conversion.

Suggestively, at *Cities of Words'* single point of contact with Marx, Cavell is absorbed not only with the theme of secularization but also with the problem of conversion. At this point, Cavell considers Marx's early "Introduction to a Critique of Hegel's *Philosophy of Right*" as a continuation of his own reflections on the manner in which Ibsen's *A Doll's House* secularizes a figure of conversion from Paul's *Corinthians*.[4]

---

[3] Marx, "For a Ruthless Criticism of Everything Existing," 15 (emphases in the original). "Die Reform des Bewusstseins besteht nur darin, dass man die Welt ihr Bewusstsein innewerden lässt, dass man sie aus dem Traum über sich selbst aufweckt, dass man ihre eignen Actionen ihr *erklärt*. Unser ganzer Zweck kann in nichts anderem bestehn, wie dies auch bei Feuerbachs Kritik der Religion der Fall ist, als dass die religiösen und politischen Fragen in die selbstbewusste menschliche Form gebracht werden. // Unser Wahlspruch muss also sein: Reform des Bewusstseins nicht durch Dogmen, sondern durch Analysierung des mystischen, sich selbst unklaren Bewusstseins, trete es nun religiös oder politisch auf. Es wird sich dann zeigen, dass die Welt längst den Traum von einer Sache besitzt, von dem sie nur das Bewusstsein besitzen muss, um sie wirklich zu besitzen. Es wird sich zeigen, dass es sich nicht um einen grossen Gedankenstrich zwischen Vergangenheit und Zukunft handelt, sondern um die *Vollziehung* der Gedanken der Vergangenheit. Es wird sich endlich zeigen, dass die Menschheit keine *neue* Arbeit beginnt, sondern mit Bewusstsein ihre alte Arbeit zu Stande bringt" (*Deutsch-Franzozische Jahrbücher*, 39).

[4] Also from the 1843–4 *Deutsche-Franzozish Jahrbücher*, cited at *Cities of Words*, 262.

Glossing Marx's text, Cavell writes, "That 'Redemption' here was interpreted as 'revolution,' and revolution as a particular form of violence, is one of the dominating facts of the bloody twentieth century." He argues that Marx's theoretical project miscarries, in other words, and that Marx's secularization has needlessly led to horrific violence. And yet Cavell acknowledges that he and the early Marx are pressing the same question: How can the figure of "redemption," or the wish for a better life, be "secularized?" In other words, how can one of the central motifs of religion be reformulated in and for political modernity? Despite his judgment and the censure that follows from it, Cavell echoes the early Marx (whom he avoids) as well as the late Wittgenstein (with whom he aligns himself) in continuously returning to the figure of waking life as a dream life, and the question of what truly waking to life requires, and of what follows from such an awakening. If conversion signifies awakening, for Cavell, this possibility is grounded in a practice of criticism that proceeds in the manner of the Hebrew prophets, as a necessary basis for a modern, secular democratic politics in the absence of community.[5] Conversion, and thus secularism, serve as the basis of a community otherwise without basis, as the acknowledgment of community's absence, and the necessity of collective action despite this absence. Conversion, here, is not imagined as conversion to an existing community but rather as the conversion of citizens necessary for collective action without community.

Leaving aside his assessment of blame for the violence of the twentieth century, Cavell's work is important because it develops a critical social theory outside the familiar horizons of specifically Marxian theory and outside also the more capacious boundaries of the tradition of critical theory that enfolds Marx. It develops a sustained, detailed, and tightly argued ethical-political response to the distinctly modern crisis of faith in the possibility of attaining a better life in a better world. If not devoid of posture and piety, this is a critical stance with a different posture and piety, and it is a stance that demands a deeper engagement and absorption within the world, rather than a rejection of it. Cavell's problem is precisely to think politics after the eclipse of hopes for another world remade through revolution, and it unfolds precisely as a politics of conversion as an alternative mode of secularism.[6]

---

[5] On prophetic discourse as a genre of political discourse, see George Shulman's *American Prophecy*.

[6] The philosopher Paola Marrati elaborates such an interpretation of Cavell in connection with her interpretation of Gilles Deleuze more clearly than anyone else. See Marrati,

This chapter will trace Cavell's reformulation of social-contract theory to show how a certain kind of conversion appears as central to the possibility of a more genuinely democratic political practice. Where the authorized image of conversion depicts the attainment of truth, certainty, and conviction in a new faith shared in fellowship with a community of belief, Cavell's work can help to draw out a more complex figure of conversion that passes through the loss of the known world, self, and community in the trial of doubt and existential isolation. By articulating an unexpected connection between criticism and conversion, Cavell's work suggests how a secularism refigured as a complex process of conversion might serve as a condition for the forms of collective politics that seem increasingly rare and imperiled in the late-modern world. Such claims – as Cavell might say – are not likely to admit of proof through argument. But they can – as Cavell might also say – be offered as an invitation, leaving readers to ask whether such claims might be worth making.

In Cavell's work, the possibility of conversion opens in a moment of disorientation, but it does not end with certainty, reconciliation, or the recuperation of wholeness suggested by dominant images of conversion, such as the authorized image of Augustine's *Confessions*. Instead, for Cavell, conversion involves folding an extraordinary dimension within the experience within ordinary life, less as a matter of critical reflection or moral turn in the Kantian tradition, and more as the creation of a crystalline structure of experience such as that outlined by Bergson and Deleuze. Cavell's interpretation of the phenomenon of conversion runs against the authorized picture, in which conversion entails a conversion to something definite, be it an established creed, church, or fold. Certainty is not necessary for conversion in this image and a network of belief is not the most useful frame in which to analyze the experience. In Cavell's view, the most important kind of conversion is one in which the subject of modern epistemology reformulates its attachments to the certainty and truth value of the networks of belief in which it is ensconced. Conversion here emerges through acknowledgment of the limits of knowledge, and reaffirmation of commitments made at and beyond these limits. In Cavell's idiom, both ethical conduct and the achievement of one's own humanity depend on renouncing the claims to certainty and finality. In its most suggestive moments, Cavell's writing hints at a process of conversion

---

The Event and the Ordinary: On the Philosophy of Gilles Deleuze and Stanley Cavell (book-length manuscript).

bound up with open-ended improvisation, through which one produces one's own individuality, negotiates the terms of one's social legibility, and assumes wider political responsibility and engagement informed by practices of criticism and dissent.

The possibility of community lies at the center of the problem – or, more precisely, the continuous and even necessary absence of community that conditions political modernity along with the persistent drive to capture, constitute, or reconstitute the missing community.[7] What conversion brings to light in connection with this problem is not merely the reconstitution of the individual subject (although that remains important) but rather the reciprocal implication of the reconstitution of the subject and the reconstitution of collective action in the absence of a community. Indeed, what is to be found here is another account of conversion, which although it acknowledges the power of narrative (under the auspices of literature), breaks fully from the form of conversion narrative, as the retrospective consolidation of an instantaneous transformation, and places narrative under the pressure of skepticism (here, under force of modern philosophy and tragedy). This chapter is divided into three sections. The first draws out Cavell's distinctive approach to criticism, argument, and conversion by considering his style of writing and the dominant themes within his work. It next turns to an example of the practice of political criticism in connection with conversion by considering a debate between Cavell and Rawls. Through a discussion of social-contract theory, it then shows how Cavell makes conversion the basis for acknowledging and navigating democratic citizenship in the absence of community.

Reading, Writing, and Argument: A First Approach at Conversion

Cavell has pursued what he calls the problem of modern skepticism throughout his philosophical career – most notably through Shakespearean tragedy, Empiricist epistemology, literary Romanticism, Hollywood film, and political theory. "Privacy," "interiority," "intelligibility," "sanity," "community," and "conversion" are among his key concerns, but neither Cavell nor his commentators have considered the connection between these concerns and the problem of modern secularism as such. This occupation with "the threat of skepticism" is grounded in Cavell's

---

[7] One could just as easily write here: "The nation, in a word, lies at the center of the problem... or re-constitute the missing nation." Or, "The People, in a word...the missing People."

interpretation of Wittgenstein's *Philosophical Investigations* and it is sustained from his dissertation, *The Claim to Rationality* (1961), through its extensive revision, *The Claim of Reason* (1979), to his latest works. Modern subjectivity according to Cavell is constituted by and suspended within a continuous threat of skepticism, which is to say that modern subjectivity is constituted through its special relation to knowledge. Modern skepticism may take one of two forms: it may claim that we cannot know the world (perhaps I am dreaming; perhaps I am nothing but a brain in a vat), or it may claim that we cannot know other minds (perhaps my neighbor is an automaton and not human at all; perhaps his tears do not express pain but are instead meant to deceive me). According to Cavell, skepticism's suggestions that we cannot know the world, that we cannot know other minds, are neither simply true nor are they simply false. Skepticism, in its fantastic and mundane forms, attends human life in modernity – it does not undo knowledge, but it reveals the essential insecurity of knowledge, and this is a fact with consequences for ethical and political life. What I would like to show here is that Cavell's suggestions for living with the insecurity of knowledge in modernity may also serve as suggestions for living with the problem of modern secularism. In my interpretation, as a response to the threat of skepticism, Cavell develops practices of philosophical criticism that might suggest an alternative image of secularism as a basis for a more genuinely democratic politics. The best way into these practices runs through Cavell's writing itself and through its approach to argumentation in the shadow of skepticism.

Although his long tenure in the department of philosophy at Harvard University lends this stance a sense of artificiality and hints at the pains that must be taken to maintain it, Cavell places himself at odds with the institutions of philosophy.[8] Artifice and theatricality, as modes of producing the extraordinary within the ordinary, constitute recurrent and fundamental motifs in his work. He presents himself as a party to "a lifelong quarrel with the profession of philosophy" and "in particular [with] the pressures of the professionalization of American philosophy."[9] His writing strains the boundaries of philosophical expression – it is in turns elliptical, gnomic, labored, self-referential, autobiographical, and digressive.[10] The irregularity of this prose alone would be enough to

---

[8] For an extended treatment of the theme of "oddness," see Stanley Cavell, "Being Odd, Getting Even."
[9] See Cavell, "The Politics of Interpretation," 31.
[10] According to Arnold Davidson, "Cavell writes not primarily to produce new theses or conclusions, nor to produce new arguments to old conclusions, but, as Kierkegaard and

assure the following types of response: According to *The Journal of Philosophy*, "even after some five hundred pages" of Cavell's magnum opus, *The Claim of Reason*, "the reader is still wondering what, if anything, has happened. Nor, I think, is he supposed to know, since the author does not know either."[11] *Mind* and *The Philosophical Quarterly* similarly record that Cavell's "self-indulgence" is an "impunity," an "irritant," and a needless "cause of suffering in his readers."[12] The *New York Times* complains that "Mr. Cavell obscures his arguments with convoluted sentences... lengthy digressions about his own previous books and lectures... [and] goes a bit too far... with what can only be construed as willful and unnecessary pretension."[13] Although the *New York Times* and many of the anglophonic philosophical establishments have often resisted challenging voices in contemporary philosophy (see the treatment of Jacques Derrida and Judith Butler), in Cavell's case, the response is in some sense warranted: these reviewers have a point. However, they understate the extent to which Cavell's writing is inseparable from the response he suggests to the threat of modern skepticism. Following his heroes – Wittgenstein and Emerson, in particular – rather than arguing one point or another, Cavell's writing is meant to help its readers probe the tenacity of their own convictions and perhaps change their minds; in other words, his writing aims to open the possibility of conversion for its readers.

The Claim of Reason's first two sentences give some idea of what vexes his readers and also show how this prose style is important to Cavell's project. The first sentence runs to 216 words, whereas the second is only 12; they are as follows:

If not at the beginning of Wittgenstein's later philosophy, since what starts philosophy is no more to be known at the outset than how to make an end of it; and if not at the opening of *Philosophical Investigations,* since its opening is not to be confused with the starting of the philosophy it expresses, and since the terms in which that opening might be understood can hardly be given along with the opening itself, and if we acknowledge from the commencement, anyway leave open at the opening, that the way this work is written is internal to what it teaches, which means that we cannot understand the manner (call it the method) before

---

the later Wittgenstein did, to excavate and transform the reader's sensibility, to undo his self-mystifications and redirect his interests" ("Beginning Cavell" in *The Senses of Stanley Cavell*, 234).

[11] Morris Weitz, "The Claim of Reason."
[12] Anthony Palmer, "The Claim of Reason"; H. O. Mounce, "The Claim of Reason."
[13] Michiko Kakutani, reviewing *Pursuits of Happiness* in the *New York Times.*

we understand its work; and if we do not look to our history, since placing this book historically can hardly happen earlier than placing it philosophically; nor look to Wittgenstein's past, since then we are likely to suppose that the *Investigations* is written in criticism of the *Tractatus*, which is not so much wrong as empty, both because to know what constitutes its criticism would be to know what constitutes its philosophy, and because it is more to the present point to see how the *Investigations* is written in criticism of itself; then where and how are we to approach this text? How are we to let this book teach us, this or anything?[14]

This first sentence concatenates nearly twenty conditioned, qualified, and interjected clauses to pose a question that could seemingly be reduced to the following eight words: "How are we to approach Wittgenstein's *Philosophical Investigations*?" But part of Cavell's point is that *Investigations* teaches its readers to cultivate resistance to their impulses to strip language of its distinctive pathways, polyphonies, cadences, hesitations, emphases, insistences, and idiosyncrasies. Much as *A Theory of Justice* and *Political Liberalism* appeal to multiple layers of reason and emotional response in disposing their readers to proceed with reasonable argumentation, *The Claim of Reason* habituates its readers to lacunae of meaning; the limits of intelligible expression; the forms of sociability, such as trust, required to proceed under these conditions; and the ethics of uncertainty required when rules are suspended and judgment itself is drawn into question.

The second short sentence supplements the first by drawing out a latent ambiguity. Repeating a single word, "this," three times in thirteen words to ask (i) how are we to approach "this text" and (ii) let "this book" (iii) teach us "this or anything" draws out the first sentence's ambivalence. Is the first sentence about approaching *Philosophical Investigations*, or is it about approaching *The Claim of Reason*, or is it about approaching something else, or is it about "anything" else? For all of their 228 words, these sentences leave this critical point unclear. A few pages later, Cavell might seem to dispel the uncertainty by writing, "I was supposed to be saying more... concerning how we should approach Wittgenstein's text," but once doubt about what "this" is has entered, a supposition at this point intensifies rather than dispels it.[15] Being "supposed to" may mean being "assumed to" or being "required to," which leads to questions such as these: Who assumed that Cavell would say more? Did the reader

---

[14] Cavell, *The Claim of Reason*, 3.
[15] Cavell, *The Claim of Reason*, 6.

assume that he was saying more? Did Cavell assume that this was what he was doing? With what reason was it assumed? Was this assumption true or false? Was he supposed to be doing it in the sense that he had an obligation to do it? If so, whence does the obligation to say more arise? And with what consequences can it be accepted or declined? None of these questions have easy answers but, in my reading, *The Claim of Reason* means to draw these questions to a reader's attention, and these questions are in some sense intended. They are important questions insofar as they thematize the artificiality and theatricality of writing, of language more generally, and of social life above all.

But how do I know that any of these questions are pertinent here and that these concerns are the most important ones? How do I know that this has anything to do with the point Cavell intends here? I can make hypotheses, supply arguments, adduce evidence, perform tests. *But can I know here?* Why would it not be better to say that Cavell opens *The Claim of Reason* with the question, "How are we to approach Wittgenstein's *Philosophical Investigations?*" I do not know. I can test my hypothesis and advance some evidence in its support. For example: Wittgenstein's *Investigations* opens with a discussion of ostension, probing how we point to, demonstrate, or indicate any particular "this." It might, therefore, seem reasonable to read Cavell's opening as an echo of Wittgenstein's. I could claim that Cavell is fascinated by this region of Wittgenstein's thought and that he treats ostension as opening problems about practices involved with the use of language: one cannot know with certainty that another has pointed to this, that, or another thing with this, that, or another intention. But that does not mean one cannot interpret another's gestures. One can, as much and as little as any text, based in part on what one is willing to allow and in part on what one is willing to offer as a response.

A receptive reader might use the same words as the *Journal of Philosophy*'s reviewer – confessing at the end of Cavell's text that "the reader is still wondering what, if anything, has happened. Nor, I think, is he supposed to know, since the author does not know either." Not at all in this reviewer's apparent spirit, such a reader might insist that the *Claim of Reason* shows a great deal about the limitations of ideas about "knowing" what has happened in this text, that situation, or the other claim. In other words, the text constitutes (through its performance) a sustained critique of the epistemological tradition that begins with Descartes. A receptive reader might be convinced of the importance of acknowledging the limitations of what can be known about oneself and others and might be moved, furthermore, to countenance the possibility that philosophy has more to say about this limit of knowledge than the modern epistemological tradition tends to allow. He or she might develop a sense for the importance of this boundary of reason for the problem of ethical and political conduct: even where I do not know, I must go on – better still, even where we do not know, precisely where we do not know, we must find a way to go on – somehow – together. I will argue that these limits of knowledge are of paramount importance for theorizing the problems of criticism, consent, and political community as a problem of conversion. Using the same words, with a different meaning, of course, is a classical part of the idea of conversion, but this kind of argument and writing leaves itself vulnerable to underappreciation.[16] When it does not achieve the conversion of interest it aims at, it may accomplish nothing at all; even when successful, its success may be difficult to account for. Cavell's writing asks for a shift in what will be legible within the discipline of philosophy, what kind of voices will be allowed to speak there, for a conversion of interest within the field.

Spanning the boundaries between what he tentatively calls Anglo-American and Continental philosophy, and between the practices of philosophy and of literature, Cavell has fashioned his own thematic idiom. His work traces and retraces a set of problems that mark out the terrain of post-Kantian philosophy, which he maps at one point in the following way:

> This fantasy of the vanishing of the human ... is a reassertion of the idea that the problem of other minds is a problem of human history ... that the problem is lived, and that this life has an origin and a progress ... The life of skepticism with respect to (other) minds will next require a history of its imagined overcomings ... The introduction of *cogitatio* [by Descartes as an early way to imagine overcoming skepticism] as the defining characteristic of mind is tantamount to the substitution of privacy for rationality as the mark of the mental ... As long as God exists, I am not alone ... [But after God's retreat] I wish to understand how the other now bears the weight of God, shows me that I am not alone in the universe. This requires understanding the philosophical problem of the other as the trace or scar

---

[16] William James emphasizes this point in his *Varieties of Religious Experience*, citing, for example, the following conversion narrative, "I took the book to my bedroom for quiet, intending to give it a thorough study, and then write her what I thought of it. It was here that God met me face to face, and I shall never forget the meeting. 'He that hath the Son hath life eternal, he that hath not the Son hath not life.' I had read this scores of times before, but this made all the difference. I was now in God's presence and my attention was absolutely 'soldered' on to this verse, and I was not allowed to proceed with the book till I had fairly considered what these words really involved."

of the departure of God. This descent, or ascent, of the problem of the other is the key way I can grasp the alternative process of secularization called romanticism.[17]

Cavell would not be the first to suggest that romanticism presents a response to secularization ("secularization" meant here in the sense of a retreat of God, or a transformation of religious faith in the North Atlantic world figured as a decline in the belief in the existence of the God of the Hebrew Bible and New Testament). Nor would he be the first to make the more specific claim that both developments (romanticism and secularization) are related to the emergence of modern epistemology and its conceptual companion, modern skepticism, or that both of these developments are related to a new way of thinking about privacy and conscience. Nor would he be alone in tying all six developments (romanticism, secularization, epistemology, skepticism, privacy, conscience) to the problem of ethics, here conceived as a problem of the responsibilities one incurs through one's ineliminable relations to others, or in thinking that this way of thinking about ethics is related to certain problems inherent in conceiving the human as, in the first case, a rational and autonomous agent. Nor would he be the first to suggest that gaining access to these problems would require one to write their history or genealogy, and that an important part of this genealogy would set modern Europe in the context of a variety of colonial and imperial relations to the rest of the world. Yet his approach to this complex of problems is remarkably consistent, creating an extraordinarily dense and self-referential network or what one might follow Bergson in calling a crystalline structure. The effect of this tends to be fascinating rather than narrowly argumentative – and this is another of the senses in which Cavell's work opens the problem of conversion as a complex process of transformation.

A first approximation of the political implications of the problem of skepticism laid out in *The Claim of Reason* and in Cavell's life of writing might run as follows: we are each separate from one another, and though we are traversed by common judgments, uses of language, and forms of life, the knowledge we can have about each other is nonetheless limited; what we would like to think of as morality emerges as we each respond to this condition, making it possible that we will treat each other with justice and without. Just as skepticism about the existence of the world and the objects within it is, in an important sense, a figment of the philosophical imagination, skepticism about one's ability to know another's mind is, in

[17] Cavell, *The Claim of Reason*, 468–70.

an important sense, constitutive of the ethical field of relations between human beings. According to Cavell, living one's skepticism entails foregoing epistemological foundations and learning not only to withstand the continuous disappointment at their absence but also to treat this absence as opening the possibility of human relations. More directly: ethical conduct depends upon accepting and responding properly to a condition in which one does not and cannot know another's mind, by cultivating generous, loving, trusting, responsive, faithful, and so forth dispositions in the absence of proof that these dispositions are appropriate.[18] Living our skepticism, here, represents dampening the human impulse to refute skepticism by establishing new foundations for knowledge, morality, community, political authority, and so forth. Cavell's late writing is largely occupied with a theory of "moral perfectionism" linked with classical images of the impetus to philosophy, such as Plato's allegory of the cave, Wittgenstein's injunction to turn investigation "around the fixed point of our true need," and Thoreau's quasi-theological demand for "awakening." It claims that these texts, along with a few others, constitute a philosophical tradition in which ethics are of primary concern and in which ethical life must be enabled and sustained by processes of conversion. At its best, this work develops an original synthesis of the fundamental ethical concern of ancient philosophy-as-system-of-ethical-self-cultivation, the imperative of psychoanalysis to treat human actions as interpretable rather than immediately transparent, the techniques of reading attentive to the myriad problems of textuality developed primarily by literary criticism and so-called Continental philosophy, and the conceptual rigor that is the pride of analytic philosophy. More than a single line of argument, this work constitutes a crystalline network of concern – a reader may not come away with new positions but may instead find his or her thought has been changed.

A certain amount of scholarly attention has already been paid to the intersection of Cavell's work with religion and theology, but not in the systematic fashion that it deserves, not in connection with the figure of conversion, and not in connection with the problem of modern secularism as it is pursued in this work. Stephen Mulhall's relatively early study, *Stanley Cavell: Philosophy's Recounting of the Ordinary*, for example, observes a studious avoidance of the topic of religion, which it reads as an assessment that the best way to acknowledge the unspeakable nature

---

[18] Cavell's analyses of Shakespeare's tragedies are helpful for understanding this point: think of the demands faced, and failed, by Lear, Leontes, and Othello. (cf. *Disowning Knowledge: In Seven Plays of Shakespeare*.)

The Wish for a Better Life 181

of God is not to speak of it. However, this ready-made image of negative-theology seems to fit Cavell's work even less well than it does Derrida's (who is certainly concerned with theology's *via negativa* but insists that deconstruction is nonetheless irreducible to negative theology). Mulhall's argument that, as he puts it, "philosophy cannot say sin" ignores the plain fact that Cavell's writing consistently recurs to theological tropes, making repeated reference to Jewish identity, God, Christ, scripture, Hebrew prophets, sacraments, and so on. Perhaps more substantially, the rhetorics of prophetic Judaism and apostolic Christianity are inextricable from Cavell's program of "moral perfectionism" and from the post-secular image of conversion that it implies.[19] More directly, Cavell's version of moral perfectionism depends upon a transformation of the self that is all but indistinguishable from (religious) conversion. Drawing out a concrete argument, Cavell's dispute with Rawls over the question of moral perfectionism can help to draw out his theory of conversion.

Cavell on Rawls and *A Theory of Justice* – a First Look at the Social Contract

Cavell touches on Rawls's work at a number of points, but his most extended discussion and his sharpest formulation of disagreement can be found in his address to the American Philosophical Association published as *Conditions Handsome and Unhandsome*.[20] The controversy turns on a handful of sentences written by Nietzsche, interpreted by Rawls, and reinterpreted by Cavell. Put this way, the point in dispute is infinitesimally small: resolving it one way or the other would yield only a negligible increase in knowledge, if any. But it is worth following in detail insofar as the way it unfolds shows something important about Cavell's argumentative practices, the problem of conversion, and a possible approach to modern secularism.

The dispute turns on the point in *A Theory of Justice*, touched upon in Chapter Four, at which Rawls takes Nietzsche as a representative of perfectionism and seeks to disqualify Nietzschean perfectionism as a moral doctrine. Rawls attributes to Nietzsche the notion that the great majority

---

[19] Stephen Mulhall, "Philosophy Cannot Say Sin," in his *Stanley Cavell: Philosophy's Recounting of the Ordinary*, 283–313.
[20] For the most extensive statement of Cavell's critique of Rawls, see *Conditions Handsome and Unhandsome*; for the most recent and most readable statement, see the chapter "Rawls," in *Cities of Words*. There is also a chapter on Rawls in *The Claim of Reason*; this, however, is directed toward Rawls's "Two Concepts of Rules" and is not immediately pertinent here.

of a society should "give value to our lives by working for the good of the highest specimens" at the expense of our less-than-highest, less-than-inherently valuable selves.[21] Presenting a passage from "Schopenhauer as Educator" as his primary exhibit, Rawls credited Nietzsche with the proposal that a society should devote its resources to producing a privileged class of great individuals. "The absolute weight that Nietzsche sometimes gives the lives of great men such as Socrates and Goethe is unusual," Rawls wrote. "At places," he added, Nietzsche "says that mankind must continually strive to produce great individuals," and he adduced the following quotation to drive his point home: "Mankind must work continually to produce individual great human beings – this and nothing else is the task ... for the question is this: how can your life, the individual life, retain the highest value, the deepest significance? ... Only by your living for the good of the rarest and most valuable specimens."[22] Rawls took the implications of this passage to be sufficiently clear without further interpretation; at least, he provided no further interpretation or consideration. Who would want to defend such a claim?

Cavell's response begins by acknowledging that, indeed, "This sounds bad."[23] But it is not as bad as it sounds. To begin, "specimens" is a poor translation of the original German, "Exemplare." The English "exemplars" is more direct and fits better, in part because it bypasses the biological connotations of the translation Rawls accepts and thereby makes less plausible the notion that Nietzsche had imagined a distinct race of men. It also hints at the special kind of relation Nietzsche is suggesting, namely, one of exemplarity.[24] In the paragraph following the one cited by Rawls, Nietzsche indicates that certain "exemplars" may lead one to feel "ashamed of oneself" on account of "one's own narrowness and shrivelled nature" and may thereby stimulate the soul's "desire to look beyond itself and to seek with all its might for a higher self as yet still concealed from it," taking the examples as guides.[25] Furthermore, the immediate context shows that the relation Nietzsche imagines toward exemplars is poorly described as the condition of the mass slavery to higher specimens. That Schopenhauer is next to absent from the text of "Schopenhauer as

---

[21] John Rawls, *A Theory of Justice*, 325.
[22] Rawls, *A Theory of Justice*, fn 325.
[23] Cavell reproduces Rawls's quotation; see *Conditions Handsome and Unhandsome*, 49.
[24] Cavell, *Conditions Handsome and Unhandsome*, 50. Cavell notes that more recent translations than the one consulted by Rawls employ "exemplar" here. Cf. Friedrich Nietzsche, "Schopenhauer as Educator," in *Untimely Meditations*, 162.
[25] Nietzsche, "Schopenhauer as Educator," 163.

Educator" gives further indication that Nietzsche does not imagine one's relation to one's exemplars to be that of slavish service.[26] To express this point in theological terms, worshiping Schopenhauer, or any other higher specimen, would be idolatrous, whereas being inspired by an exemplary figure to enlarge "one's own narrowness and shrivelled nature" is to "consecrate oneself to culture."[27] Tracing out the implications of this line of thought – touching as it does the workings of criticism, culture, theology, and a variant of moral perfectionism indebted chiefly to Romanticism – has occupied Cavell for his career; but although it may be difficult to see the full meaning Cavell attaches to Nietzsche's sentences, that Nietzsche did not mean what Rawls says he did is relatively plain.

Rawls never published on the topic of Romanticism, the broad cultural movement under which Nietzsche is most often subsumed, and to my knowledge neither took any serious interest nor claimed expertise in it. But it is still fair to ask how Rawls could fail to notice that Nietzsche was an even stronger critic of the state's intervention in education and in culture than himself. It is strange that Rawls imagined Nietzsche to have been "directing society to arrange institutions and to define the duties and obligations of individuals so as to maximize the achievement of human excellence in art, science, and culture," when, in the essay Rawls cites to support this claim, Nietzsche is adamantly opposed to any such thing.[28] Nietzsche writes that "precisely those forces at present most actively engaged in promoting culture do so for reasons they reserve to themselves" and that "whenever one now speaks of the 'cultural state', one sees it as facing the task of releasing the spiritual energies of a generation to the extent that will serve the interests of existing institutions: but only to this extent," so that the state can only produce "misemployed and appropriated culture" and not the true culture that Nietzsche admires.[29] It would be difficult to imagine that Rawls would disallow the promotion of culture insofar as it contributes to the stability of the institutions of governance, but Nietzsche is averse even (and precisely) to the promotion of culture for such purposes. There are a few more things to notice about Rawls's interpretation of Nietzsche. He offers as a basis for his reading

---

[26] In Cavell's words: "the author of that text ["Schopenhauer as Educator"] is not consecrating himself to Schopenhauer – Schopenhauer, as everyone notes, is scarcely present in the text" (*Conditions Handsome and Unhandsome*, 53).
[27] For "idolatry" and the "theology of reading," cf. *Conditions Handsome and Unhandsome*, 53, 57; "The Politics of Interpretation"; and *The Senses of Walden*, 63–4.
[28] Rawls, *A Theory of Justice*, 325.
[29] Nietzsche, "Schopenahuer as Educator," 164, 165.

of Nietzsche G. A. Morgan's *What Nietzsche Means*, a text distinctly colored by the perception of Nietzsche's responsibility for the Nazi regime current at the time of its publication and more than thirty years old by the time of *A Theory of Justice*'s publication.[30] He credits "J. R. Hollingsdale" as Nietzsche's translator rather than R. J. Hollingdale. These latter are again small points, but they argue a certain inattention on Rawls's part, and I take Cavell's point to be that ethical and political implications follow from this kind of inattention.

The crux of this disagreement, then, has much less to do with Nietzsche's, Cavell's, and Rawls's conceptions of perfectionism than it does with their respective approaches to reading; to writing; to philosophy, theory, and criticism; and to agreement, disagreement, consent, and dissent more generally. The crux of the quarrel lies in the presumed moral and political sufficiency of the arguments accomplished in *A Theory of Justice* to their own aims. It is not only a dispute over the limits of knowledge but also about the means, ends, limits, and possibilities of public argument. Cavell affirms the common assessment of *A Theory of Justice*'s importance as a central contribution to the field of political philosophy, having placed the tenets of liberal governance on firm analytic ground. He gives, in his own words, "all honor... to Rawls for articulating the ground of the right of and the respect for and the responsibility toward difference (the value of freedom), and the ground of the moral irrelevance of difference (the value of equality)."[31] What emerges as a problem, however, is satisfaction with the criteria of justice Rawls outlines. Cavell suggests that perfectionism, his shorthand for a continuous process of conversion, is a necessary supplement to any given theory of justice insofar as perfectionism inspires responsiveness toward claims that cannot as yet be accommodated in current terms of justice.[32]

When Rawls denies standing to individuals who would make claims on bases other than those articulated by his *Theory of Justice*, the injustice of that exclusion calls the standing of his own theory into question, for to close the terms of justice in advance is to deny the possibility that

---

[30] See G. A. Morgan, *What Nietzsche Means*.
[31] Stanley Cavell, *Philosophy The Day after Tomorrow*, 187. Although much of this honorific is retracted a few lines later: "these defenses [against what Cavell calls "moralism" made by Kant, Rawls, and Mill] may come too late in a current moral crossroads, before our societies have largely interiorized the moral vision of such thinkers."
[32] More properly speaking, Cavell offers "Emersonian Perfectionism" or, synonymously, "Moral and Political Perfectionism."

these terms and the commitments they support may themselves need to be changed. It is also to foreclose the possibility of a continued process of transformation in which these terms will be transmuted – to deny, in short, the complex process of conversion. Cavell expresses the concern this way:

> The reservations and reinterpretations I express... [with respect to Rawls] must concern this matter... of how and where the conversation of justice stops. Earlier the moment of the failure of conversation presented itself as a refusal of conversation; here it presents itself rather as a denial that conversation has been offered... But what if there is a cry of justice that expresses a sense not of having *lost* out in an unequal yet fair struggle, but of having from the start been *left* out... Rawls... seems to be denying precisely the competence of expressions claiming a suffering [perpetuated by a condition in which]... the mass of the individual members of society have been deprived of a voice in their histories.[33]

Cavell suggests that liberal democracy, particularly as Rawls imagines it, reproduces highly specific conditions in which its citizens are not only denied a role in determining the conditions of governance but are also deprived of their voices.

Rawls seeks to demonstrate the reasonableness of society's basic institutions sufficiently well for all members of society to agree to them, to consent to them, and to be bound to obey their dictates. He articulates the "principle of legitimacy" and the related "duty of civility" that follow in this way:

> Our exercise of political power [defined as coercive power] is proper and hence justifiable only when it is exercised in accordance with a constitution the essentials of which all citizens may reasonably be expected to endorse in the light of principles and ideals acceptable to them as reasonable and rational. This is the liberal principle of legitimacy. And since the exercise of political power itself must be legitimate, the ideal of citizenship imposes a moral, not a legal, duty – the duty of civility – to be able to explain to one another on those fundamental questions how the principles and policies they advocate and vote for can be supported by the political values of public reason.[34]

Cavell's critique presses on the concept of legitimacy from within a liberal theory by claiming, to use a distinction that will be elaborated in the next section of this chapter, that *A Theory of Justice* locks many – if not all – of its citizens in a position of tacit consent to the terms of the social contract. A consistent theme in Cavell's work is that the expressive capacity of a

---

[33] Cavell, *Conditions Handsome and Unhandsome*, xxxvii–xxxviii.
[34] Rawls, *Political Liberalism*, 217.

specifically human voice is threatened in modernity, and the dispute we are tracing here might be reframed in light of that concern such that the central questions become: When does the procedural discourse of justice rob citizens of their voices? When it does rob people of their voices, how is the condition of forced silence to be replaced by one in which people find their voices? Rawls never replied to Cavell's criticism in print nor, as Cavell reports their exchanges, was he able to meet this criticism in private – a fascinating failure of communication, which raises a series of questions about whose voice, if anyone's, is denied through this exchange.[35]

What is at stake here has, at any rate, little to do with Nietzsche's work per se but rather with the tendencies of philosophical and political discourses to silence voices through claims to knowledge. That phenomenon has certainly been recognized before – the critique of metaphysical dogmatism, for example, lies at the basis of Kant's critical project – but Cavell suggests the need to become attuned to the insistences of one's own commitments as well as to the specific tonalities of others' claims, and to do so with an openness to the possibility of conversion, for doing so places oneself and one's world at stake. In his engagement with Rawls, Cavell seizes on moments of closure that resist this kind of transformation – this is what links the remark about being "beyond reproach" with the short and dismissive passages on Nietzsche. The fault with Rawls's theory of justice accented here is its foreclosure of any further conversion on the part of those who accept it.

That may not sound like much of a critique, and it may not appear to revitalize democratic theory in a time of crisis. Apparently worse still, Cavell counts "snobbery," "conformity," and lack of "seriousness" among the most pressing problems in contemporary politics. He implies that Rawls's work is at best unsuited to addressing these problems and

---

[35] I thank Frances Ferguson for alerting me to the possibility that it is Cavell here who stifles Rawls's voice, demanding in effect more than the other is obliged to give. Cavell reports on their exchange as follows: "Of course I asked John Rawls, and of course, collegially, he agreed, to read a late draft of Lectures 1 and 3 [of Cavell's Carus Lectures, published as *Conditions Handsome and Unhandsome*, which critique Rawls's *Theory of Justice*]. In the two long and full conversations we devoted to them, the topic that most interested both of us was whether *A Theory of Justice* denies anything I say, whether it doesn't leave room for the emphases I place on things." After these "two long and full conversations," however, Cavell was apparently left without an answer to the question: "[I]f it is this easy for a perfectionism to accommodate itself to *A Theory of Justice*, why has Rawls bothered carefully to rule out the extreme form of the doctrine, associated by him with the name of Nietzsche, which on its face fails to get started in a (democratic) theory of justice?" (*Conditions Handsome and Unhandsome*, xxii, xxiii).

at worst inclined to contribute to them. This at first seems faint next to some other possible criticisms of Rawls, including the following: (i) Due in large part to his intervention, the academic field of political philosophy has been colonized by arcane and politically irrelevant work, which serves to distract intellectual labor from its most pressing tasks. (ii) Lacking an adequate intellectual defense, the most admirable impulse of his work – its commitment to reduce society's irrational and needless cruelty, to improve the egalitarian quality of democratic institutions – has been underrepresented in political discourse. (iii) The redistributive thrust of *A Theory of Justice* has been undercut by the largely accomplished retrenchment of welfare, dismantlement of public institutions, and increased openness of a globalizing economy underway at least since its publication, so that the direction of the theory no longer matches that of society. (iv) Given these conditions, the increasing juridicalization of politics he endorses further entrench the powers, privileges, and protections of property at the expense of individual persons and their communities. (v) His early endorsement of rational choice theory has contributed to the eclipse of political considerations by economic ones within public discourse undermining the bases of collective action and political self-determination. (vi) His theory is insufficiently attentive to liberal tendencies toward imperialism, thus obscuring ongoing global injustices. However, Cavell does not pursue any of these lines of criticism, seemingly avoiding many of what could be called the marquee issues in contemporary political thought.

If the terms that Cavell proposes do not appear to have much purchase either on the highly complex social formations of modern politics or on the increasingly complex theoretical vocabularies that have been developed to engage these conditions, this may be because what is at stake in his work is not so much a matter of producing knowledge as it is of changing minds. Cavell's claim that ordinary language philosophy should not be seen "as an effort to reinstate vulgar beliefs, or common sense, to a pre-scientific position of eminence, but to reclaim the human self from its denial and neglect by modern philosophy" begins to address this concern.[36] To put it more forcefully, social criticism should not aim to produce knowledge – rather, it should aim to change minds, an aim common to the Hebrew prophets, to Marx, and to Cavell. The "denial and neglect" of the human self in philosophical modernity includes a denial that conversion forms the basis for a range of ethical and critical practices.

---

[36] Cavell, *The Claim of Reason*, 154.

It would be difficult to connect the six criticisms of Rawls outlined previously with the problem of conversion because they are not directed toward anyone in particular – Rawls, political theorists, readers, citizens. Although they are addressed to specific phenomena and trends, they do not seem to have been made from any particular position: they contribute to our knowledge of contemporary political predicaments without pressing for the acknowledgment of one's place in or responsibility for them.

Cavell explains how his criticism follows Emerson and Nietzsche, departs from Rawls and Kant, and connects with the problem of conversion in the following passage, worth quoting at length:

[There are two main features of Emersonian-Nietzschean perfectionism that place it in an uneasy relationship to modern philosophy] "(1) A hatred of moralism – of what Emerson calls "conformity" – so passionate and ceaseless as to seem sometimes to amount to a hatred of morality altogether (Nietzsche calls himself the first antimoralist; Emerson knows that he will seem antinomian, a refuser of any law, including the moral law). (2) An expression of disgust with or disdain for the present state of things so complete as to require not merely reform, but a call for a transformation of things, and before all a transformation of the self."[37]

Cavell continues on the next page:

This in turn is to be heard against John Rawls's impressive interpretation of Kant's moral philosophy in which he presents Kant's "main aim as deepening and justifying Rousseau's idea that liberty is acting in accordance with a law that we give to ourselves," and emphasizes that, "Kant speaks of the failure to act on the moral law as giving rise to shame and not to feelings of guilt."[38] A text such as Emerson's "Self-Reliance" is virtually a study of shame, and perceives what we now call human society as one in which the moral law is nowhere (or almost nowhere) in existence... It is a violent perception of a circumstance of violence. How do we, as Emerson puts it, "come out" of that? How do we become self-reliant? The worst thing we could do is rely on ourselves as we stand – this is simply to be the slave of our slavishness... We must become averse to this conformity, which means convert from it, which means transform our conformity, as if we are to be born (again).[39]

These remarks map the connections between a form of critique that seeks to open the possibility of revolutionary change, "a call for a transformation of things," prepared by but irreducible to the conversion of the self, "before all a transformation of the self." Within the terms of this critique, it is not so much the moral law that is to be suspended, on account of

---

[37] Cavell, *Conditions Handsome and Unhandsome*, 46.
[38] Rawls, *A Theory of Justice*, 256.
[39] Cavell, *Conditions Handsome and Unhandsome*, 47.

its complicity in the reproduction of injustice; better yet, within these terms, the moral law is to be seen as already suspended, "is nowhere (or almost nowhere) in existence," leaving only violence, "a circumstance of violence." If a just moral community remains the operative ideal in this vision, every existing community obstructs this ideal. If shame serves for Rawls and Kant as an index of one's failure to act in accordance with the moral law, for Nietzsche and Emerson according to Cavell, shame at one's conformity to an (always necessarily) unjust law serves as a starting point for the transformation of oneself, as a process of conversion away from such law, and toward a more just formulation itself unimaginable or unintelligible within the conjunction in which one finds oneself.

Cavell's critical idiom is, perhaps, more subtle and insightful than it might first appear. "Snobbery" might diagnose a privilege enjoyed by citizens of contemporary North Atlantic liberal democracies, who reap the benefits of an unjust global distribution of goods, and participate in a conspiracy (often of silence and ignorance) against the rest of the world to ensure the continuation of this distribution. "Conformity" might diagnose the uncritical acceptance of the norms that regulate conduct and produce identities and the enforcement of such norms against others (again, often in silence and ignorance). It diagnoses the saturation of individuals by power and the production of a variety of shamelessness that does not so much distort ethical judgment as foreclose its possibility by supplying ready-made forms of moral law. "Seriousness," in its turn, identifies one way of imagining the distinctive possibilities of a modernity in the shadow of skepticism, in which art, philosophy, ethics, and politics must (finally) become responsible for themselves in the sense of confronting, acknowledging, and transforming their own conditions. As a transformation of the self required to entertain new possibilities for living, conversion might be imagined as overcoming snobbery and conformity to begin living seriously.[40] Seen this way, Cavell's idiom covers much of the same ground as the six alternative lines of criticism suggested previously. It differs, however, by drawing the critic him- or herself into question as part of the object of criticism: Am *I* a snob?, and How could *I* not be?, What might *I* do to become something other than a snob?, and so on. It calls for giving an account of oneself and for conceiving practical responses and concrete pathways of transformation. It is this ethical impulse that Cavell opposes to Rawls's vision of an individual's life lived "beyond reproach."

[40] See, e.g., Cavell, "The *Investigation*'s Everyday Aesthetics of Itself," 372–3.

But how can democratic life be imagined as something more "serious" than the periodic, reasonably reliable, and more-or-less transparent popular election of representative officials? How might learning to speak Cavell's idiom change anything – what contribution does its figure of conversion as the outcome of a serious reckoning with the dangers of snobbery and conformity make to political thought? In what ways does the adoption of a religious figure of conversion contribute to refiguring the possibilities of secular critique? How might the modern imaginary of secular liberal democracy be inflected by the problem of conversion as Cavell asks us to imagine it? Cavell lays emphasis alternately on *America* and on *democracy* in his more explicitly political texts. The title of a recent text, *This New Yet Unapproachable America*, suggests, however, that the nation and the form of politics he imagines under these terms have *not yet* been realized, nor perhaps will they ever be. Cavell's reflections on American national identity and democratic practice are premised on the constant thought that neither is yet what it can and should be: Simon Critchley has suggested that America might read as "*Amerique à venir*" and democracy as "democracy to come" in Cavell's texts by way of comparison with the late work of Jacques Derrida, and this observation registers something important about Cavell's work, although it would require a careful study to trace the relation between their work.[41] Cavell notes that the "emphasis of perfectionism," which can be read as an emphasis on conversion, as he conceives it, should "be taken as part of the training for democracy... as preparation to withstand not its rigors but its failures, character to keep the democratic hope alive in the face of disappointment with it."[42] It is the promise of a sustainable faith in democracy at a time when democratic forms of governance appear increasingly insufficient to the challenges of late modernity, including globalization, transnational pluralization, and emerging economic and ecological crises. These problems are pursued most clearly in Cavell's revision of the theory of the social contract, to which we now turn.

Cavell on Locke's Second Treatise – a Conversion of the Social Contract

Theories that ground the power and authority of government in a figurative contract established between the individual members of a political community are among the hallmarks of secular modernity. In his political

---

[41] Simon Critchley, *Very Little... Almost Nothing*, 148. See Cavell's *Philosophical Passages: Wittgenstein, Emerson, Austin, Derrida*; and Roger V. Bell, Jr., *Sounding the Abyss*.
[42] Cavell, *Conditions Handsome and Unhandsome*, 56–7.

writings, Cavell returns continuously to this familiar – indeed, archly canonical – topic of social-contract theory, but he produces a radical reinterpretation of the social contract and, with it, a radical reinterpretation of secular modernity.[43] His argument further democratizes the theory of the social contract, perhaps paradoxically, by interweaving the problem of consent with practices of social criticism that echo prophetic speech and aim at effecting a particular kind of conversion. To appreciate Cavell's intervention here, it will help to sketch a preliminary picture of social-contract theory, for the very idea of a social contract is deeply overdetermined – it is polysemous, crystalline in Bergson's sense, and mysterious in the extreme, because it has been defined so many times. Nonetheless, a fair amount of what is generally said about social-contract theory can be summarized in the following seven points:

(1) Traditionally, the classical social-contract texts find their bookends in John Locke's *Two Treatises on Government* and John Rawls's *A Theory of Justice*. Although there is considerable pressure to expand these boundaries, to include Hobbes at the very least and possibly a great deal more, for the purposes of many contemporary contractarians, these points limn the canon.

(2) Conceptually, theories of the social contract detail the internal relations of consent, legitimacy, and obligation. Together, these elements form a constellation of concepts that renders government's enforcement of law just in some cases and unjust in others.

(3) Mythically, the social contract marks Western modernity's transition from the long tutelage of Christian political theology to claim for the people an authority to establish and, if need be, to reestablish the conditions of social organization. It is in this sense a revolutionary doctrine, announced in Locke's *Second Treatise*, and enacted in Jefferson's declaration of independence.[44] If not complete independence, the theory of the social contract is taken to mark the relative

---

[43] See, e.g., *The Senses of Walden, The Claim of Reason, Conditions Handsome and Unhandsome*, and *Cities of Words*.

[44] Jeremy Waldron states the key points covered by this imagined transition as follows: "the idea of social contract... expresses in a clear and provocative form a view... that the social order must be one that can be justified to the people who have to live under it... [And] the Enlightenment impulse on which this is based is the demand of the individual mind for the intelligibility of the social world. Society should be a *transparent* order, in the sense that its workings and principles should be well-known and available for public apprehension and scrutiny... [rather than] shrouded in mystery, and its workings should not have to depend on mythology, mystification, or a 'noble lie.'" Jeremy Waldron, "Theoretical Foundations of Liberalism," 146.

independence of political principles from divine principles and to mark a key point in the transition from rule by divinely ordained kings to representative self-government.[45]

(4) Allegorically, the social contract may nonetheless be seen as a continuation of the Hebrew Bible's figure of a covenant with God, in which the letters of this compact are amended but the spirit retained. John Winthrop's seminal sermon, "A Model of Christian Charity," as an alternative to Jefferson's declaration, is a reminder of this.

(5) Institutionally, and in large measure through its recodification of private property, the social contract constitutes a basis for the enmeshed legal and economic structures that would enable the patterns of individual acquisition, transfer of property, development of industry, establishment of colonies and empires, expansion of trade, and explosion of capital that mark the past three centuries of European and American history.

(6) Theologically, theories of the social contract have tended to inscribe God's design within human reason. Prior to their articulation, creation was seen to express God's design in a single continuous, great chain of being, which encompassed everything from the heavens through the social order to the earth itself.[46] As this image of nature fell into abeyance and faith in divine revelation was attenuated, the mind came to be seen as possessing sufficient light to reconstruct the dictates of natural law, from natural rights, so that an image of the proper moral and social orders could be reproduced on the basis of human reason.

(7) Politically, the articulation of the social contract accompanied new arrays of power attuned to producing self-regulating individuals fit for assemblage in social machineries of increasing sophistication, pliability, and productivity. Matching the theological production of a new, rational soul, societies governed by the social contract created a new, regulating soul. As Michel Foucault's aphorism that "the soul is the effect and instrument of a political anatomy; the soul is the prison of the body" implies, societies arranged by the social contract produce individuals who bear rights and accept duties in new and increasingly self-regulating ways.[47]

---

[45] See Edmund S. Morgan, *Inventing the People*.
[46] See Arthur O. Lovejoy, *The Great Chain of Being*.
[47] Michel Foucault, *Discipline and Punish*, 30.

To go a bit further, it should be noted that the theory of the social contract is a thoroughly political theory in the sense that it has been contested since the moment of its modern articulation. Insofar as one takes Locke's *Two Treatises of Government* (1689) to mark its beginning, the theory of the social contract is born in controversy engaging both the concrete social conflicts unfolding between crown and parliament, court and country, James II and William III, from the Exclusion Crisis through the Glorious Revolution, as well as the more abstract theologico-political question of the patriarchal right of kings, as well as a global context marked by the clashes of European powers and their deeper alliance in deriving the fruits of colonial plantations from the foregoing labors of exploration and settlement. If it was born in Locke's text, then it was born dialogically into theoretical controversy as well, for Locke's text is itself constructed as a reply to Robert Filmer's theory of patriarchal authority. And from the time of its birth, the theory has received numerous answers, in numerous national-philosophical traditions, many of which have themselves become key canonical texts, from David Hume's "Of the Original Contract," to Jean-Jacques Rousseau's "Discourse on the Origin of Inequality," to Friedrich Nietzsche's *Genealogy of Morals*.

Cavell moves this traditional problem into a new register by using the figure of the social contract to confront the depth of the problems of modern subjectivity and, by extension, modern secularity. *The Claim of Reason* registers not only the abeyance of faith that conditions modernity but also the abeyance of faith in the sufficiency of the positive use of reason that marks its culmination; this text traces precisely the deficiencies of modern philosophy (as it develops through empiricism into a centrally epistemological theory) that lodge it within the problematic double horizon of skepticism (with respect to the world and with respect to other minds). As a result, *The Claim of Reason* also presses open possibilities for rethinking an expressly modern faith that emerges at the limit of modern skepticism. Cavell's serial remarks on the social contract translate his philosophical investigations of the emergence of modernity through an epistemological adjustment haunted by the problem of skepticism to the problems of political founding, order, and community.

Hanna Pitkin's influential interpretation of Locke's theory of the social contract sets out a traditional interpretation against which it will be much easier to follow Cavell's argument.[48] Pitkin's essay works on the level of

---

[48] This essay was divided into two parts, as follows: "Obligation and Consent I" and "Obligation and Consent II."

conceptual analysis to address a then-growing body of arguments that sought to discredit the theory of the social contract by showing that its apparent foundation, the idea of individual consent, is insufficient to secure either obligation or legitimacy. Pitkin tries to rescue the theory by reframing its problem. She allows that granting and revoking consent cannot alone account for obligation: reflection on the everyday grammar of promising and contracting shows that revoking one's consent after making a promise or entering a contract does not, in fact, dissolve one's obligations, for a promise and a contract can *only* mean something insofar as they exclude this possibility. The example of the Nazi regime shows that consenting to a wrongful authority is not sufficient to produce legitimate obligation. In short, revoking consent does not dissolve obligation and granting consent does not produce it. It follows that neither legitimacy nor obligation can rest on the unqualified consent of the governed. Having conceded these points, Pitkin's task is to provide a new explanation of the connections among consent, legitimacy, and obligation.

Although obligation does not stem from the consent of the governed, she argues that it stems from the legitimacy of government, which can be assessed independently of the subjective presence or absence of individual consent. Pitkin argues "that your obligation depends not on any actual act of consenting, past or present, by yourself or your fellow citizens, but on the character of government. If it is a good, just government doing what a government should, then you must obey it; if it is a tyrannical, unjust government trying to do what no government may, then you have no such obligation."[49] She does not imagine that judging whether government is just or tyrannical will be easy or that the criteria for this judgment will be readily forthcoming. Instead, articulating the proper criteria becomes the essential task of political judgment, which implies that such judgments may be difficult but not impossible. For Pitkin, the question of consent will, at most, be part of a test applied in judging the goodness of government and thus the legitimacy of political obligation: following this test, one asks if government is such that "rational men considering all relevant facts and issues would consent" to it, and one

---

[49] Pitkin, "Obligation and Consent II," 39. She continues, anticipating Rawls's formulation of the Original Position: "Or to put it another way, your obligation depends not on whether you have consented but on whether the government is such that you *ought* to consent to it, whether its actions are in accord with the authority a hypothetical group of rational men in a hypothetical state of nature would have (had) to give to any government they were founding."

lets their imagined answer measure the legitimacy of their obligation to obey the government in question.[50] There will also need to be other tests because the questions submitted for political judgment are not easy ones. They cannot be resolved automatically, and Pitkin invokes Wittgenstein's remark that "there are a hundred reasons; there is no reason" for arriving at a particular judgment.[51]

It is not clear which passage of Wittgenstein's Pitkin is paraphrasing here, but it may have been the same that Cavell had in mind when writing, "What *reason* did I have for assuming that? A hundred reasons; no reason."[52] Perhaps a hundred passages, no passage. Perhaps both have Emerson's "Self-Reliance" in mind: "He has not one chance, but a hundred chances."[53] Wherever this locution came from, the critical point is that all hundred of Pitkin's reasons serve to measure the extent of one's obligation to obedience. And where Pitkin differs from outright critics of the social-contract theory by inclining more toward finding that one's obligation is in order, she and they both take establishing one's obligation to obedience as the chief stake in the theory of the social contract. As the problem is stated here, consent is always something to be extracted from political subjects, or to be produced in them, or if they prove too recalcitrant for either, to be attributed to them against their will. Such is the standard relation established between consent and obligation both by its supporters and its critics.

Like Pitkin's, Cavell's interpretation of Locke's theory of the social contract hinges on the problematic status of consent in the text of the *Second Treatise*, but it rejects outright the centrality of obligation to the theory. In this sense, it is extremely idiosyncratic. Cavell notes that "the received view, to which I still know of no exception, is that Locke is weak or confused or dishonest at this crucial point [consent] of his theory," but whereas Pitkin sets Locke's apparent confusion in order, Cavell resists the implication of the received view, noting that Locke's writings in general are composed of "an extraordinary texture of arguments at once commonsensical and mysterious," which may be the "secret of Locke's fantastic influence in the century [centuries?] following his."[54] Rather than reconstructing Locke's argument, Cavell's interpretation intensifies its paradoxes.

[50] Pitkin, "Obligation and Consent II," 39.
[51] Pitkin, "Obligation and Consent II," 47.
[52] Cavell, *The Claim of Reason*, 317.
[53] Ralph Waldo Emerson, "Self-Reliance."
[54] Cavell, *Cities of Words*, 62, 55.

Cavell claims Thoreau as an ally in rejecting theories that make obligation the central point of political reflection. A passage from *The Senses of Walden*, which is situated within a longer reflection on the problem of social-contract theory, within a longer-still reflection on his practice of interpretation as finding out a text's sense rather than imposing one upon it, is helpful here.

> I do not wish to impose a political theory upon the text of *Walden*. On the contrary, if the guiding question of political theory is "Why ought I to obey the state?" then Thoreau's response can be said to reject the question and the subject. The state is not to be obeyed but, at best, to be abided. It is not to be listened to, but watched. Why ought I to abide the state? Because "it is a great evil to make a stir about it." A government, however, is capable of greater evil, "when its tyranny or its inefficiency are great and unendurable" (CD, 8). How do you know when this point has been reached? Here the concept of conscience arises, upon which secular, or anyway empiricist philosophy has come to grief: what can conscience be, other than some kind of feeling, of its essence private, a study for psychologists? – as though the "science," that is to say knowledge, that the word "conscience" emphasizes can at most register a lingering superstition. *Walden*, in its emphasis upon listening and answering, outlines an epistemology of conscience.[55]

The imposition of theory is abjured here, and a turn is made toward the claims of conscience, which can however no longer be taken as private but instead become the subject of epistemology and thus once more public, with an orientation toward assessing "the nature or quality of our relationship to one another" as manifest in our capacity to express consent to this relationship.[56] This is an extraordinarily dense passage, touching as it does on obedience, secularism, the public/private distinction, conscience, and knowledge as epistemology, and although the rejection of obligation may be the most important point here, it is worth touching on some of the others as well. Like Pitkin's argument, Cavell's claim here turns on understanding consent as an act of judgment, a judgment more precisely about when a government is so bad as to be illegitimate. It is at the point of this judgment, for Cavell, that secularism (as a form of philosophical empiricism) "comes to grief," for it cannot make judgments about the legitimacy of government backed by certain knowledge. Beyond certain knowledge, secularism as empiricism sees only private feelings, for it lacks an adequate "epistemology of conscience." In reading *Walden*, Cavell

---

[55] Cavell, *The Senses of Walden*, 88.
[56] Cavell, *The Claim of Reason*, 268.

finds such an epistemology outlined in Thoreau's practices of listening and answering; in his larger philosophical project, the central problem of such an epistemology lies in the "acknowledgment" of others, which although it cannot find a basis in certain knowledge itself constitutes a basis for ethical conduct and for justice.

Cavell's interpretations of Locke, Rousseau, and Thoreau constitute a distinctive mode of argument: he does not take them simply as partners in conversation, nor does he attempt to reconstruct the historical contexts of their claims, nor does he aim at rationally reconstructing their theories. The import of Cavell's interpretations here lies both in his arguments about these texts and in the mode of argumentation he performs in reading them, just as it did in his engagement with Rawls treated in the previous section.[57] A rejection of the obligation-consent nexus as the pivot of the *Second Treatise* happens to be congruent with a great deal of current historical scholarship according to which this text should be read primarily as an argument against tyranny, against the usurpation of government, and only secondarily, if at all, as an account of how legitimate government, and therefore obligations to government, derive from the consent of the governed. Cavell's argument, however, is not precisely reducible to this interpretation; it seeks instead to set these two possible lines of argument, one about tyranny and the other about consent, into a new relationship. In doing so, and as part of its articulation of a complex figure of conversion, it also works to refigure the humanist conceptual constellation of the adult-rational-autonomous-citizen, and the relation between faith and politics inscribed within the idea of modern secularism as separation.

The sensibility underlying Thoreau's stance as a "sojourner" in civilized society, who "abides" government, invokes and refigures a stance toward secular authority recognizable from Paul's *Letter to the Romans*, Augustine's *City of God*, and Luther's letter "On Secular Authority," through to Bunyan's *Pilgrim's Progress* and beyond. A compelling argument can be made that each of these texts authorizes secular governance to dispose of everyday matters that are indifferent from the perspective of salvation and registers a sense of Christian alienation from the world. However, as the operative figures of god, law, salvation, and perdition are

---

[57] Another example of the importance of a mode of engagement is Cavell's recent "Companionable Thinking," which treats the problem of eating animals as it is raised in John Coetzee's *Elizabeth Costello*, but which also performs a certain kind of philosophical engagement between Cavell and Cora Diamond.

naturalized or "secularized," and the kingdom of god is brought within the earthly kingdom in Thoreau (at least in Cavell's reading of *Walden*), the pilgrim's stance is likewise reimagined. In this new picture, the state is not to be abided while one waits for the next state as a life to come, but the redemption through rebirth is instead "secularized" in the following precise sense: everyday life becomes the only site in which to figure salvation, and abiding the state must therefore be seen as conducing to this transformation. Secularization here figures the transformation of the problem of obedience into the problem of conscience.

Stepping back again, arguing against the centrality of obedience radically alters the generally received problem of social-contract theory. Or, as it may be better to say, it turns one around with respect to the problem. Thoreau's rejection of obedience as the central figure of political thought suggests a sense that the theory of the social contract is badly stated as a theory of obligation. Instead, the real "problem – at once philosophical, religious, literary, and, I will argue, political – is to get us to ask the questions, and then to show us that we do not know what we are asking, and then to show us that we have the answer."[58] And the real problem, therefore, in thinking through the meaning of the social contract, just as it is the problem in thinking through living and writing in *Walden*, is the same as that of the classical Hebrew prophet whose "problem, initially and finally, is not to learn what to say to" his or her people because "that could not be clearer" for "everyone is [already] saying, and anyone can hear, that this is the new world, that we are the new men; that the earth is to be born again; that the past is to be cast off like a skin; that we must learn from children to see again; that every day is the first day of the world; that America is Eden" and, as Locke could add, that all the world is America.[59] The problem is to find that the customary uses of these words are somehow wrong or insufficiently serious, and the suggestion that what is needed is learning to say these words in a new way. (Again, learning to say the same words in a new way as a way to figure conversion.[60]) This is a vision of political theory as social criticism and social criticism as an internal critique that directs society back to its more original commitments – a political theory, in other words, in the style of

---

[58] Cavell, *Walden*, 47.
[59] Cavell, *Walden*, 11, 59. More precisely, Locke writes in his *Second Treatise*'s famous chapter, "On Property," that "in the beginning all the world was America, and more so than that is now; for no such thing as money was any where known."
[60] This holds from William James's *Varieties of Religious Experience* to Susan Harding's *The Book of Jerry Falwell*.

the Hebrew prophets, crystallized with but not simply reducible to that style.⁶¹

In this view, the words of the social contract are good enough words to go on using, and their import is exceedingly familiar. Taken rightly or wrongly as a basis for the American revolution, and of a liberal theory of politics, the social contract runs as follows:

> The essential message of the idea of a social contract is that political institutions require justification, that they are absolutely without sanctity, that power held over us is on trust from us, that institutions have no authority other than the authority we lend them, that we are their architects, that they are therefore artifacts, that there are laws or ends, of nature or justice, in terms of which they are to be tested. They are experiments.⁶²

In this vision, politics consists in further experimentation, and a proper theory of politics cannot aim to justify existing political institutions because such institutions will never be perfectly just. It would instead formulate a plan for enacting the collective transformation of these institutions. The terms of the social contract are simple, as simple as the commands entailed by the Abrahamic covenant with God, or as simple as the practical dictates of Reason identified by Kant, but they are everyday as mystified and as little honored, such that the blessing of freedom is everywhere transmuted into the bonds of slavery:

> Society remains as mysterious to us as we are to ourselves, or as God is. That we are the slave-drivers of ourselves has not come about "for private reasons, as [we] must believe" (I, 10). It is an open realization of what we have made of the prophecy of democracy. It is what we have done with the success of Locke, and the others in removing the divine right of kings and placing political authority in our consent to be governed together. That this has made life a little easier for some, in some respects, is a less important consequence than the fact that we now consent to social evil. What was to be a blessing we have made a curse. We do not see our hand in what happens, so we call certain events melancholy accidents when they are the inevitabilities of our projects (I, 75), and we call other events necessities because we will not change our minds.

The problem is that as its inheritors, we have never become accustomed to using the words of the social contract as they might be used and that we have therefore never truly become their inheritors and never matched their revolutionary import.

---

⁶¹ See Sacvan Bercovitch and Perry Miller for the classic accounts of the Jeremiad's Puritan heritage, and George Shulman, Andrew Murphy, and James Morone for more recent accounts.
⁶² Cavell, *Walden*, 82.

Inheriting a potentially radical legacy of the revolution, or meeting the prophetic demands of the idea of democracy, opens here as a problem of conversion insofar as no new knowledge is required for the transformation that is sought and insofar as a change in disposition is needed sufficient to allow the same words to be spoken with a new meaning. It is more than ironic that Locke's revolutionary theory should be taken only to have replaced a hereditary king with a representative form of government that leaves the structures of obligation, legitimacy, and consent unmodified. Mysteriously, having deposed their king, the people remain in a relation of needless obeisance to their institutions of governance, without any clear "sense that the mystery is of our own making; that it would require no more expenditure of spirit and body to let ourselves be free than it is costing us to keep ourselves pinioned and imprisoned within 'opinion, and prejudice, and tradition, and delusion, and appearance.'"[63] The lesson here is quite simple and has already been taught, again and again, but "to learn that we have forgotten this is part of our education which is sadly neglected."[64]

Learning what has been forgotten about the revolutionary and antityrannical doctrine of the *Second Treatise* involves learning to find one's way through the thorniest sections of the text's arguments about consent, for in this interpretation, the revolutionary potential of the social contract is obscured and mystified within the terms of consent. This interpretation undermines generally accepted views that the distinction between tacit and express consent is dishonest, incoherent, or otherwise unacceptable and suggests instead that the revolutionary import of the theory depends on the accuracy and salience of that distinction. According to an interpretation such as Pitkin's, even in the absence of their express consent to government, tacit consent can be attributed to individuals, and this form of consent is meant to justify their obligation to obedience to government. In Cavell's interpretation, the only road to full membership in a political society, with its attendant rights and duties, runs through expressing consent to the political conditions of one's life, but even where one means to have actively and expressly consented to the terms of society, one cannot be certain of succeeding in this, in having managed to achieve a society with one's fellows, and one therefore remains at constant risk of isolation, voicelessness, captivity, or, as Locke puts it, of remaining in a tacit condition, as a foreigner in one's own land. In this light, the

[63] Cavell, *Walden*, 78.
[64] Cavell, *Walden*, 82.

force of the *Second Treatise*'s argument about consent anticipates the claim of Rousseau's *Social Contract* that "the social contract is nowhere in existence, because we do not will it; therefore the undeniable bonds between us are... [made] privately and in secret... [so that] the logic of our position is that we are conspirators." In other words, the distinction between tacit and express consent is to be taken as an indication of the standing possibility that the social contract is invalid and inoperative; in the more hyperbolic terms suggested by Shakespearean tragedy or classical Hollywood melodrama, this indicates the possibility that we are both imprisoned and insane, for "If this is false, it is paranoid; if it is not, we are crazy."[65]

The claim in section 119 of Locke's *Treatise* that merely traveling on the highway is a gesture sufficient to constitute one's consent to be governed has incited enormous criticism throughout the literature, and with good cause. This remark constitutes a blot on the theory of the social contract as a theory of legitimate obligation based on consent, but Cavell treats this point as the crux of the theory, requiring interpretation. Section 119 reads in full:

Every man being, as has been showed, naturally free, and nothing being able to put him into subjection to any earthly power, but only his own consent, it is to be considered what shall be understood to be a sufficient declaration of a man's consent to make him subject to the laws of any government. There is a common distinction of an express and a tacit consent, which will concern our present case. Nobody doubts but an express consent of any man, entering into any society, makes him a perfect member of that society, a subject of that government. The difficulty is, what ought to be looked upon as a tacit consent, and how far it binds – i.e., how far any one shall be looked on to have consented, and thereby submitted to any government, where he has made no expressions of it at all. And to this I say, that every man that hath any possession or enjoyment of any part of the dominions of any government doth hereby give his tacit consent, and is as far forth obliged to obedience to the laws of that government, during such enjoyment, as any one under it, whether this his possession be of land to him and his heirs for ever, or a lodging only for a week; or whether it be barely travelling freely on the highway; and, in effect, it reaches as far as the very being of any one within the territories of that government.[66]

Locke seems to argue that "barely travelling freely on the highway" regulated and maintained by government is sufficient to indicate that one consents to this government, that one acknowledges its legitimacy even if

---

[65] Cavell, *Walden*, 87.
[66] John Locke, *Second Treatise*, 347–8.

only silently, and that one is therefore obliged to obey its commands. It also seems clear that any consent given with such ease and inadvertence, or any consent that would be so difficult to avoid giving, must either be empty or ill-formed – suspect at any rate. Section 119 of the *Second Treatise* says that lodging, traveling, or merely finding oneself present within the territory of a government makes one subject to the laws of that government and, given that laws, for Locke, roughly amount to penalties, this is a harsh fact.[67] As Cavell puts it elsewhere, this might open "a violent perception of a circumstance of violence."[68]

But if Locke's argument about tacit consent is objectionable, this cannot merely be on account of the fact that law must be backed by force. The idea that if one wishes to travel on the highway, one should expect to find oneself subject to the rules of the road, seems clear enough.

Being subject to the penalties of law, itself, does not account for the objections commonly felt toward this section. Finding oneself subject to penalties is not at all surprising, perhaps not even objectionable: the proposition that government should maintain order when a significant number of individuals within its jurisdiction stand beyond the reach of its penalties strains the imagination. It would be difficult, at best, to imagine a government that would require the consent of its subjects at the point of applying the penalties of law. As Locke puts the matter, such an arrangement "cannot be supposed, till we can think, that rational creatures should desire and constitute societies only to be dissolved."[69] There must then be a different kind of problem here. What is disturbing about Locke's claim that traveling on the highway amounts to tacit consent is the further idea that granting such consent entails something more than becoming subject to penalties – the idea that consent transforms mere force into right. Having argued that man is born free and followed this with another argument that only consent can ground a determinate range of obligations that temper this freedom, Locke seems to have gone on to say that any act ("barely travelling freely on the highway") will be counted as consent. It follows both that one's natural freedom is much less secure and that the obligations one incurs are themselves much less freely entered than they had at first seemed. The distance between a

---

[67] Recall Locke's definition of political power at the opening of the *Second Treatise*, "Political power, then, I take to be a *right* of making laws with penalties of death, and consequently all less penalties, for the regulating and preserving of property, and of employing the force of the community, in the execution of such laws, and in the defence of the common-wealth from foreign injury; and all this only for the public good" (268).

[68] Cavell, *Conditions Handsome and Unhandsome*, 47.

[69] Locke, *Second Treatise*, 333.

government based on the consent of the governed and a government based on patriarchal authority or prerogative seems much diminished if one's tacit consent is in fact given with every action that one takes, short of open rebellion. In either picture, obligation remains effectively without limit so that one is obliged to accept whatever government does, or else to undertake a revolution, or to enter exile, either because one is born in such subjection or because all of one's actions can be construed to enter one into such subjection. To some extent, of course, these pictures seem to be more or less empirically accurate images of many forms of citizenship as passive subjection to government within a large number of polities – perhaps within any and every heretofore existing polity – but that sort of empirical observation does not change the fact that something seems to be wrong with a normative aspect of Locke's argument.

What if there is something wrong instead with the approach taken immediately above, in which the theory of the social contract is deployed as a form of justification for government? And what if it were seen neither as a justification for government nor through what might loosely be called a "Jeffersonian" inversion of this approach, as a justification for permanent revolution? What if it were to be seen as a theory of conscience and as the basis for a practice of criticism that tests the quality of one's society and of one's own place within it? Such an approach would diverge from the avenues taken by other interpreters, who perceive the inadequacy of the notion of tacit consent formulated in the *Second Treatise* but seek to develop new ways of thinking about consent that would better answer to the agreed-upon problems of legitimacy and obligation. At this point, Cavell follows Thoreau in rejecting the centrality of obligation and in shifting the problem.

The idea of tacit consent is ordinarily taken as a weak point in Locke's argument because it fails to provide as convincing a ground for obligation as express consent, but this very disparity between tacit and express consent might be viewed as the crux of the theory and not just a wrinkle in its fabric. Cavell's argument turns on noticing this disparity and elaborating its consequences. To begin, textual scrutiny would seem to bear out the claim that tacit and express consent do *not* function as equivalent terms, nor are they interchangeable. The text of the *Second Treatise* clearly marks and maintains the distinction between these forms. Section 121 reads:

Since the government has a direct jurisdiction only over the land, and reaches the possessor of it, (before he has actually incorporated himself in the society [by giving his express consent]) only as he dwells upon, and enjoys that; the obligation any one is under, by virtue of such enjoyment, to *submit to the government, begins and ends with the enjoyment*; so that whenever the owner, who has given nothing but such a *tacit consent* to the government, will, by donation, sale, or otherwise, quit the said possession, he is at liberty to go and incorporate himself into any other common-wealth; or to agree with others to begin a new one, *in vacuis locis*, in any part of the world, they can find free and unpossessed: whereas he, that has once, by actual agreement, and any *express* declaration, given his *consent* to be of any common-wealth, is perpetually and indispensably obliged to be, and remain unalterably a subject to it, and can never be again in the liberty of the state of nature; unless, by any calamity, the government he was under comes to be dissolved; or else by some public act cuts him off from being any longer a member of it.[70]

If section 119 was at pains to show how easily tacit consent is entered, section 121 is at similar pains to show how easily tacit consent is revoked. Furthermore, this passage sharply distinguishes one's tacit consent, which may be revoked at any time as it "begins and ends with the enjoyment" of land, from one's express consent, which once given makes one "perpetually and indispensably obliged to be, and remain unalterably a subject" of a commonwealth. Tacit consent is entered and revoked with ease, but express consent, once entered, is binding for as long as a government lasts.

The two forms of consent, then, draw out to very different sides of government. The relation of tacit consent places an individual in an indirect political relationship with the *territorial state*. "Government" is conceived here as that which has "a direct jurisdiction only over the land," and an individual is brought into a relation with government so conceived when he or she enters competing claims to use or "enjoyment" of the land. The relation of express consent, however, places an individual in a direct political relationship with others as members or subjects of government conceived as a *common*wealth. "Government" is conceived here as an entity that "incorporates" individuals in a relation that might be "dissolved" but that is not mediated by any relation to land or territory. Locke's argument here might be said to trace a distinction between nation and state without bringing it forward for explicit thematization. In this sense, its terms track what is now in some ways more clearly recognized as a tension between the state regulation of territory and the national integration of individuals.

One key difference between these terms registered in Locke's text is that tacit consent places one in a relation of submission to government's

---

[70] Locke, *Second Treatise*, 349 (emphases in the original text).

laws, whereas express consent places one in a relation of membership in society. Part of the burden of the *Second Treatise* is to show that being born in a commonwealth does not suffice to make one a subject: indeed, this is a key part of Locke's argument with Filmer's theory of patriarchal authority, developed at length in the *First Treatise*. In light of that larger argumentative context, section 119 is ordinarily taken to answer the question, "If not birth, what then makes one a subject of the commonwealth?," by invoking the notion of tacit consent. The general sense of dissatisfaction with Locke's concept of tacit consent is in turn connected to its apparent failure to fulfill this argumentative purpose. However, section 121 makes clear that tacit consent does not bind one to the commonwealth in the same way as express consent. In other words, it implies that the idea of tacit consent is not deployed to answer this question; or, perhaps more accurately still, it implies that the argument of the *Second Treatise* does not seek to resolve this question. Through tacit consent, one becomes "obliged to obedience to the laws of that government" but not a member of the commonwealth.[71] By maintaining the distinction between the two forms of consent, it becomes possible to see that although an obligation to obey laws emerges almost inevitably along with the territorial state, this does not exhaust the question of whether one consents to be a party to government, whether one can be seen as a full member of society, and whether one accepts the authority of both as legitimate and binding for oneself. The social contract, for Cavell, does not ground obedience to government: territorial states must exact obedience to the law with or without contract, with or without consent, if they are to exist at all. Instead, the contract articulates a question about the quality of one's society and one's government conceived as a community in which full, adult members exercise their voices.

In this view, the question addressed in section 119 would be, "What makes a person a member of a political community?"[72] And section 122 shows that tacit consent does not suffice for that; in fact, it implies that this is the most important part of the distinction between tacit and express consent. Emphases in the following are Locke's:

[S]ubmitting to the laws of any country, living quietly, and enjoying the privileges and protection under them, *makes not a man a member of that society*... And thus we see, that *foreigners*, by living all their lives under another government,

---

[71] Locke, *Second Treatise*, 347–8.
[72] Cavell, *Cities of Words*, 63.

and enjoying the privileges and protection of it, ... do not thereby come to be *subjects or members of that common-wealth*.[73]

Contrary to the drift ordinarily assigned to it, rather than suggesting that tacit consent is meant to fulfill the same function as express consent in authorizing government, section 122 *explicitly precludes* this possibility: in the absence of express consent, one is subject to the penalties of law, but one is not a member of society. Express consent and tacit consent only converge insofar as participation in the life of society can be reduced to submission under laws. From this perspective, a theory of the social contract does not serve to explain the legitimacy of obligations – *one always has a hundred reasons, perhaps no reason, for heeding the law* – or as Bergson would say, *life* itself obliges one to have obligations. The social contract serves rather to mark the difference between participating in the life of a political community and being merely subject to its laws.

Granting one's tacit consent to the law remains as difficult to avoid as ever, but this interpretation emphasizes another problem, namely that one lives as a "foreigner" in one's own country when one cannot find a way to express consent. The concept of tacit consent, then, renders the problem of alienation as political subjection to the penalties of a law one has had no part in producing and as lacking a voice or place in political society altogether. Insofar as the effective institutions through which one would register express consent to governance are lacking, even citizens may only submit tacit consent to government, rendering them "foreigners" or sojourners or pilgrims in their own lands. Historical context suggests that express consent would not have been the least mysterious or elusive for Locke and that it refers rather to the possibility of swearing an oath of allegiance. The interest of Cavell's interpretation lies in the difficulty, perhaps impossibility, of effectively swearing such oaths today. This interpretation avoids attributing to the *Second Treatise* what Cavell calls the "epistemologically stupid and politically heartless" argument that tacit consent suffices to render government legitimate, and it opens a series of more difficult questions about the legitimacy of modern government.[74]

Tacit consent acknowledges the basic condition of one's subjection to law, an inevitable condition so long as there are governments that promulgate law. The distinction between tacit and express consent, however, emphasizes that submitting to law without an effective voice in

---

[73] Locke, *Second Treatise*, 349 (emphases in the original text).
[74] Cavell, *The Claim of Reason*, 25; *Cities of Words*, 64.

its creation is a common condition but also an alienated and therefore problematic one. Cavell's interpretation of the social contract centers on what he calls the "standing mystery" of expressing and withdrawing consent within contemporary political societies. If he suggests that a citizen must own his or her voice, that suggestion in turn requires that we take seriously the role of ideas of ownership in Locke's text and in our lives. If one can own a voice, one might also be able to lose, sell, buy, or trade voices. The value of one's voice might fluctuate. Credit may be required to secure a voice. For Locke, for Cavell, and for us, the concept of ownership is enmeshed within economic discourses, and I take it that Cavell frames citizenship in terms of owning one's voice to foreground the ways in which modern lives are so intimately governed by constructs of the economy (property, money, commerce, credit, debt – *capital*). To say that one's citizenship depends upon owning a voice is to suggest that the concept of ownership, and the discourses that couch it, are to be interrogated. Thoreau employs a similar strategy in the opening chapter of *Walden*, entitled simply "Economy." As Cavell points out, this chapter produces "visions of captivity and despair" made vivid as Thoreau's prose "turns into a nightmare maze of terms about money and possessions and work, each turning toward and joining the others."[75] Thoreau and Cavell are concerned with showing the consequences of an economic discourse that has spilled its banks and overrun social, political, moral, and even religious life. It is often suggested that this condition is distinctive of late-capitalism, a recent phenomenon endemic to the articulation and expansion of neoliberalism over the last four decades.[76] Thoreau and Cavell suggest that the problem is, rather, perennial, but whichever perspective one adopts, their texts work to foreground this problem, to show how deeply enmeshed language and economy are, in order to produce

a brutal mocking of our sense of values, by forcing a finger of the vocabulary of the New Testament (hence of our understanding of it) down our throats. For that is the obvious origin or locus of the use of economic imagery to express, and correct, spiritual confusion: what shall it profit a man; the wages of sin; the parable of talents; laying up treasures; rendering unto Caesar; charity.[77]

This kind of writing aims to correct "spiritual confusion" through conversion. It seeks to motivate an intellectual sense that there is something

---

[75] Cavell, *Cities of Words*, 88.
[76] See David Harvey's *A Brief History of Neoliberlism* and, for a longer time frame, Karl Polanyi's *The Great Transformation*.
[77] Cavell, *Cities of Words*, 89.

wrong with a discourse that holds one captive. In this case, the problem is an economic discourse that would overrun the proper terrains of moral, theological, and political discourses. In the case of the social contract, it is a discourse of obligation that would overrun the proper space of politics. From this perception of wrongness, it seeks to motivate disgust with oneself and one's world as it is constituted by such discourses sufficient to demand their transformation – as redemption, revolution, and conversion. Criticism here seeks to motivate, in other words the following kind of apprehension:

> We labor under a mistake. What will save us from ourselves is nothing less than salvation. // The second major strategy I said *Walden* uses to cut into the circling of economic terms is to win back from it possession of our words. This requires replacing them into a reconceived human existence. That it requires a literary redemption of language altogether has been a theme of my remarks from the beginning; and I have hoped to show that it simultaneously requires a redemption of the lives we live by them, religiously or politically conceived, inner and outer.[78]

The intention is not to choose words without political significance but rather to choose significant words in dire need of resignification. In this light, the question, *Do you own your own voice?*, asks you to think about how deeply your life is permeated by economic discourse. Cavell cites yet another philosophical precedent for this procedure:

> [B]ecause it is natural for us to frame our ideas of personal rights in terms of private ownership, Nietzsche, like Thoreau, frames his instruction in terms of possessing something, coming into possession of something, *in order to wrest our notion of ownership from our grasp.*[79]

The hands grasping notions of ownership, whose hold one should like to see broken, are ours, just as the finger that finds its way down our throats must be. Conversion here depends on a tumbling of old interests, a loosening of fictions, a disavowal of shared valuations.

If it does not uncritically repeat existing discourses of property, a theory of the social contract based on the ownership of a voice might seem liable to another shortcoming: that of neglecting the forms of social and political power that condition the exercise of one's voice. In this case, Cavell's theory might seem as blind to the effects of power in the formation of identity and right as Locke's theory is often taken to be. And yet, such blindness seems unlikely in light of *The Claim of Reason*'s painstaking investigation of the necessarily public face of even the most

---

[78] Cavell, *The Senses of Walden*, 92.
[79] Cavell, *The Claim of Reason*, 384 (emphasis added).

intimate bonds of private psychic interiority. Once again, Cavell does not so much ignore the forms of power that condition modern subjectivity as he reframes the problem. A brief comparison with Hume's text, "Of the Original Contract," is helpful here.[80] Hume suggests that theories of the social contract misrepresent the structures of authority and allegiance when they base the obligation of obedience on a promise to obey. He argues the pointlessness of conflating the fidelity implied by keeping promises with the allegiance implied by maintaining obedience – promising and obeying, fidelity and allegiance, are necessary parts of social life, but they are constituted by distinct practices. For Hume and Cavell, no less than for Bergson, obligation is something every child learns in the course of growing into a culture – it is a mere ensemble of habit. The benefits of allegiance to government are something that every rebelliously minded adult must weigh, but none of these philosophers think that allegiance requires a philosophical explanation, let alone a formal social contract. *There are a hundred reasons for each allegiance, and perhaps no one reason.* But where Hume sees only contradiction and obscurity in the theory of the social contract, Cavell suggests that this theory brings something important into view. Indeed, part of "the training for democracy ... as preparation to withstand not its rigors but its failures, [and] character to keep the democratic hope alive in the face of disappointment with it" depends upon facing an abhorrent condition of tacit consent, if not owning one's voice, then beginning to own one's lack of voice.[81]

The distinction between adults and children is no less ancient, protean, problematic, and important than the distinctions between humans and animals and between the civilized and the savage.[82] Throughout the modern liberal tradition, more specifically, the figure of childhood forms the background against which adulthood is constructed – children are subjected to rule because of their imperfect capacity for reason, whereas adults are to govern themselves according to the dictates of reason. Locke's *Thoughts on Education* suggest that the figure of childhood is not a passing theme and that it has direct bearing on the distinctions he draws among modes of authority, education, and liberty. In a different vein, the *Second Treatise*'s chapter "Of Paternal Power" both criticizes

---

[80] David Hume, "Of the Original Contract."
[81] Cavell, *Conditions Handsome and Unhandsome*, 56–7.
[82] Childhood forms a subtheme of *The Claim of Reason*'s reflections on the acquisition and use of language, and the human/animal distinction figures prominently in Cavell's recent reflections on J. M. Coetzee's work in his "Companionable Thinking." On the philosophical history of the human/animal distinction, see Jacques Derrida's recent *The Animal That Therefore I Am*.

and exploits the metaphorical fecundity of childhood in dissecting what Locke characterizes as patriarchal theorists' political-theological abuse of *Exodus*' injunction to "honor thy father." Setting these specific examples aside, it is difficult to express how pervasive and generative the figure of adulthood is: the "age of reason," for example, refers both to a point in an individual's life generally placed between the ages of seven and twelve at which the faculty of reason establishes itself and to the broad cultural enlightenment of the seventeenth and eighteenth centuries.

The text of the *Two Treatises* layers one story about outgrowing paternal power with another story about outgrowing patriarchal authority, emplotting both as conversion narratives that track the transformation from childhood to adulthood and moving back and forth between individual and social, natural and political, evolutionary and revolutionary registers.[83] The structure of the argument is crystalline in Bergson's sense, and Cavell works similarly when he suggests that becoming an adult requires a second – a political – education, which in turn is figured as an awakening, or rebirth, or conversion.

In the face of the questions posed in Augustine, Luther, Rousseau, Thoreau ... we are children; we do not know how to go on with them, what ground we may occupy. In this light, philosophy becomes the education of grownups. It is as though it must seek perspective upon a natural fact which is all but inevitably misinterpreted – that at an early point in a life the normal body reaches its full strength and height. Why do we take it that because we then must put away childish things, we must put away the prospect of growth and the memory of childhood? The anxiety in teaching, in serious communication, is that I myself require education. And for grownups this is not natural growth, but *change*. Conversion is a turning of our natural reactions; so it is symbolized as rebirth.[84]

According to Cavell, the social contract discloses politics as a field of education distinct from the field in which children are taught a language and introduced into a culture. Contrasted against these scenes of instruction, politics is figured as a field for the education of adults and education is figured as the openness to conversion.

Finding one's voice and learning to express consent through a certain kind of participation in the political life of the commonwealth stands in the same relation to the ordinary condition of tacit consent as the poetic use of language stands in relation to its ordinary use. The exercise of one's own voice in poetry or politics requires turning back on the "natural"

---

[83] See especially chapters 6 and 8.
[84] Cavell, *The Claim of Reason*, 125.

uses of words and patterned responses learned as children. "One might think of poetry as the second inheritance of language," Cavell claims, "if learning a first language is thought of as the child's acquiring of it, then poetry can be thought of as the adult's acquiring of it, as coming into possession of his or her own language, full citizenship."[85] Learning the rules or obligations of language is the task of children: in this view, the standard interpretation of the social contract as producing obligation pictures adults as mere adepts in the tasks of childhood. Learning obedience, in other words, comes as a matter of course; what is wanted is an explanation of how obedience can be tested, transmuted, or converted into the ownership of one's own voice.

One produces poetry in one's own language and truly becomes an adult only on the condition of conversion; becoming an adult requires a second kind of task, departing from and returning to the rules and obligations of childhood as artifacts. Whatever doubts one might have about Cavell's readings of Locke, the gesture of returning to one's inherited beliefs and commitments as artifacts to be subjected to critical and responsible judgment tallies precisely with the spirit of Locke's *Essay* and *Letter*.[86] Assessing one's habits, beliefs, obligations, and so on as artifacts does not imply that they could be dispensed with at will. It does, however, mean that attaining to ethical conduct, self-knowledge, and full political citizenship will depend on something like a movement from prose to poetry.[87] This applies equally to and is exemplified in the work of reading and writing political theory. For students of the tradition of political thought, the texts written by canonical thinkers such as Locke, Kant, Emerson, Thoreau, and Rawls, to return to an earlier register, have become the fingers of our hands best turned down our own throats. In other words, Cavell suggests that our interest has never been in Locke but only in our inheritance of Locke, only in our reading of his texts, only in changing our relation to the tradition he represents, only in waking ourselves from the dreams about this tradition that we inhabit. Rousseau's vision of human sociability, for example, may be keener than Locke's, but it is the latter's vision of politics as the effective management of property – what he calls the "business of civil government" – that must be effectively turned back on the social order, which it has helped to produce at this precise historical moment. In this vein, Cavell compares the figure of tacit consent

---

[85] Cavell, *The Claim of Reason*, 189.
[86] See Nicholas Wolterstorff, *John Locke and the Ethics of Belief*.
[87] See Judith Butler, *Precarious Life*, 26–7.

to Emerson's figure of "secret melancholy," Thoreau's figure of "quiet desperation," and Rousseau's figure of humanity in chains.[88] These figures are employed in radical criticism, and it might be shocking to find Locke's notion of tacit consent in their company. Turning oneself and one's fellows loose from secret melancholy and quiet desperation were the tasks of Emerson's and Thoreau's transcendentalism – they layered literary, philosophical, political, and religious resonances just as powerful as those implied by Rousseau's legislator, that saint, that god, who would come to make our chains legitimate. In each case, conversion is an apt figure for the response needed. Cavell's interpretation of the *Second Treatise* asks that it be taken as a form of social criticism no less serious than Thoreau's, Emerson's, or Rousseau's, directed not only at patriarchal authority but also at a politics that fails to construct a more genuinely democratic society within existing institutions. In this reading, the theory of the social contract is important precisely where it shows how wrong our lives are – that we live in tacit consent – and how far we remain in need of conversion. Whereas authorized histories, to recall the distinction introduced in reading *Confessions*, posit a moment of revolutionary change or conversion in the past, at the threshold of modernity, at the declaration of independence, Cavell's theory suggests that revolution or conversion is a problem for the present, that the problem of transformation, change, or conversion imposes continuous tasks.

The final step in Cavell's interpretation is to refashion the connection between the *Second Treatise*'s concept of consent and its concluding thoughts on the dissolution of government. The constitution of express consent is always doubtful: the very existence of the public must always remain open to question; its terms are unsettled and continually open to failure or repudiation; it is essentially without guarantee; it lives only insofar as its members acknowledge it to live, only insofar as they find themselves able to stir it to life. Although it is not yet clear what giving express consent would entail, it must entail leaving (or transforming) the condition of tacit consent. What is at stake in giving one's express consent is claiming full membership in society: membership is precisely not in question in the case of tacit consent, which Locke thematizes as the condition of children, primitive people, and foreigners. In the absence of express consent, it is doubtful that a "Politick Society" exists: as Cavell

---

[88] Cavell tends to say "silent melancholy," words that I do not know Emerson ever to have published together. In "New England Reformers," however, Emerson writes of "secret melancholy." Thoreau's phrase can be found in the first chapter of *Walden*, "Economy."

puts the matter, "so far as I am in doubt whether I have, or how we have, given consent, I am so far in doubt whether my society exists, whether it speaks for me and I speak for it. And it seems to me what Locke's wavering [in particular, his wavering between express and tacit consent] indicates is his sense that this doubt is never permanently resolved."[89] To think that one could say either that consent exists or does not exist by inspecting the private consciousnesses of citizens or a record of their past statements is to imagine this relationship falsely – it is to lack a true epistemology of conscience. There is no way, as Cavell has it, to verify the presence or absence of consent: "I've suggested in effect that you cannot tell whether consent has been given to a society by examining the individual members of that society to determine whether they have – or remember having – given their consent to it."[90] The quality of consent, and thus the existence of society, must perpetually be left open to doubt – the suggestion is that society here, as we are inclined to imagine language everywhere, should be imagined as a thin net stretched over an abyss.[91] Lacking knowledge, precisely, we must proceed together or not at all.

Locke's argument builds across two books and forty chapters to his concluding statement on "The Dissolution of Government." The text cites many possible causes of such dissolution, the most readily memorable being that "*Governments are dissolved*... when the Legislative, or the Prince, either of them act contrary to their trust... [and] *endeavour to take away, and destroy the Property of the People*, or to reduce them to Slavery under Arbitrary Power," at which point the people are "absolved from any farther Obedience."[92] Cavell follows Locke, and interpreters such as Pitkin, in asking how one might know that government has become bad enough to absolve citizens of their ties:

The tyranny or inefficiency of government can become unendurable. How do you know when this point has been reached? Here the concept of conscience arises, upon which secular, or anyway empiricist philosophy has come to grief: what can conscience be, other than some kind of feeling, of its essence private, a

---

[89] Cavell, *Cities of Words*, 68.
[90] Cavell, *Cities of Words*, 60.
[91] Cavell, *The Claim of Reason*, 178. Cavell notices in *The Claim of Reason* that at times, "we begin to feel, or ought to, terrified that maybe language (and understanding, and knowledge) rests upon very shaky foundations – a thin net over an abyss." Of course, as Cavell has it there, this is a fantasy brought on by the epistemological search for solid foundations. All the same, it is not a mere fantasy; Cavell also notices that it comes with a certain necessity – we are fated, it would seem, to seek foundations, even if there are none to be found.
[92] Locke, *Second Treatise*, sections 221, 222.

study for psychologists? – as though the "science," that is to say knowledge, that the word "conscience" emphasizes can at most register a lingering superstition, *Walden*, in its emphasis on listening and answering, outlines an epistemology of conscience.[93]

The problem of consent is conjoined here to the problem encountered by modern philosophy – the key problem that runs through Cavell's work, that of the ethical-political register that opens at the limits of secular reason. We cannot know these things about other minds, about society, even about our own minds, but we must no less act, one might say, on faith: in good faith, in accord with our senses and sense that the whole world is America (a promised land) and that America is not the land we have promised ourselves. This is not a matter of knowledge, for the words of the prophets are old and clear. It is a matter instead of conversion.

Locke begins his last chapter by noting that "He that will with any clearness speak of the *Dissolution of Government*, ought, in the first place to distinguish between the *Dissolution of Society*, and the *Dissolution of Government*."[94] This mirrors the distinction between full membership in a society and subjection to its laws, and in perfect crystalline form it mirrors the distinction between express and tacit consent. Locke imagines that society might be dissolved in the case of foreign conquest and writes that:

> Whenever society is dissolved, 'tis certain the Government of that Society cannot remain. Thus Conquerors Swords often cut up Governments by the Roots, and mangle Societies to pieces, separating the subdued or scattered Multitude from the Protection of, and Dependence on that Society which ought to have preserved them from violence.

He then suggests that:

> there wants not much Argument to prove, that where the *Society is dissolved*, the Government cannot remain; that being as impossible, as for the Frame of an House to subsist when the Materials of it are scattered, and dissipated by a Whirl-wind, or jumbled into a confused heap by an Earthquake.[95]

And yet one of the persistent dangers – perhaps one of the constitutive facts – of the politics of the modern nation-state is precisely what Locke refuses to countenance here, what he considers an impossibility: the state

---

[93] Cavell, *The Senses of Walden*, 88.
[94] Locke, *Second Treatise*, section 211.
[95] Locke, *Second Treatise*, section 211.

form persists today, indeed flourishes, in the apparent absence of a society, or a people, sufficiently well-constituted to authorize it.[96]

Cavell's interpretation intensifies and tarries with the problem that interpreters such as Pitkin try to resolve, that it is necessarily impossible to know – once and for all, with certainty – whether one's government is good enough to support and, what is more, whether or not a community (what Locke calls Society, what other theorists call "a people") exists such as to make this determination. One's rebirth or conversion into political adulthood – paradoxically, *full citizenship* – takes the form of acknowledging, which is to say learning to live with and act within, this condition. This would require coming to recognize and withstand the failures of (the false promises of) democracy, withstanding that is to say the fact of one's tacit submission to the law and one's complicity in and responsibility for the law, and nonetheless maintaining faith in the possibility of modern democracy as the effective contestation of power in the absence of community. According to Cavell, in the modern political world, the wish for a better life begins here. By Locke's lights, this would likely be unreasonable, by Rawls's unnecessary. This is on the one hand a secularized image of conversion – for it is precisely a conversion toward this world, an awakening to the true dimensions of what has always lain before us, such that as the young Marx had it, "mankind begins no *new* work, but consciously accomplishes its old work." Perhaps more important, this figure of conversion shows something about the remaining possibilities of secularism itself. It becomes possible in this light to view secularism not as a formation separate from religion, not as a formation constituted through its difference from religion, but rather as a special kind of openness to the artificiality of moral, political, and religious institutions, to the artificiality of those institutions that remain indispensable as they continue to disappoint us. It would require not merely an openness to this artificiality but also an openness to the fact that changing such institutions will require changing oneself. Such an idea of secularism as conversion, then, would not project this change into a mythic past but rather posit an openness to change at the very heart of democratic governance in the present, as a condition imposed by the challenges of collective political life given the unknowability of other minds within conditions of deep pluralism. To understand secularism as, in part, a process of conversion

---

[96] The constitution of a people is one of the problems in modern political thought in general and in theories of representative government in particular. For a recent and trenchant engagement with the problem, see Jason Frank, *Constituent Moments*.

away from certainty and toward creative and potentially transformative experimentation may be one way to begin accepting the challenges of collective action in the absence of moral, political, religious community that conditions modern democratic practice.

Bibliography

Bercovitch, Sacvan. *The American Jeremiad*. Madison: University of Wisconsin Press, 1978.
Bodin, Jean. *Les Six Livres de la République*. 1576.
Butler, Judith. *Precarious Life: The Powers of Mourning and Violence*. New York: Verso, 2006.
Cavell, Stanley. "Being Odd, Getting Even (Descartes, Emerson, Poe)," in *In Quest of the Ordinary: Lines of Skepticism and Romanticism*. Chicago: The University of Chicago Press, 1988: 105–29.
Cavell, Stanley. *Cities of Words: Pedagogical Letters on a Register of the Moral Life*. Cambridge, MA: Belknap, 2004.
Cavell, Stanley. *The Claim of Reason: Wittgenstein, Skepticism, Morality, and Tragedy*. New York: Oxford University Press, 1979.
Cavell, Stanley. "Companionable Thinking," in *Philosophy and Animal Life*. New York: Columbia University Press, 2009: 91–126.
Cavell, Stanley. *Conditions Handsome and Unhandsome: The Constitution of Emersonian Perfectionism*. Chicago: University of Chicago Press, 1990.
Cavell, Stanley. *Contesting Tears: The Hollywood Melodrama of the Unknown Woman*. Chicago: University of Chicago Press, 1996.
Cavell, Stanley. *Disowning Knowledge: In Seven Plays of Shakespeare*. New York: Cambridge University Press, 2003.
Cavell, Stanley. "The *Investigation's* Everyday Aesthetics of Itself," in *The Cavell Reader*, ed. Stephen Mulhall. Cambridge, MA: Blackwell, 1996: 369–89.
Cavell, Stanley. *Must We Mean What We Say? A Book of Essays*. Cambridge: Cambridge University Press, 1969.
Cavell, Stanley. *Philosophy the Day after Tomorrow*. Cambridge, MA: Belknap, 2005.
Cavell, Stanley. *A Pitch of Philosophy: Autobiographical Exercises*. Cambridge, MA: Harvard University Press, 1994.
Cavell, Stanley. "The Politics of Interpretation," reprinted in *Themes Out of School: Effects and Causes*. San Francisco: North Point Press, 1984.
Cavell, Stanley. *Pursuits of Happiness: The Hollywood Comedy of Remarriage*. Cambridge, MA: Harvard University Press, 1981.
Cavell, Stanley. *The Senses of Walden: An Expanded Edition*. Chicago: University of Chicago Press, 1992.
Coetzee, John. *Elizabeth Costello*. New York: Viking, 2003.
Connolly, William E. *The Ethos of Pluralization*. Minneapolis: University of Minnesota Press, 1995.
Critchley, Simon. *Very Little ... Almost Nothing: Death, Philosophy, Literature*. New York: Routledge, 1997.

Davidson, Arnold. "Beginning Cavell," in *The Senses of Stanley Cavell*. Richard Fleming and Michael Payne, eds. Lewisburg, PA: Bucknell University Press, 1988.
Derrida, Jacques. *The Animal That Therefore I Am*. New York: Fordham University Press, 2008.
Emerson, Ralph Waldo. "Self-Reliance," in *The Collected Works of Ralph Waldo Emerson*, vol. 2. Cambridge, MA: Belknap, 1979: 25–52.
Emerson, Ralph Waldo. "New England Reformers," in *The Collected Works of Ralph Waldo Emerson*, vol. 3. Cambridge, MA: Belknap, 1983: 147–70.
Foucault, Michel. *Discipline and Punish: The Birth of the Prison*. New York: Vintage, 1995.
Frank, Jason. *Constituent Moments: Enacting the People in Postrevolutionary America*. Durham, NC: Duke University Press, 2010.
Harvey, David. *A Brief History of Neoliberlism*. Oxford: Oxford University Press, 2005.
Hume, David. "Of the Original Contract," in *Hume: Political Essays*. Cambridge: Cambridge University Press, 1994: 186–201.
James, William. *Varieties of Religious Experience*. New York: Library of America, 1990.
Kakutani, Michiko. "Review: Pursuits of Happiness," *New York Times*, February 9, 1982.
Locke, John. "Second Treatise," in *The Two Treatises of Government*, Peter Laslett ed. Cambridge: Cambridge University Press, 1960.
Lovejoy, Arthur O. *The Great Chain of Being: A Study of the History of an Idea*. Cambridge, MA: Harvard University Press, 1976.
Maritain, Jacques. *Man and the State*. Chicago: University of Chicago Press, 1951.
Marrati, Paola. *Gilles Deleuze: Cinema and Philosophy*. Baltimore, MD: Johns Hopkins University Press, 2008.
Marx, Karl. "M. an R." *Deutsch-Franzozische Jahrbücher*. Paris: Arnold Ruge and Karl Marx, 1844.
Marx, Karl. "For a Ruthless Criticism of Everything Existing." Robert Tucker, ed. *The Marx-Engels Reader*. New York: W. W. Norton & Company, 1978: 12–15.
Miller, Perry. *Errand into the Wilderness*. Cambridge, MA: Belknap, 1956.
Morgan, Edmund S. *Inventing the People: The Rise of Popular Sovereignty in England and America*. New York: W. W. Norton & Co., 1988.
Morgan, G. A. *What Nietzsche Means*. Cambridge, MA: Harvard University Press, 1941.
Morone, James. *Hellfire Nation: The Politics of Sin in American History*. New Haven, CT: Yale University Press, 2003.
Mounce, H. O. "The Claim of Reason," *The Philosophical Quarterly*, vol. 31, no. 124 (July 1981): 280–2.
Mulhall, Stephen. "Philosophy Cannot Say Sin," in *Stanley Cavell: Philosophy's Recounting of the Ordinary*. Oxford: Clarendon, 1994: 283–312.
Murphy, Andrew. *Prodigal Nation: Moral Decline and Divine Punishment from New England to 9/11*. New York: Oxford University Press, 2009.

Nietzsche, Friedrich. "Schopenhauer as Educator," in *Untimely Meditations*. Daniel Breazeale, ed. Cambridge: Cambridge University Press, 1997: 125–194.
Palmer, Anthony. "The Claim of Reason," *Mind*, vol. 91, no. 362, April 1982: 292–5.
Pitkin, Hanna. "Obligation and Consent I," *American Political Science Review*, vol. 59, no. 4, December 1965: 990–9.
Pitkin, Hanna. "Obligation and Consent II," *American Political Science Review*, vol. 60, no. 1, March 1966: 39–52.
Polanyi, Karl. *The Great Transformation*. Boston: Beacon Press, 1957.
Rancière, Jacques. *Disagreement: Politics and Philosophy*. Minneapolis: University of Minnesota Press, 1999.
Rawls, John. *Political Liberalism*. New York: Columbia University Press, 1993.
Rawls, John. *A Theory of Justice*. Cambridge, MA: Harvard University Press, 1971.
Shulman, George. *American Prophecy: Race and Redemption in American Political Culture*. Minneapolis: University of Minnesota Press, 2008.
Thoreau, Henry David. *Walden*. New York: Library of America, 2009.
Waldron, Jeremy. "Theoretical Foundations of Liberalism." *The Philosophical Quarterly*, vol. 37, no. 147, April 1987: 127–50.
Weitz, Morris. "The Claim of Reason." *The Journal of Philosophy*, vol. 78, no. 1, January 1981: 50–6.
Wolterstorff, Nicholas. *John Locke and the Ethics of Belief*. Cambridge: Cambridge University Press, 1996.

Conclusion

From *Supernovas* into *The Deep*

Secularism as Conversion, a Conversion of Secularism...

As a contribution to the task of thinking critically and constructively about the possibilities of democratic politics in a contemporary global context, this book set out to contest a key component of modern democratic thought: secularism. *It argues that secularism is not a matter of separating "church & state" but rather of transforming the interrelated fields of religion and politics, and it suggests that this transformation should be understood as a process of conversion.* Secularism is already widely understood as the outcome of a process of conversion insofar as it is figured as the outcome of a process of secularization through which the modern West has freed itself from religion, for secularization narratives are patterned by a particular image of conversion as a break between a present and its irreconcilable past, between the new man and the old, between a secular modernity and its religious past. That narrative pattern, however, has never been critically examined as a conversion narrative, and examination shows that this narrative form does not exhaust the tradition from which it is drawn. Beginning with a canonical source, Augustine's *Confessions*, and working through Locke, Rawls, and Taylor, as well as Bergson and Cavell, the chapters of this book articulate a more complex, crystalline form of conversion that lies obscured beneath the surface of the familiar image, and they use this alternative image of conversion as the basis for imaging secularism differently. This book argues that the possibilities for democracy can be enhanced by moving from implicit to explicit understandings of secularism as conversion, and of conversion as a complex, crystalline process.

The figure of conversion, it turns out, is deep, ambivalent, and involuted. An authorized image of instantaneous change adorns its surface.

It is an image of change that separates the old and the new while it brings certainty and security. Yet a complex and ambivalent process of transformation lies beneath this surface, proceeding in fits and starts with reversals, hesitations, and inconsistencies, layering new habits, practices, and partial identifications unevenly upon old habits, practices, and identifications. Beneath its *authorized* surface, conversion is *crystalline*: it is an elaborately structured process of growth that proceeds through the self-organizing accumulation of fractured layers, generating and regenerating intricate forms. This process and structure are often rendered invisible beneath the static appearance of their smooth surface. As smooth – as seductive – as its authorized surface may be, secularism too conceals a crystalline process of transformation. This conclusion will briefly review that argument, show how it differs in fundamental ways from what is emerging as today's leading account of secularism, and explain why that difference matters in contemporary politics.

Secularism's *Authorized* and *Crystalline* Forms

The layered structure of conversion accounts for the apparent contradiction at the heart of the modern secular imaginary: namely, that a metaphoric "wall of separation between church & state" persists as its cornerstone despite our full knowledge that this metaphor is insufficient. Secularism is much more than separation, for it helps to constitute both religion and politics in their modern forms. And it is also much less than separation, for religion and politics have never been separate in practice. More fundamentally, the metaphor of a "wall of separation" is insufficient insofar as the image of separation obscures the process nature of secularism, obscures the sense in which secularism continues to transform the shape of human relations as it continually remakes religion and politics, and obscures the ways in which religion and politics remake one another. The idea of a separation between church and state is insufficient to secularism in much the same way as conversion narratives are insufficient to the complex processes of conversion they represent. The layers of conversion – authorized narrative of separation on the surface and crystalline process of transformation in the depths – may be analytically distinct, but they are practically entwined and mutually reinforcing. There is no experience of conversion without the retrospective narrative that names it, both consolidating and catalyzing the transformation. Conversely, there would be no change to experience as conversion, no event worth retrospective narration, without an underlying process of transformation. As a process of conversion, secularism enfolds both the authorized strictures of separation and the complex, or crystalline, process of transformation. Authorized surface emerges from and conceals crystalline depths: despite its apparent insufficiency, the authorized narrative remains inextricable from the process it represents, and upon which it depends, such that an apparent contradiction within the modern secular imaginary reveals the crystalline structure beneath its surface.

Where Augustine's *Confessions* presented the best text in which to study the layered structure of the conversion process, John Locke's *A Letter Concerning Toleration* presented one of the best texts with which to begin translating this layered structure into the field of political contestation. Locke's arguments must be seen to work on two levels: on the surface of his argument, Locke advocates the clear separation of religion and government; in the rhetorical grain of this text, Locke intermixes the theological and the political, the religious and the civil, within a process of conversion that enables and sustains the argument of the surface. The rhetorical work of the *Letter* is but one instance of the myriad moments of public contestation that contribute to the complex process of conversion and that over time have established a once implausible image of separation as the authorized emblem of secular modernity. Conversely, the authorized image of separation played hyperbolic and proleptic roles within the rhetorics that catalyzed and regulated the process of transformation underway. Surface and depth in the *Letter*, analytically distinct but linked in practice, support one another, spurring a process that would make the idea of secularism as separation plausible in later generations, a process that would transform political and religious life to the extent that they may have even approximated secularism as separation in some times and places.

Locke's *Letter* presents an argument for the authorized image of secularism as separation, but it also presents a different mode of secularism as a crystalline process of transformation in which the argumentative resources of both "religious" and "political" discourses are mobilized together to challenge and ultimately change some of the basic parameters of public life. It contributes to an authorized literature of statecraft insofar as it articulates the rationality of governance, restricting it to the disposition of things and the facilitation of the public good. At the same time, it registers an exemplary instance of democratic citizenship, addressing and seeking to renegotiate existing patterns of social domination by publicly contesting the requirements of conformity to Anglican doctrine and practice. The installation of "toleration" within British political culture began before Locke's intervention and continued long after it, but it should be seen as a transformation of both "religious" and "political" life. Toleration, rather than the break from religion that the authorized story of secularism suggests, emerged as a transformation of religion and politics, which would reroute many of religion's public claims while shifting the targets of political power. Locke's participation in the politics of early modern secularism, then, cannot be reduced to the exclusion of religion (qua forced conversion) from politics but must also be seen as a practice of publicly contesting and renegotiating the roles played, and powers exercised, by religious and political actors within collective life. Secularism here carries the authorized valence of a modern discourse of state regulation, and the crystalline dimension of an open-ended process in which individuals and communities practice a deeply democratic mode of citizenship precisely by working to renegotiate the institutions that regulate their lives.[1]

Where *Confessions* and the *Letter* trace some early outlines of the authorized and crystalline forms of conversion and of modern secularism, these outlines are later retraced with precision in the work of John Rawls. Where Locke's letter marks a relatively early point in the formation of modern secularism, a point at which the separation of church and state is emerging as a mere possibility, Rawls's work represents the apex of this form, a point at which separation has become a deeply engrained, default assumption. Rawls's argumentative style and rhetorical voice, no less than the propositional content of his work, are exemplary of the late-twentieth century's authorized discourse of secularism: although he explicitly disqualifies theology as a political discourse (as a species of comprehensive doctrine inadmissible in public debate over essential matters), he presents his arguments as the culmination of the Euro-American social contract tradition, abjuring the originality of his claims and denying the possibility that accepting them would require his interlocutors' conversion. My reading shows, however, that Rawlsianism depends upon the work of conversion, even while it disavows and actively works to obscure that fact. Despite the presumption in favor of separation that it expresses, disavowed "religious" forms permeate Rawls's work, forms which are evident in the reception of his work as "miraculous," and

---

[1] My distinction between a modern discourse of state regulation and a deeply democratic mode of citizenship tracks James Tully's distinction between the "modern," "civil," and "cosmopolitan" on the one hand and the "diverse," "civic," and "glocal" forms of citizenship on the other. I am inspired by and indebted to Tully's discussion of democratic citizenship in his *Public Philosophy in a New Key*; see especially vol. 2, chap. 9.

in the acceptance of Rawls himself as a "saint." Although much more subtle in this respect than Locke's *Letter*, Rawls's work likewise reflects processes remaking the basic parameters of public life, reforming the ethical dispositions of participants within political (and intellectual) life, and reconstituting the forms that sustain communities.

Once more, Rawls contributes to recodifying the practices of public argumentation appropriate to modern, rule-governed citizenship. His advocacy of a particular, cosmopolitan ideal of public reason, to the extent that it has been effective, constrains the practices and possibilities of democratic citizenship in ways that touch upon both "religious" and "secular" dimensions of public life. At the time in which Rawls was writing, within many late-twentieth-century Euro-American contexts, a commitment to such an ideal of public reason and the form of modern citizenship that attends it may have been all but fully naturalized, all but seamlessly authorized. Attention to the process of conversion that sustains it, however, reveals how it is nonetheless premised upon a transformation of the self, including the cultivation of particular habits, dispositions, and dimensions of character and a transformation of community that attends these changes. Where the principle of separation rises as a small, fragile bubble from within the turbulent welter of transformation that is Locke's *Letter*, Rawls's writings project an image of separation as accomplished fact. The luminous surfaces of Rawls's texts, however, obscure the transformations that sustain them – although glimpses appear at their seams. Where Augustine, Locke, and Rawls present portraits of conversion and secularism in their dominant Western forms, Bergson and Cavell actively probe the depths of conversion, providing the resources with which to imagine secularism in new ways – the problem to which we turn now.

Secularism's Possible Futures: Authorized and Crystalline Forms

The twenty-first century is proving to be a time of profound crisis within the modern secular imaginary, and its cornerstone, "the separation of church & state," is under assault from all sides. A Rawlsian discourse that grounded secularism in the promise of finally separating politics from religion, and thus defined its authorized form at the close of the twentieth century, is sliding now into eclipse – at least, at many of scholarship's leading edges. There is today a broad-based movement to actively reimagine the possibilities of secularism within a wide range of Euro-American and global contexts. And although this movement has constituted a relatively open field to date, Charles Taylor appears poised to supersede

Rawls as the new authoritative philosopher of modern secularism, based in large part on the reception of his book, *A Secular Age*. It is true that there are serious differences between the images of secularism projected by Rawls and Taylor, true that a choice between them matters, and true that their differences deserve careful attention insofar as the relative ascendance of one or the other image will carry real consequences for the lives governed by one or the other mode of secularism. Nonetheless, it would be well to hesitate within the present moment in its very uncertainty about the basic meaning of secularism, in order to contemplate the contingency, contestability, and consequentiality of whatever new formations of secularism will be authorized and deployed as this moment passes. In the terms developed in this book, an authorized mode of conversion resists, obscures, and obstructs responsibility for – and experiments with – transformation, whereas the crystalline mode plunges one directly into a process that transforms both religious and political life at their points of intersection. In what follows immediately, I use Taylor's project to provide contrast for my own and to consider the implications of our differences.

Where twentieth-century secularization theory imagined that modernity remade religion in its image, differentiating religion from other fields and rendering it private, Taylor suggests instead that religion has made modernity, more precisely that the transformation of Western Christianity produced Euro-American modernity. In his story, the emergence of a modern secular public, and a modern secularized religion, is premised upon the conversion from a naive religiosity to a reflective one, upon the conversion to a new kind of religion. The key engine of modernity is what Taylor calls a "supernova" effect constituted by an explosion of intellectual and spiritual difference within early modern Christianity.[2] This supernova raises pluralism to a new power and qualitatively transforms social life: the proliferation and collision of faiths that it eventuated, according to Taylor, both threatened to undermine faith itself and made a new mode of faith possible.[3] Modern belief became more "reflective" as it moved from the background to the foreground of experience, and it became "fragile" as it stood foregrounded as one possibility among others in the wake of European Christianity's fragmentation, of the increased visibility of world religions, and of the emergence of atheism as a public possibility.

---

[2] Taylor, *A Secular Age*, 299.
[3] On the condition of deep pluralism, see especially William E. Connolly, *Pluralism*.

A supernova of pluralization is a useful image, and a relatively uncontroversial account of the explosion of difference that characterizes the epistemological condition of modernity, but the framing of "religion" within Taylor's account is much more controversial – it is even deeply problematic in some respects. For Taylor, religion grants believers access to the experiences of "fullness" and "power," to an experience of "faith" that derives from the connection with a transcendent God and that is unavailable to unbelievers – in his account, unbelievers often experience "confusion" and feelings of "exile" because they lack the sense of fullness that attends faith.[4] Taylor makes a series of crucial substitutions here and throughout his text: belief is substituted for the experience of fullness and power; the experience of fullness and power is substituted for faith; faith is substituted for Western, reformed Christianity; Western, reformed Christianity is substituted for Christianity; Christianity is substituted for religion. Through this series of substitutions, "religion" in *A Secular Age* is consistently reduced to "belief."[5] For at least a generation, the discipline of religious studies has recognized this reductive gesture as a central feature of the modern concept of religion. Theologians have noticed something like it for much longer. But if belief functions as the authorized emblem of modern religion, this concept of religion has been roundly criticized by scholars as the parochial projection of assumptions particular to Protestantized Christianity, by theologians as an inadequate expression of Christian tradition, and to an extent by Taylor himself insofar as he is critical of the tendency toward "excarnation" at work within modern Christianity.[6]

Insofar as the reduction of religion to belief follows from assumptions deeply engrained within the background of modern Euro-American intellectual and spiritual culture, it can be difficult to recognize. But the criticism of this reduction is straightforward and compelling once articulated: the concept of "belief" is insufficient to capture the constitutive importance of ritual and communal practice to most, if not all, religious traditions. Although it may be difficult to define "religion," an adequate

---

[4] Taylor, *A Secular Age*, 5–6.
[5] Taylor works with a concept of religion whose lineage can be traced through Mircea Eliades' *The Sacred and the Profane*, William James's *The Varieties of Religious Experience*, and Friedrich Schleiermacher's *On Religion: Speeches to its Cultured Despisers*. For influential criticisms of this concept, see Masuzawa, Fitzgerald, and Asad. As seen in the first chapter's discussion of James's *Varieties*, the authorized modern concept of religion as belief can literally be drawn from the authorized image of conversion coined in Augustine's *Confessions*.
[6] See especially Taylor, *A Secular Age*, 614–5, 753, 771.

definition must acknowledge the centrality of performance to religion: contemporary scholarship reminds us that *religion is something people do (usually together in a group)*. Insofar as representing religion goes to the heart of modern secularism, Taylor's reduction of religion to belief is enormously consequential. Viewed from a slightly different perspective, if the variety of "religious" practices around the globe are actually converging upon a modern Western form of religion centered on belief, it remains necessary to explain – or at least acknowledge – the different starting points, rates of change, and current extent of those processes of transformation.

Taylor's theory reframes the emergence of modern secularism, but in doing so it uncritically deploys a particular and a particularly controversial conception of religion as belief. Returning to his account, because the experiences of fullness and power that epitomize religion become precarious in "a secular age," and because belief itself becomes "fragile," Taylor argues that it is necessary to buttress belief against the cosmic winds that threaten to sweep it away, and he attempts to do so by re-narrating the history of modernity. Facing an epistemic supernova, Taylor retrenches: he encloses religion within belief, he encloses belief within the individual, he encloses the individual believer within secularism, and he encloses secularism within a Euro-American tradition. As he retrenches, he doubles down on authorized narratives that separate and secure belief and identity: on a large scale, the story of modernity is told as Latin-Christendom's conversion into Euro-America; on a small scale, this story is told to support individuals who continue to believe in the midst of a "secular age" of rampant unbelief. This response secures the place of Protestantized Christianity within the landscape of Euro-American secularism: it renders a particular kind of religion – a form of religion equated with belief – compatible with secular modernity. It refuses, however, what may be the most pressing challenge posed by the intersection of religion and politics today: How can forms of religion that are irreducible to private belief be accommodated within and perhaps make distinctive contributions to the public life of pluralistic constitutional democracies?

Although there is much to appreciate in Taylor's supernova thesis, there is much to dissent from in the response he recommends to this condition. I imagine that Bergson would have appreciated Taylor's image of a supernova, for he admired and, indeed, imitated Lucretius' use of cosmological metaphors as tools of philosophical, ethical, and political suasion. If a great cosmic wind blows against us, carrying away old forms, Bergson would suggest that humanity can only be achieved under such conditions by plunging into an ever-renewed process of transformation rather than seeking to retreat with Taylor into the security of an authorized narrative. Faced with a supernova of change – as he surely was in interwar Europe – Bergson recommended the practice of mystics who "open their souls to the oncoming wave," opening themselves to the new, becoming otherwise in the process, and diving into the depths of a crystalline process of conversion.[7] Taylor consigns conversion to a secure place within the modern image of religion, wherein it signifies the experience of conversion to a specific religion, accompanied (if authentic) by the special experiences of fullness and power that attend belief, but Bergson and Cavell pursue concepts of conversion that transcend the boundaries of "religion" so conceived. The authorized form of conversion sets the pattern for Taylor's vision of secularism: it is a form that simplifies, consolidates, secures, and closes determinate religious and political institutions. The crystalline form sets the pattern for the alternative vision I would propose: it is a form that exposes complex formations, renders the constitutive parts of these formations mobile, and opens religion and politics to mutual transformation.

I imagine that Catherine Keller might also appreciate Taylor's invocation of a supernova, for she too draws upon cosmological imagery in constructing a postmodern, feminist theology of creation. But if she might agree that our world is shaken by the force of a supernova, Keller's work suggests that Taylor does not follow this figure far enough. Refiguring the astro-physical theory of "the big bang" as "the big birth" and interpolating it within the book of *Genesis*, Keller crystallizes a wide range metaphoric registers (scientific, feminist, religious) when she asks her readers to contemplate how:

A strange "dark energy" pushes the universe infinitely out. In a centrifugal expansion that is paradoxically without center, glamorous conflagrations of star death glide along on the same momentum with nurseries of nebulae incubating fetal stars. The galaxies interlace like a circulatory system: the nonlinear geometry of chaos is figured everywhere. Astronomers, who had once focussed upon "jewel-like lights that moved in eternally recurring patterns," must confront the possibility that the starry galaxies and their creatures are "barely more than flecks of froth on a stormy sea of dark matter." Darkness upon the deep.[8]

Keller adds "depth" to Taylor's supernova theory. Whereas Taylor's supernova unfolds within the immanent frame of a secular age, in Keller's

---

[7] Taylor, *A Secular Age*, 754; Bergson, *Creative Evolution*, 99.
[8] Keller, *Face of the Deep*, xv.

view, "the deep" figures an unmasterable generativity that both makes and unmakes every given plane of immanence. The figuration of the deep invoked in Keller's most recent work resonates with the crystalline depths of conversion, and her much longer-held argument that "separation and sexism have functioned together as the most fundamental self-shaping assumptions of our culture" suggests the urgency, and perhaps the difficulty, of formulating alternatives to the authorized image of separation.[9] This is not to say that Keller's work should be read as a direct engagement with, much less a refutation of, Taylor's work. But their juxtaposition can begin to show concretely how Taylor's authorized narrative of modern secularism obscures alternatives, and that pattern can be traced further by following the authorized narrative's consistent elision of feminist scholarship.[10] I cite here briefly three landmark contributions to the study of secularism rooted within feminist literatures that are elided by the authorized narrative:

1. Taylor's portrayal of secularity as the reflective emancipation from naive faith should be tested against Saba Mahmood's painstaking analysis of the uncritical attachment to the value of freedom within theories of secularism. Her careful ethnographic delineation of practices of ethical cultivation endemic to religious life, more precisely women's participation in the Egyptian Mosque Movement, suggests that ethical subjects are deeply implicated in the transformational process of conversion, and that this process is irreducible to the categories of reflective emancipation or naive domination.[11] This work argues that the normative ideal of freedom from (religious) constraint inscribed within the authorized narrative of secularism obscures the multifaceted dimensions of ethical life that underpin freedom in concrete contexts.
2. Taylor's construction of a hermetic, Euro-American narrative for modern secularism should be problematized in the light of Adriana Cavarero's argument that the narratives constituting one's unique individual identity are always constructed with and for another.[12]

---

[9] Keller, *From a Broken Web*, 2.
[10] On feminism's complex intersection with secularism, see, e.g., Lila Abu-Lughod, "Do Muslim Women Really Need Saving? Anthropological Reflections on Cultural Relativism and Its Others"; Judith Butler, "Sexual Politics, Torture, and Secular Time"; and Joan Wallach Scott, "Sexularism" and *The Politics of the Veil*.
[11] Saba Mahmood, *The Politics of Piety*.
[12] Adriana Cavarero, *Relating Narratives*.

The opening page of Taylor's *Secular Age* symptomatically consigns "almost all other contemporary societies (e.g., Islamic countries, India, Africa)" to the margins of its narrative, indiscriminately confining a constellation of states, a nation-state, and a continent within parentheses in a spectacular example of exclusion from the authorized narrative of secularism. Following Hannah Arendt, Cavarero argues that one can never craft the story of one's own life in complete independence from others, for this elides the relational nature of the self and the fact that one's identity is essentially public rather than private. Extending this argument suggests that telling the story of Euro-America's "secular age" as the story of its emergence from "Latin Christendom" necessarily distorts by eliding Euro-America's relationships with the rest of the world. In fact, the global future of secularism is not a marginal question, and secularism itself should be opened to rearticulation and transformation as it collides with and takes root within the world's manifold religious traditions. To translate the Euro-American problematic of secularism into global terms, it will be necessary to acknowledge and include Euro-America's others in constructing the narratives that constitute the identity of secularism, but authorized narratives block such acknowledgment.

3. Taylor's construal of the secular as an epistemological background that sets the conditions for the freedom of belief should be tested against Gauri Viswanathan's historical analyses of the concrete constraints placed on believing individuals and their communities by the secular state, more precisely the constraints placed on women with respect to conversion in the context of colonial and post-colonial India.[13] Such testing reveals both that the institutional formations of secularism distribute religious freedom unevenly and, more subtly, that secularism's institutional forms are inherently constraining. The point is not that one should try to imagine governance without constraint, for that makes very little sense, but rather that it is important to render constraints visible so that they can be assessed and, where necessary, contested and reformed. Once more, the authorized narrative's conflation of secularism with freedom elides the constraints that are internal to secularism itself.

To refigure "secularism" as a crystalline process of transformation would help to pry this key term of contemporary democratic theory loose from

[13] Gauri Viswanathan, *Outside the Fold*.

the authorized narratives that hold it so tightly and may thus allow an ever-larger range of scholars and activists working in an ever-wider range of traditions to participate in an essentially democratic process of assessing, contesting, and reshaping the actual formations of modern secularism.

Where Rawls was ultimately uneasy about the role of Christian faith in philosophy and public life, Taylor modifies the authorized narrative of secularism to reconcile it with Christianity: he draws secularism, the prodigal child, back home to the warm embrace of its Christian father. Although there are many strong connections between Euro-American secularism and Western Christianity, casting these connections as the necessary and essential core of modern secularism as such avoids the most significant challenge for reimagining secularism today. To respond adequately to the rapid pluralization that is among the chief sociological characteristics of our time, in part a consequence of globalization, in part a consequence of a variety of politics of recognition, "secularism" should be reimagined as a viable possibility for individuals and societies whose practices exceed the patterns of Protestant(ized) Christianity and whose religions exceed the confines of private belief.

The understanding of secularism as a crystalline process that I propose explicitly acknowledges that religions have appropriate roles within public life in democratic societies, and it is distinctly attuned to the accelerating pace of change within modernity. Where authorized narratives suggest that individuals and societies are to convert from "religion" to "secularism," the crystalline model proposes that secularism should be understood as a conversion of both the "religious" and the "secular" or "political." It is an open rather than a closed process: the practices that sustain democratic political life, and the practices that sustain religious life, in this view, must be conceived of as hybridized, evolving, and overlapping traditions.[14] These fields of practice have always overlapped and intersected, and their intersection has always been contested. Although the privatization of conscience and the reconstitution of religion as a matter of individual belief are specific to the dominant forms of Western Christianity, and to the authorized narrative of secularism, the necessary intersection and contestation of "religious" and "political" practices at

---

[14] As Jeffrey Stout pithily notes in his recent and incisive book on grassroots democracy, *Blessed Are the Organized*, "if one subtracted the churches from IAF [the Industrial Areas Foundation] and other similar organizing networks, then grassroots democracy in the United States would come to very little" (5). In more general terms, religious institutions and communities often overlap extensively with popular democratic politics.

their points of intersection are much more nearly universal in historical and global senses. For the idea of "secularism" to be of use for anything more than managing Protestant(-ized) Christianity within an established constitutional order, it should be understood as the site where a variety of religious and political practices mutually reshape one another. What a crystalline theory opens secularism to, above all perhaps, is the persistence of multiple religious pasts within the present and to the enfolding of an ever-greater multiplicity of present religious forms within a possible secularism of the future.

The Conversion of Secularism

A series of steps must be taken to move from the authorized image of secularism as the separation of church and state toward a theory of secularism as crystalline conversion. First is the recognition that modern secularism is imagined to separate "the secular" from "the religious," within the terms of an authorized narrative of conversion. This is true when Rawls imagines a "post-metaphysical" secularism to have surpassed the age of public, doctrinal conflict, and when Taylor imagines a reflective "secular age" to have grown from naive Christianity. The modern secular imaginary is, in fact, governed by the authorized terms of this conversion narrative. Second is the recognition that the image of separation is insufficient to account for the work of transformation within a process of conversion, so that beneath the image of secularism as separation are continuous, if rough and uneven, patterns of contestation, imbrication, and exchange. Our age is, in fact, not a secular age but instead one marked by the co-presence of faiths, traditions, and practices – naive, reflective, evangelical, reformed, orthodox, reconstructed, secular, lay, clerical, atheist, pantheist, animist, and so forth ad infinitum – a deep pluralism that can only be flattened upon the plane of Taylor's supernova with significant violence. Third, if secularism is a process of crystalline conversion that works through accretion and transformation rather than separation, this increasingly globalized phenomenon will enfold new layers, dimensions, forms, and possibilities as it grows beyond Euro-American contexts. Perhaps the most grievous limitation of Rawls's and Taylor's theories of secularism is their foreclosure of the sense that secularism faces continuous transformation and that it has lived and will continue to live within this transformation, rather than within any particular configuration.

Modernity may well be a supernova born of the deep – within late modernity, in any case, global politics is marked by paradox, tension, and transformation in abundance as the familiar political forms of European modernity stagger into an uncertain global future.[15] Late modern social conditions intensify the problems addressed by modern political thought at every turn: where the always uneasy conjunction of nation, state, sovereignty, and democracy with the traditional social contract's themes of obligation, legitimacy, and consent produced many of political theory's signature conceptual dilemmas, our times threaten to overrun these, in particular as Euro-American forms are at once projected further around the globe and at the same time parochialized within the deep pluralism of global traditions. We are called to think and act with deep intellectual uncertainty in the face of profound sociological change. If Bergson and Cavell – this book's two key imaginative resources – are by no means equal to the task of taming this theoretical and sociological complexity, they are pertinent precisely for their insistence that human knowledge will remain ever insufficient to the ethical and political problems that face us. Alleviating injustice requires, Cavell insists, acknowledgment rather than knowledge. Justice requires humanity to continuously outstrip its own boundaries, Bergson insists, riding intuition and creative emotion. Bergson and Cavell both work creatively within religious traditions, understanding these traditions as dynamic and mutable, and drawing upon them to create new possibilities within the tradition of political thought. For both, and for me in reading both, the point is not so much to convert to a new perspective but rather to effect a conversion of the modern secular imaginary.

Secularism alone, in its authorized modern form, cannot be made to bear the blame for life's permeation by power, nor can it be expected, even in crystalline form, to answer for the apparent insufficiency of political power to address the threats to life's continuation in the future. Indeed, problems of that order must be referred to the whole complex of "globalization," "representative government," or "the political" rather than to secularism. Secularism – *authorized* or *crystalline* – is no answer. But with that said, secularism as we have known it in Rawls's formulation, and as we are coming to know it in Taylor's, obstructs many possible responses to these problems, and its authorization obscures that fact. Cavell and Bergson suggest that the work of crystalline conversion will issue at best in modest change: for Cavell, it might aid in withstanding the disappointments of democratic life, and for Bergson, participation in

---

[15] For a probing analysis of the uneasy persistence of modern political formations within the contemporary condition, see especially the account of "post-Westphalian" sovereignty in the first chapter of Wendy Brown's *Walled States, Waning Sovereignty*.

Conclusion 233

the world's ceaseless change and creativity is a necessary precondition for doing more than merely surviving our circumstances. To approach secularism as a site of creative transformation at the juncture of religion and politics may only be to remove one barrier to the kind of genuinely democratic and deeply pluralistic politics this world needs, but that would still be something. To dive beneath the authorized image into secularism's crystalline depths is to accept the instability, the fragility, the transience of identities and institutions – "religious," "political," and "secular" – in this world as a possibility, as the site for the emergence of truly democratic forms of self-determination. Beneath the elaborate concrete formations of modern secularism, a process continues to unfold in which we are transformed, and the nature of our relations to those around us are transformed, and the communities that sustain us are transformed – change happens here, for better and for worse, but it is of critical importance to grasp the dynamic nature of secularism as a precondition for actively, intelligently, and responsibly intervening to direct its course.

Ours is not "a secular age" in any special or privileged sense. We are neither more nor less secular than our forebears have been or our heirs will be – for secularism is a process, and secularity does not mark a degree of separation from religion but instead names one's relation to "religion," a concept that refers to yet another set of practices that shift in time. One key story of modern secularism, the story of toleration, is told as the exclusion from public life of forced conversions to Christianity. Another is told as the transformation of Christianity. There is an overabundance of stories, an overdetermination of Christianity, a supernova of narrative, but there is no one special relation between modern secularism and Christianity, and there is no special story of modern secularism's genesis from the deep: there are a hundred relations, no relation; a hundred stories, no story. The legal, administrative, and cultural institutions of modern secularism mark and patrol the boundaries of the public sphere against religion, but this is only a small part of modern secularism. Modern secularism, as Cavell suggests it should, may come to describe the acknowledgment of the continual absence of political community and the awakening to one's responsibility for this absence, for continuing in the face of this absence, for becoming, paradoxically, stateless democratic citizens. Public reason is but one face of secularism. Secularism, as Bergson suggests it should, may also come to express a faith in the possibilities of collective life that unfold among radically different constituents, a collective life based not on knowledge, a collective life without public reason, a collective life borne upon the wish for a better life that compels people to act together, precisely where they lack public reasons for doing so, precisely in the face of their disappointments with the institutions of democracy. This would be one possible secularism as an expression of faith in democracy in the face of democracy's constant failures. Secularism as a condition of the political wish for a better life within this world, as faith in the possibility of transforming this world, alongside or within but not after, not beyond every other faith, as a process of becoming otherwise than one is, along with a community that may not yet nor ever be: a secularism irreducible to "religion" or "politics."

In the end, I have tried to do two main things with the figure of conversion: I have used it to explain why we tend to imagine modern secularism in the way that we do, and I have used it to suggest how we might imagine modern secularism otherwise. This is a moment of profound crisis within and reconsideration of the authorized discourses of modern secularism and, with them, the authorized images of "the religious" and "the secular." There is a seam, perhaps more, perhaps no more. It may be the case that Taylor's image of secularism as the culmination of Christian tradition will be sewn over the worn fabric of Rawls's image of secularism as a post-metaphysical exclusion of religion from public life, in which case one authorized narrative will simply recede beneath another. But secularism may also be poised to move in another direction, to become a name for one of the key processes of transformation that determines, and redetermines, the tenor of public life by forming, and reforming, the ways in which a society's constituent members relate to one another, by forming and reforming individual lives through an essentially democratic process that contests existing social forms – as a process of conversion whose authorized narratives are always crystallized within processes that remake individuals in their relation to communities. The authorized course appears, as yet, the more likely, perhaps the certain course: the conversion from one stable form of secularism to another. But – in *the twinkling of an eye*, as the *turning of a mood or a cheek*, on this *our refractory planet* . . . – there might also be an opening for the conversion of secularism itself as part of the crystallization of a more democratic future.

Bibliography

Asad, Talal. *Formations of the Secular: Christianity, Islam, Modernity*. Palo Alto, CA: Stanford University Press, 2003.

Asad, Talal. *Genealogies of Religion: Discipline and Reasons of Power in Christianity and Islam*. Baltimore, MD: Johns Hopkins University Press, 1993.

Bergson, Henri. *Creative Evolution*. Mineola, NY: Dover, 1998.

Brown, Wendy. *Walled States, Waning Sovereignty*. New York: Zone Books, 2010.
Butler, Judith. "Sexual Politics, Torture, and Secular Time," in *Frames of War: When Is Life Grievable?* New York: Verso, 2009: 101–136.
Caputo, John. "Spectral Hermeneutics: On the Weakness of God and the Theology of the Event," in Gianni Vattimo, John Caputo, and Jeffrey Robbins, eds., *After the Death of God*. New York: Columbia University Press, 2009: 47–88.
Caputo, John. *The Weakness of God: A Theology of the Event*. Bloomington: Indiana University Press, 2006.
Cavarero, Adriana. *Relating Narratives: Storytelling and Selfhood*. New York: Routledge: 2000.
Connolly, William E. *Pluralism*. Durham, NC: Duke University Press, 2005.
Eliade, Mircea. *The Sacred and the Profane: The Nature of Religion*. New York: Harcourt, Brace, 1959.
Fitzgerald, Timothy. *The Ideology of Religious Studies*. New York: Oxford University Press, 2000.
James, William. *The Varieties of Religious Experience*. New York: Library of America, 2010.
Keller, Catherine. *Face of the Deep: A Theology of Becoming*. New York: Routledge, 2003.
Keller, Catherine. *From a Broken Web: Separation, Sexism and the Self*. Boston: Beacon Press, 1986.
Mahmood, Saba. *The Politics of Piety: The Islamic Revival and the Feminist Subject*. Princeton, NJ: Princeton University Press, 2005.
Masuzawa, Tomoko. *The Invention of World Religions, or, How European Universalism Was Preserved in the Language of Pluralism*. Chicago: University of Chicago Press, 2005.
Schleiermacher, Friedrich. *On Religion: Speeches to Its Cultured Despisers*. Cambridge: Cambridge University Press, 1988.
Scott, Joan Wallach. *The Politics of the Veil*. Princeton, NJ: Princeton University Press, 2007.
Scott, Joan Wallach. "Sexularism," in *The Fantasy of Feminist History*. Durham, NC: Duke University Press, 2012: 91–116.
Stout, Jeffrey. *Blessed Are the Organized: Grassroots Democracy in America*. Princeton, NJ: Princeton University Press, 2010.
Taylor, Charles. *A Secular Age*. Cambridge, MA: Belknap Press, 2007.
Tully, James. *Public Philosophy in a New Key*, vol. 1 and 2. Cambridge: Cambridge University Press, 2008.
Viswanathan, Gauri. *Outside the Fold: Conversion, Modernity, and Belief*. Princeton, NJ: Princeton University Press, 1998.

Index

Abu-Lughod, Lila, 228n10
affect, 112, 134, 149–150, 162
  creative emotions, 120–122
  guilt and shame, 55–56, 155, 158,
    161–162, 163
  theory of, 121n53
Agamben, Giorgio, 136n9
Anidjar, Gil, 76n9
Ansell-Pearson, Keith, 124
argument, 19
  and Cavell, 181
  critical, 20–21
  history of political thought, 20–21
  "knock-down," 19
  normative, 20–21
  public, 19, 223
Aristotle, 33
  Poetics, 33–34
  Rhetoric, 150–151
Asad, Talal, 9, 144n28, 225n5
Audi, Robert, 21
Augustine, 13, 14, 20, 21, 22, 23–24,
    30–68, 75, 99, 126, 129, 145,
    197
authority, interpretive, 47
autobiography, 46–51
  and Rawls, 160–164
  split subject, 48–49, 54–55, 97–98

Bennett, Jane, 124
Bergson, Henri, 20, 21, 22, 24–25, 26,
    97–129, 132, 226–227, 232–233
Blumenberg, Hans, 6

Boyarin, Daniel, 53n38
Brown, Peter, 51n34, 50–52, 61n49, 62,
    63, 65
Brown, Wendy, 36n12, 232n15
Buddhism, 13
Bunyan, John, 197
Butler, Judith, 175, 228n10

Caputo, John D., 98n3
Casanova, José, 6n9, 21n38
Cavarero, Adriana, 228–229
Cavell, Stanley, 20, 21, 22, 25–26, 141,
    151, 162, 168–216, 232–233
Chadwick, Owen, 21
character formation, ethical, 3, 44, 50–51,
    222–223
Christianity, 4–5
  and American political culture, 11
  and Augustine's milieu, 61–62
  and Bergson, 24, 98
  and conversion, 13–14, 15, 30–31
  as family-resemblance concept, 14
  as foundation of modernity, 6, 14
  and Locke, 85–86
  protestantized, 81, 90, 230
  secularization of, 6
  and Taylor, 31–32, 38, 225–226, 230
Clark, Gillian, 51–52
Coetzee, J. M., 197n57
community, 12
  absence, 169, 171, 172–173, 212–213,
    214–216, 233
  membership, 206, 212–213

community (cont.)
  reorientation, 3, 12, 50–51, 61–62, 74, 169, 222–223
Confucianism, 13
Connolly, William E., 19, 19n32, 144n29, 224n3
conscience, 81, 85, 86–87, 135, 178–179, 196–197, 203, 212–214, 230–231
consent, 191
  express, 200–201, 203, 204, 206, 210–211, 212–213
  and poetry, 210–211
  tacit, 185, 200–207, 212–213
contract, social, 142–144, 171, 190–216
conversion, 12–18, 30, 109–110, 138–139, 168–169, 219
  exclusion of, 4, 18, 24
  forced, 17–18, 82–83
  multiplicity of, 60
  narrative, 3, 23, 34–35, 47–48, 59, 60–61, 73–76, 210, 219–221
  as perfect story, 34
  and writing, 17, 50–51, 60–61, 178, 208
Courcelle, Pierre, 40–41, 46–47
Critchley, Simon, 190

Dante, 48–49
Davis, Kathleen, 76n9
deconstruction, 14, 102
Deleuze, Gilles, 102n7, 104, 124, 127–128
democracy, 1–2, 4, 7–8, 18, 94, 164–165, 171, 174, 190, 199–200, 212, 214–216, 219, 232–234
  citizenship, 94, 173, 221–222, 223
  practices, 137–138, 169, 171
Democritus, 101
Derrida, Jacques, 53n38, 104, 175, 181, 190
Dewey, John, 141
discontinuity, 12, 23–24, 32, 38, 49, 67–68, 74, 97–98, 127–128, 135, 219–221
  and conversion narratives, 42, 43–44
  and narratives of secularism, 21–22
discourse, economic, 207–208
Dreisbach, Daniel, 2n3
Durkheim, Émile, 5–6, 36, 98, 133n4

Eliade, Mircea, 225n5
Emerson, Ralph Waldo, 175
Enlightenment, 143

Epicurus, 101
exemplarity, 158–159, 182–183

faith, 26, 37, 40, 91, 133–134, 171
  and Bergson, 123, 125
  and Rawls, 133–134, 158
Ferguson, Frances, 186n35
Fitzgerald, Timothy, 225n5
Foucault, Michel, 16, 17, 44, 104, 192
Frank, Jason, 215n96
Freccero, John, 48–49, 54–55, 59

Gauchet, Marcel, 21, 35
Godard, Jean-Luc, 127–128
Goodchild, Philip, 98n3
governance, 81–82
  democratic, 94
  rationality, 81–82, 221–222
Grosz, Elizabeth, 124
Guerlac, Suzanne, 104n13
Gutmann, Amy, 141

Habermas, Jürgen, 8, 21, 73
habit, 105, 110–111, 114–116, 208–209
  and institution, 118–119
Hadot, Pierre, 15, 46–47
  and conversion, 15–16, 17
Hampshire, Stuart, 141, 150
Hart, H. L. A., 142
Hauerwas, Stanley, 7
Hegel, G. W. F., 21, 31n4
Hirschkind, Charles, 16n29
Hobbes, Thomas, 139, 139n13, 143
Hume, David, 20, 139, 140n14, 208–209
Hunter, Ian, 16–17
Huntington, Samuel, 76n9

identity, 104, 105–106, 125–126, 128–129
  and depersonalization, 110, 112, 120, 123
  and faith in modern secular liberalism, 134
  narrative, 3, 12, 34–35, 37
ideology, 7, 18
  secularist, 7
imaginary, modern secular, 2, 3, 13, 14, 18, 32, 57, 71–77, 92–93, 109, 113, 219–221
  crisis in, 26, 223–224, 234
Islam, 13

James, William, 41, 42–45, 151, 159–160, 176n15, 179n17, 225n5
Jefferson, Thomas, 77, 203
  "wall of separation between church & state," 2, 71, 91, 220
Judaism, 13

Kant, Immanuel, 21, 101, 143, 143n27
Keller, Catherine, 98n3, 227–228

Lefort, Claude, 136n9
liberalism, 71–74, 76–77, 132–134, 164–165, 185–186
Locke, John, 19, 20, 21, 23–24, 26, 32, 71–94, 136, 137, 139, 139n13, 143, 190–216, 221–222
Lucretius, 100–101, 108, 226
Lukacs, Georg, 22
Luke, 53–54
Luther, Martin, 8, 14, 47, 126, 197

MacIntyre, Alasdair, 7
Mahmood, Saba, 16n29, 228
Man, Paul de, 39, 48, 48n29, 79
  irony, 39–40
Marrati, Paola, 124, 171n6
Marshall, John, 78
Marx, Karl, 22, 26, 103, 168–172, 187, 215
Masuzawa, Tomoko, 225n5
McClure, Kirstie, 78
Mill, John Stuart, 141
miracle, 138–139, 148
Morrison, Karl, 39n18, 40n19
Mulhall, Stephen, 180–181
Murray, Molly, 39n18, 101n6

narrative, 18, 33–35
  account of secularism, 21, 35, 63, 68, 73–74
  in Augustine and Taylor, 23–24, 31–32
  authorized, 18
Nietzsche, Friedrich, 143, 143n27, 181–189, 208
Nock, Arthur Darby, 41–42

obligation, 113–119, 191, 193–197, 198–199, 206, 208–209
  and consent, 191, 205
Orthodoxy, Radical, 6–7

Paul, 14, 30, 40n19, 47, 63, 75, 126, 170, 197
  and conversion, 38–39, 40
perfectionism, 152–154, 162, 181–189
  and democracy, 190
Pitkin, Hanna, 193–196
Plato, 30, 31n3, 101, 137, 180
pluralism, 19, 19n32, 26, 94, 128, 214–216, 224n3, 224–225, 230–231, 232–233
Pogge, Thomas, 160–162
political-theology, 13, 90–91, 92, 98, 133n4, 164–165
  and Rawls, 144–145
  and the social contract, 191–192
Popper, Karl, 71–73
Possidius, 64–65
Proast, Jonas, 80, 82
process, crystalline, 12, 21–22, 23, 24, 32, 44–61, 76–77, 97
prophecy, 169, 171, 181, 187, 191, 198, 199–200

Rawls, John, 7, 9, 19, 20, 21, 25, 30, 32, 71–73, 99–100, 132–165, 181–188, 222–223
  "above reproach," 162–163, 186, 189
reason, public, 26, 158, 162, 223, 233
Reformation, Protestant, 8, 9
rhetoric, 19, 23, 24, 25, 46, 78, 79, 83–84, 85, 89–90, 92, 149, 164–165, 181, 221, 222–223
  and Locke, 77–92
  and pretense, 87–88
  and zealotry, 88–89
  and Rawls, 149–158, 160
  and conversation, 154–157
Ricoeur, Paul, 33n7, 144n29, 149–150
Rorty, Richard, 7, 20n35
Rousseau, Jean-Jacques, 122, 137, 143, 144–149
  and paradox of founding, 122, 144–149, 157, 164–165
Ryan, Alan, 140

saint, 25, 138–139, 164–165
  and Bergson, 126–127
  and Rawls, 25, 132–134, 136, 149, 158–159, 222–223
Sandel, Michael, 142
Schleiermacher, Friedrich, 225n5

Schmitt, Carl, 6, 133n4, 143, 144n27
Scott, Joan Wallach, 228n10
secularism, 1, 5–12
    as crystalline conversion, 1, 19, 21–22, 32, 63, 68, 86, 93–94, 231, 234
    and democracy, 2
    as separation, 1, 3, 5, 21–22, 23–24, 26, 63, 73, 74, 76–78, 92, 221
    as transformation, 1, 2, 21–22, 26, 76–78, 83–85, 93–94, 219–221, 233
secularity, 8–9, 233
    and negotiation, 85
secularization, 5–8, 197–198
sensibility, 3, 74–75, 76, 83–84, 91, 92
Shulman, George, 171n5
skepticism, 170, 173, 174, 179–180, 193
Spinoza, Baruch, 47, 133n4, 135, 139, 139n13
stammer, 105–106, 127–128
    and Augustine, 105–106
    and Bergson, 108–109
    and creative emotions, 121
Stock, Brian, 50–52
Stout, Jeffrey, 7–8, 230n14
Strauss, Leo, 133n4
surface, authorized, 1, 13, 21–22, 23, 26, 38–45, 63, 97–98, 134–135, 172–173, 221
    and *Confessions*, 39

Taylor, Charles, 21, 30, 51n34, 73, 223–231
    A Secular Age, 31–32, 35–38, 66–68
    as conversion narrative, 38, 67–68
    "knock-down" argument, 19
    "supernova" effect, 224–228
theology, 14
    exclusion of, 135–136, 222–223
    as genre, 46–47
    and Locke, 84
    and Paul, 14, 40
    and the social contract, 192

theory, critical, 168–172, 198
    and Cavell, 189–190
Thoreau, Henry David, 180, 195–197, 207–208
Tocqueville, Alexis de, 10–12
toleration, 4, 9, 71–74, 76–77, 233
tradition, 1
    Augustinian, 1, 3
    Christian, 7, 17, 52
    democratic, 7
    Enlightenment, 17
    epistemological, 177
    Greek, 15, 17, 52
    Jewish, 15, 52
    minor, 17
    philosophical, 15, 170
    Roman, 15
    secular, 52
transformation of the self, 12, 17, 24, 74, 169, 181, 188–190
Tully, James, 78, 81, 224n2

universe, conception of, 100–103, 226–228

violence, 89, 171, 188–189, 202, 214
Viswanathan, Gauri, 229
Vries, Hent de, 24n39

Walker, William, 79
Walzer, Michael, 71–73
Weber, Max, 5–6, 36
White, Stephen K., 164n68
Williams, Bernard, 156, 156n53, 157n54
wish for a better life, 168–169, 233–234
    as redemption, 170–171
Wittgenstein, Ludwig, 161, 169–170, 180
    family-resemblance, 14
    Investigations, 175–177
Wolin, Sheldon, 135, 141
Wolterstorff, Nicholas, 19n34

Zerilli, Linda, 79